BUILDING RESILIENCE

ROD WARNER

kr publishing

2018

Endorsements

"*Building Resilience* is a must read if you're looking for a way to turn your adversities into the opportunity to grow. This book packs a punch when it come to the principles and steps to become more resilient. It's filled with practical insights, reflective exercises, tips, tools, stories, strategies and surveys to help you find meaning, purpose and joy despite the set-backs, curve-balls, trauma, tragedy and disappointments that life inevitably tosses at all of us from time-to-time. Learning how to make meaning of the past, cope with the current day-to-day challenges, and build hope and strength for the future is the key to fulfillment and personal effectiveness. This is required reading for all as we navigate tough times and work on doing so with confidence and hope."

Prof Shirley Zinn: CEO of Shirley Zinn Consulting, director of Boards, and bestselling author of "Swimming Upstream".

"In the volatile, unpredictable and demanding world we live in today, resilience can go a long way to shield individuals against burnout and positively prepare them to cope with life. Whether you are an individual facing hardship, leading a team through stormy seas, or simply want to help your children build essential life skills, you will find practical examples, advice and information in this book to guide you."

Dr Renate Scherrer, Managing Director: JvR Consulting Psychologists

"*Building Resilience* is a welcome addition to the 'library' of Positive Psychology literature. As a self-help book on coping with adversity, the content speaks to a broad audience, including people across all spheres of life, parents, teachers, leaders and work teams. Moreover, practitioners in the field will find this book a valuable practical handbook for resilience counselling and facilitating workshops on resilience for adults and children. Resilience as a core theme of the book is highly-relevant to the contemporary chaotic context in which uncertainty, life's disruptions and constant change prevails. The book provides practical exercises and application tools for adults, teams and children that can be applied in everyday living circumstances to regain and sustain a sense of thriving and wellbeing amidst life's challenges. The book is enriched with personal anecdotes and case studies which make it easier for readers to understand the power of resilience. Based on the practical life experiences of the author, I have no doubt that readers will benefit from the book."

Melinde Coetzee (DLitt et Phil), Professor in Industrial and Organisational Psychology, University of South Africa

"In the new world of work, resilience is without doubt a competitive advantage. It's seldom to find a book that's deeply grounded in latest theory yet written in a practical manner. This book doesn't belong on your bookshelf, but in your backpack. This is masterpiece that tackles an important topic in a deep and thoughtful manner."

Dr Rica Viljoen, Henley Business School, Managing Director: Mandala Consulting

"With the rate of change, coping and surviving is no longer sufficient, what is required is to develop and nurture the ability to thrive, and to be unconsciously competent at handling challenges with the same ease as one breathes. Warner builds a relationship with the reader, by connecting in an authentic way through stories and exercises. "This book offers practical tools to show building resilience is an easy life skill to develop in oneself and to teach to others. I highly-recommend it for your personal journey ahead!"

Ashnie Muthusamy, Group Manager: Talent Management, Sun International

"Inspiring and applicable throughout one's lifetime."

Fred Irumba, science teacher, Jakindaba Senior Secondary School

"Easy to implement at work and home. The results are remarkable!"

Brent Beilinsohn, Manager, Old Mutual Investment Group South Africa

"Mind blowing! Implementing these practical exercises has made me a better person"

Fanuel Kakuiya, Senior Superintendent, South African Police Services

This book is dedicated
to my dear wife, Lyn,
who epitomises resilience
in the face of debilitating myalgic encephalomyelitis.

Thank you for putting up with me for the two and a half years
it took to write this book, which took precedence over
our holidays, house maintenance, daily chores
and every conversation.

First published in 2012
Second print in 2018

ISBN: 978-1-86922-745-6 (Printed)
ISBN: 978-1-86922-746-3 (ePDF)

Published by KR Publishing
P O Box 3954
Randburg
2125
Republic of South Africa

Tel: (011) 706-6009
Fax: (011) 706-1127
E-mail: orders@knowres.co.za
Website: www.kr.co.za

Printed and bound: Tandym Print, 1 Park Road, Western Province Park, Epping, 7475
Typesetting, layout and design: Orchard Publishing
Graphic illustrations: Devine Dezine
Cover design: Ralf Broemer
Editing and proofreading: Anne Taylor
Project management: One Life Media cc
Project management for KR Publishing: Cia Joubert, cia@knowres.co.za

Contents

Acknowledgements

Cindy Warner-Dobrowski, whose guidance led me to specialise in the area of resilience, and for advice on the chapter: Building Resilient Children.

Jerry van Niekerk, who was my first Building Resilience Workshop client, and who, through the Ilima Trust, made the workshops available to local and provincial government administrations.

Mthandazo Mango, for challenging me to assist teams to become resilient and to thrive.

Stephanie Vermeulen, who encouraged me when I was suffering from the dreaded writer's block.

Tim Warner, for proof-reading articles and chapters of the book, and making suggestions for improvement in the kindest possible way.

Anne Taylor, who, as editor, transformed my tortured sentences into some sort of coherent sequence.

Barbara Elion, for project managing the manuscript through various stages into its final form, and for building an index.

Bronwyn Clur for marketing advice, sage beyond her years.

The many people who attended Building Resilience Workshops and suggested improvements to the exercises.

The 76 people who participated in my research on resilience, telling me the most amazing personal stories of how they triumphed over some of life's adversities and struggled with others.

The Positive Psychology movement, whose work inspired this book, including the leading lights such as Martin Seligman, Barbra Fredrickson, Christopher Peterson, Sonja Lyubomirsky and Rashid Tayyab – to mention just a few.

Introduction

A fork in my path

My mobile phone rang just as I had taken my seat on a flight from Cape Town to Durban on my way to run the Comrades Ultra Marathon the following day. It was a colleague in my company's human resources department. 'Return to head office the day after the race,' she blurted.

'That's not possible,' I responded with some irritation. 'I set up important negotiations with Durban clients several weeks ago and cannot cancel them.'

'You don't understand,' she replied. 'This isn't a request. It's an instruction.'

I worked for a very large financial institution which had recently decided to demutualise and seek a stock exchange listing. The 147-year-old organisation was undergoing very rapid and far-reaching changes as it struggled to change its very soul from a mutual society to a public-listed entity. One of the changes was an extensive cost-cutting exercise that extended across all the organisation's businesses. What this really meant was that staff were to be retrenched, so, having had this conversation, I was now deeply concerned about the security of my own job.

I flew on to Durban and ran the 79 km race the next day, all the time doing my best not to think about what waited for me on my return home.

Back at head office the following day, and while walking to the meeting room where I was to report, I reflected on the success of the business operation I headed. It had been established seven years earlier by my predecessor and its income had more than doubled each year for six consecutive years. The previous year there had been 'only' a 50 per cent increase. The automated retirement fund administration, for which I was also responsible, was regarded as best in its class in South Africa.

Surely I couldn't be retrenched?

The meeting room door was closed – an ominous sign. The executive and three senior officials faced me from behind a table.

My worst fears were realised. In a few sentences I had been retrenched.

I was asked to sit, and one of the senior officials carefully read from a prepared statement which, basically, said that they were very happy with the long and faithful service that I had given the company, but unfortunately...

I was asked if I had anything to say and, stunned, I could only relate that I was concerned about the negotiations I had cancelled in Durban. I wanted to strategise how best to rescue the deal. The officials made polite comments and then asked me to go into the adjacent meeting room, where a psychologist wished to talk to me.

In a daze I walked out. As I closed the door I overheard a gale of laughter, quickly hushed. In the adjacent room a psychologist asked me what had happened, how I felt and what was I going to do now. The questions were more annoying than helpful. It felt as though the organisation was putting a tick in the box labelled 'Offer employee assistance' rather than providing anything meaningful to assist me.

I really did need assistance, but not what was being offered by the psychologist. Most pressing was the urgent need to replace my salary. I was almost fifty years old, in a country where transformation pressures made finding a job, for a white male, very difficult. With the economy in a downturn, I certainly was going to need a great deal of help.

I had to inform my family what had happened and explore with them what this meant for our lifestyle. I wanted to ensure that my anxiety and fear for the future did not spill over into their lives. My wife Lyn was bedridden and I wanted to make sure the additional strain did not exacerbate her illness. I also needed to talk to my two daughters about what this meant for the promises I had made to them to finance their university studies for as long as they studied.

At work, I was given eight weeks to find an alternative position in the organisation. I tried to do this while continuing to run my old job. The entire organisation was, however, going through the same cost-cutting exercise, and so there were few new openings.

At the back of my mind I was sure the organisation would realise there had been a dreadful mistake, and someone would come rushing back to ask me to stay. Finally it dawned on me that this was not going to happen. I dried my tears and left, still not quite believing what had happened.

In the course of struggling to find a job with another organisation, I was told that affirmative action, my age and my deep experience made finding formal employment extremely difficult. So I set up my own business in training, teambuilding and change management. I undertook assignments for various large organisations, including the one that had just retrenched me.

After a few years, I was very busy and earning well. Lyn's health had improved to the point that she was no longer bedridden, although she had a long way to go to full recovery. My daughters were busy with their tertiary studies. 'Well," I thought, 'if this is the alternative to having a highly pressurised corporate job, it's not so bad at all.'

And that's when the wheels fell off.

The government passed affirmative action legislation which meant that organisations would only use people from previously disadvantaged backgrounds for their outsourced work. Overnight, my assignments dried up. My skin colour was a liability – which was not offset by my skills and experience. So, once again, I was suddenly without work and income.

Fed up, I decided to change my career. I cashed in our savings, extended the mortgage on our home, and purchased a small business in Cape Town. It was a courier company using motorbikes and vehicles for local deliveries.

I'd been warned that buying a small business is buying trouble. So I paid a firm of auditors to carry out a comprehensive due diligence study. They found little of concern, and so I proudly took possession of my business on the first of the month – which was a Tuesday. By Thursday afternoon I had a query. I called the seller, but he said that he was really busy, and would I please phone back on the weekend?

Come Saturday, there were several more puzzling issues. I was feeling really uneasy. Imagine my horror when I finally established that the seller had moved overseas, and was not contactable. Then the truth came out. Many of the motorbikes were fraudulently registered, with several sharing the same photocopied license disk, and a large measure of the profitability had been based on bribery and corruption of officials.

The wheels had fallen off once again!

Resilience is the ability to cope in the face of difficulties and emerge from adversity, stronger and more resourceful. At work, it is the ability to remain task-focussed and productive, when experiencing tough times. Most important, resilience enables one to continue to experience joy, to grow and even thrive in the face of life's challenges.

It took eighteen months of dispiriting work to sort out the mess, and get the business back on to a legal basis. By then it was much smaller and less profitable. I eventually sold it at a significant loss, mighty relieved just to get out of it.

While sorting out the business, I spent many sleepless nights thinking about my life and what had happened to me. I knew that, ideally, I should be turning my adversities into growth experiences, to bounce back and thrive. I wanted to live a life of fulfilment and joy, and be able to deal with this adversity as just one of several that we all encounter during our life's journey.

In other words I wanted to be resilient.

I decided to try to understand more about this concept called resilience. Surely there must be a body of research about how to get through difficult times in the easiest and quickest way? I wanted to use that information to help myself, and if I could find things that worked for me, then perhaps I could help other people by teaching them those things too. It could become a new business for me.

I did a thorough search of the academic literature on resilience. I found a great deal of information on resilience with regard to post-traumatic stress disorder, depression, significant traumatic events and extremely trying circumstances. But they were not really relevant to me, as, fortunately, my situation did not encompass such crises.

So I undertook my own study of how ordinary people deal with day-to-day hassles and disappointments, as well cope with the trauma, catastrophes and grief that we all encounter in our journey through life. This enabled me to identify seven constructs of resilience which I later reframed as the principles and steps of resilience. But more than locate theoretical concepts, it was really important for me to find and to develop practical exercises to enhance resilience. This I did over several years and gradually found what works for me. I also found exercises that, while not working for me, worked for other people.

The next step was to develop workshops to assist other people to develop their resilience. I have many years of experience in developing workshops and facilitating learning, but even so, it took many iterations of design before I settled on the present format of the workshops. Now the typical comment from delegates at the end is 'what I have learnt will change my life'.

One of the big changes was to reduce the duration of the workshop from four days to two. But what should I do with all the wonderful material that I had developed for my workshops and which I could no longer use because of the time factor? And how should I respond to people who had asked for additional exercises or for a different application – all of which I had?

The answer was to write this book in which I would include all the background, stories and exercises that are not covered in the official workshop. Writing a book would also enable me to incorporate stories of coping and thriving told by people who attended the workshops.

Why resilience is important

We all want to live life with joy and fulfilment. We all want to be happy and have our dreams fulfilled. Meeting this basic human need is probably the most common goal all people on earth have.

Yet, when you look at the people around you, and even when you reflect on how you live your own life, it's apparent that it's very easy to live a life without joy and fulfilment. This is so well expressed in the opening lines (see left) of M. Scott Peck's book, *The Road Less Travelled*[1].

'Life is difficult. This is a great truth. One of the greatest truths.'

It's not easy to achieve our goals and to live our lives the way we want to. It's only once we truly understand and accept that living is fundamentally about struggling that we can rise above the struggle. The very act of accepting and being at peace with the idea that we have to struggle allows us to turn our attention to what we can achieve, rather than focus on the unfairness, injustices and difficulties of everyday life.

There is an inherent irony in the idea of experiencing difficulties and obstacles in life and accepting that this struggle is ongoing and part of human existence. The irony is that, although we all would like to avoid problems and challenges in our lives – and, indeed, we go to great lengths to do so – it's only in the face of real challenges that we develop as human beings.

It may seem surprising to consider adversity as an opportunity for growth. However, think about times when you've grown and developed the most in your life. For example, consider the occasions at work, when you have been thrown in at

You don't grow and develop during good times: you grow and develop during difficult times.

the deep end or have been promoted and have struggled to cope. Or in your home life, when minor catastrophes have occurred. Coping with difficulties inevitably means you are forced out of your comfort zone and have to grow and develop. Facing and coping with difficulties has, no doubt, made you a better and more rounded person.

And that's the irony about difficulties and struggling. Although no one wants to experience them, tough times do have benefits – if you are able to learn from them[2]. Without experiencing some level of difficulty in childhood, our ability to withstand more severe difficulties later on in life is impeded[3]. Difficulties and struggles stretch and force us to cope and recover and, in so doing, help us grow stronger and develop capabilities as human beings.

What you will find in this book

The book is structured in three parts. Part One gives background information about resilience. It starts off by describing how resilience works and explains some myths about it. Then my research is outlined, which resulted in the identification of the personal building blocks of resilience, and which led to the identification of the principles and steps of resilience. Finally, a questionnaire is presented, which enables you to assess your resilience.

Part Two details the seven principles of resilience, with each principle described in a chapter. At the end of each of the chapters there are exercises for you to complete, in order to enhance your resilience in that area.

Part Three contains two specific applications of resilience. There is a chapter on building resilient teams at work, which is aimed at team leaders who want to build powerful teams that can cope and thrive in the face of organisational change and difficulties. There is also a chapter on building resilience in children, which contains exercises to assist children develop resilience to cope with the challenges they will inevitably face at school and at home.

Throughout the book, practical exercises and application tools are included, to assist you to apply the concepts to your own situations. **Take the time to write your answers to the questions.** A good idea is to dedicate a journal for this purpose. Formulating written responses to the questions will help crystallise your ideas which will help you get the most from this book. In this way, the book will be both a source of reference and a development tool.

Building resilience is not a quick process and you need to be patient with yourself as you learn new ways of thinking, reacting and connecting. But be assured, if you work through this book and complete the exercises, your resilience *will* be enhanced.

Ready to start?

Each of the chapters is designed to be self-contained. So you can start at any place that catches your fancy. If you would like my advice, start by completing the questionnaire about your resilience in Chapter 1, before you read the rest of the book. This will help you see where you are now and, at the end of the book, you can take the questionnaire again and see how your resilience has been improved. It's always encouraging to have confirmation that you are growing and developing.

Good luck with enhancing your resilience and improving the way that you experience and enjoy your life.

ENDNOTES

1   Peck, M.S. 1990. *The road less travelled: a new psychology of love, traditional values and spiritual life.* London: Arrow.

2   Dienstbier, R.A. 1989. Arousal and physiological toughness: Implications for mental and physical health. *Psychological review,* 96:84–100.

3   Meichenbaum, D. 2003. Stress inoculation training. *In* W. O'Donohue, J.E. Fisher & S.C. Hays (eds.). *Cognitive behaviour therapy: Applying empirically supported techniques in your practice.* Hoboken, NJ: Wiley and Sons. 124–139.

PART ONE

1

How resilience works

We all experience tough times. No matter how wealthy, slim, good-looking or clever we are, there will be times when we struggle. Sometimes the struggle will involve dealing with minor irritations and, at other times, it will involve having to cope with significant adversity. However we look at it, life is full of difficulty, obstacles and crisis.

Some of us even feel we have become better human beings because of the struggles we have faced. What, then, is this ability to cope with tough times and get through them? It's called resilience. We all have some resilience, and the more we know about fostering the capacity for resilience, the easier it is for us to build this inner strength and buffer.

Let's now read how Sipho learnt through adversity.

Sipho learns through adversity

Sipho was on the fast track. He had been identified as having the potential to move into the senior management ranks of his organisation within three years. As a young, ambitious graduate from the University of Cape Town's Graduate School of Business, he had excellent qualifications but lacked experience. He was reluctant to acknowledge areas where he lacked the in-depth knowledge of some of his longer-serving peers. In addition, he tended to be critical of other people – from top management to the most junior employee – and he would not hesitate to voice this using his intellectual superiority. In the process, he often humbled others with his razor-sharp insights and wit. His colleagues and staff complained among themselves that he was arrogant. They described him as 'distant, unapproachable and insensitive'.

His wife had a very busy professional career and was frequently away on business. Their young children suffered benign neglect from their parents who, despite their best intentions, did not spend quality time with them.

The issue with children came to a head at a parent-teacher conference, when the teachers told them that their children were not coping at school and that behavioural problems were starting to occur. The teachers also mentioned that the children had complained that their parents were too busy to spend time with them. Sipho and his wife were aghast. On the advice of the school counsellor, they held a family meeting with the children to discuss the problems. The elder of the two angrily told her father that he was never around, never cared about them. The only time he spoke to her was to criticise and be nasty. She told him that he preferred to work on his laptop at home rather than play with them.

The younger daughter complained that he didn't read to her at night, as he was always too tired, or was watching TV and didn't want to be disturbed. She said he didn't love her any more, at which point both children burst into tears and ran, sobbing, to their rooms.

Sipho's wife turned to him and said her best friend, whose husband worked in the same organisation as Sipho, had let slip that Sipho was regarded as a bully at work and that he was unlikely to be promoted further in the organisation.

Sipho was devastated. He had no idea that his interactions were viewed so badly. He was very angry and said that everyone was making things up. He blamed his family for being over-sensitive and talking behind his back. Furious, he had several confrontations with his colleagues, as well as with his wife, and again with his children. Through the angry words and harsh things that were said, he slowly came to realise that he needed to change.

Over the next few months, Sipho began to change the way he related to his colleagues and his loved ones. This wasn't easy for him. He often felt exasperated and confused. Nevertheless, he persisted in trying to find new ways of voicing his opinions. He tried hard to understand how what he said affected other people. He tried to listen more and to ask questions. At home, he set aside time in the evenings for his wife and children. Over the weekends he allocated individual special time for each of the three and spent time with them alone.

Sipho wasn't always successful. But, increasingly, he got it right more times than he got it wrong. Gradually, he changed his relationships with the people around him and, in particular, with the people he loved.

Today he will tell you that he is a different person, which is backed up with some relief by what others say of him.

Facing unpleasant truths and then having to deal with them is tough. Yet, it was precisely because Sipho recognised his failings that he was able to change, develop and grow as a person. The tough times he went through had a definite benefit for him. They enabled him to become a better person.

Everyone has the ability to deal with the most difficult of circumstances and rise above them. Everyone, also, has the ability within them to experience joy, happiness and fulfilment in their lives, even in the face of obstacles, disappointments and setbacks. In most instances you can't change what is happening to you, but you have choices in how you react. Fortunately, everyone possesses this ability to choose *how* to react in really difficult times.

Recovery from adversity – as well as living a happy and fulfilling life – is actually hastened or hampered by the choices you make.

Fortunately, everyone possesses this ability to choose how to react in really difficult times.

We call this resilience.

We quickly recognise resilience in people who survive disasters such as tsunamis and bombings, or admire it in people such as Richard Branson – people who achieve great success in business, despite significant obstacles. It is a condition of mental hardiness that enables us to bounce back, after experiencing stressful life events, such as significant change, stress, adversity and hardship.

To sum up, resilience is your ability to cope with the hassles associated with daily living as well as your ability to overcome stress, hardship and even trauma. It enables you to deal with the unsettling changes you experience in life, as well as having to adapt and cope in your job with organisational pressures and changes. Having resilience enables you to avoid despair, depression and other psychological disorders that are so often associated with living through troubled and difficult times.

The most important aspect of resilience, though, is that it enables you to live your life in the face of all these difficulties in such a way that you experience happiness and fulfilment and emerge stronger than before.

Reaching for resilience in your everyday life

This is where magic can happen in your life. When you are in the depth of despair and in the dark night of adversity; when you are really struggling, having resilience enables you to emerge from horrible times and become stronger and more resourceful than before. Resilience is a natural and common process of coping and enjoying life that we all have available to us.

The upside of living through really challenging times is that we can get through them and be a better person on the other side. We can emerge from these dark times, having coped, been healed, and ultimately thrive at a new level of living.

We all need resilience in our personal lives. We all want to live with joy, happiness and fulfilment. We all yearn to experience life free from worry and fear. To be able to deal with the tough times that come from normal daily living, and despite this, really enjoy being alive. We need resilience to be able to bounce back, cope and thrive.

Resilience, in an organisational or work setting, is the ability to remain task-focused and productive, while experiencing tough times. It is the bedrock of employee alignment to organisational performance.

At work you also need resilience. You need it to cope with organisational pressures and change, such as new priorities, major change initiatives, new technologies, mergers and even downsizing, all of which are common events.

How does the process of resilience work?

Everyone experiences periods in life that they have been 'up' and periods when they have been 'down'. When significant adversity strikes – such as loving relationships ending, children going off the rails, debt becoming uncontrollable, major illness striking or losing a job – predictably, you become less resilient and you enter dark depths of despair. [1]

The process of how adversity is experienced with resilience is shown in the diagram on the next page, in a series of phases[2]. The diagram shows four phases of coping after the experience of some significant adversity, with the final phase incorporating living with enhanced resourcefulness and strength. Although the progression is shown as linear, for the sake of clarity, in reality, people experiencing significant adversity report spiralling back and forth through the four phases over the passage of time.

Everyone has some degree of resilience. We have all learned to cope with difficulties and setbacks, put them behind us to a greater or lesser extent and to move on. Some days are better than others, but on the whole, one's resilience remains fairly constant day-to-day. This is indicated on the left of the graph as 'usual conditions'.

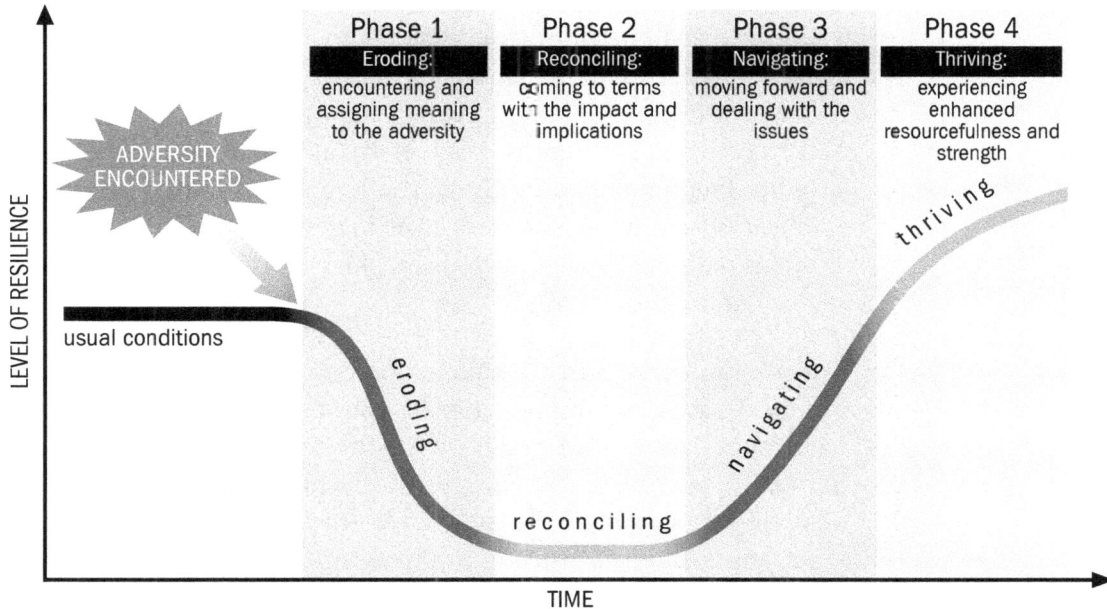

	Phase 1	Phase 2	Phase 3	Phase 4
	Eroding:	Reconciling:	Navigating:	Thriving:
	encountering and assigning meaning to the adversity	coming to terms with the impact and implications	moving forward and dealing with the issues	experiencing enhanced resourcefulness and strength

ADVERSITY ENCOUNTERED

LEVEL OF RESILIENCE

usual conditions

eroding

reconciling

navigating

thriving

TIME

Experiencing adversity with resilience

PHASE 1: ERODING

Every now and again some really significant adversity strikes and your world is turned upside down. Sometimes these adversities loom large on the horizon and when they arrive, they confirm your worst fears. At other times, severe adversity strikes unexpectedly and the suddenness and shock makes the experience even worse.

At such times when a significant adversity is encountered, there is an immediate eroding of your resilience as you struggle to cope with and deal with the issues. It sometimes feels as though a huge black cloud has obscured the sun and everything has suddenly become dark. All you can see is pain and sorrow. As you become caught up in the negative issues and start to understand the implications, it's easy to feel overwhelmed and defeated. You try to make sense of what has happened and why it has happened to you. There appears to be no logic or fairness in the bad things that happen, often to the very best people.

PHASE 2: RECONCILING

With time, the initial shock wears off and you begin to understand and experience the implications of the adversity. It's no longer how bad you think it will be – it's experiencing how bad it actually is. You experience the depths of adversity as you become immersed in what has happened, with all the negative consequences and implications. Your resilience is at its lowest. You struggle to come to terms with the changes in your life. Just getting through each day seems a mountain to climb.

Life seems to be mostly taken up with just dealing with the practical issues and implications of what has happened. You adjust to circumstances and get on with the tasks required for daily living. This involves accepting what has happened and what can't be changed, starting with the process of becoming reconciled to what has happened and the implications. With severe adversity, life changes and you realise things will never be the same. As a consequence, your future will be different from what you had expected.

PHASE 3: NAVIGATING

With time you are able to move forward and deal with the implications of the adversity. This phase involves trying out new things and finding the best way forward. Sometimes it feels like taking two steps forward and one step back, but the important thing is the movement in the direction of healing and connecting, again, to your meaning in life. It's about letting go of the past and trying to live with a changed future. It's about trying to find joy and happiness in your life, despite what has happened.

While no one wants to experience tough times, it is only through them that we have the chips on our shoulders knocked off and we get to see, with greater clarity, the really important things in our lives. We grow and mature in tough times, not in easy times.

PHASE 4: THRIVING

The fourth and last phase in dealing with a significant adversity is that of thriving, with enhanced resourcefulness and strength. The experience of going through the dark night of adversity forces you to think about what is really important in your life. Life's big questions are confronted and changes in attitude, behaviour and lifestyle are the result. In this way you emerge from the adversity stronger than before.

Personal growth and development requires our usual state to be disrupted. Adversity achieves this and initiates a process of change. Horace the Roman thinker is reputed to have said: 'Adversity has the effect of eliciting talents which, in prosperous circumstances, would have lain dormant'. After a life-disrupting change, you cannot go back to how things were – you will become stronger or weaker; better or bitter. In this way, resilience can be viewed as the life force (necessary) to overcome adversity. (to) heal and to strive towards self-actualisation and flourishing[3].

Experiencing adversity with impaired resilience

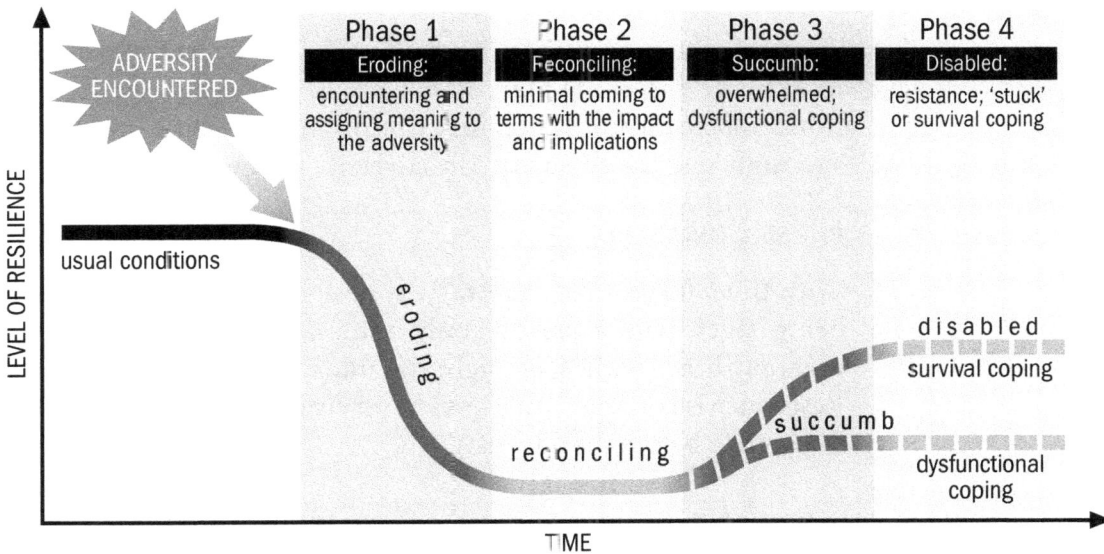

Experiencing adversity with impaired resilience

But what happens if you experience similar adversity without resilience or with impaired resilience? The answer is that you go through a similar process but with fewer positive outcomes.

The graph below 'Experiencing adversity with impaired resilience' shows going through the same adversity as I have discussed but, in this case, with less personal resilience[4]. As with the previous graph, the sequence is more a series of forward and backward spirals over time than a straight line progression.

PHASE 1: ERODING

The first phase is identical for people with all levels of resilience. Unfortunately, resilience does not insulate one from experiencing tough times.

PHASE 2: RECONCILING

For people with limited resilience, however, problems arise when they try to come to terms with adversity, its impact and implications. They struggle to find or assign meaning to what has happened.

PHASE 3: SUCCUMBING

Typically, the person with less resilience feels overwhelmed and, in extreme cases, life loses its meaning. It is very easy for this to translate into dysfunctional coping. In this sense, they have succumbed to the adversity. The adversity has beaten them.

PHASE 4: DISABLED

With time, further recovery may, at best, only lead to a feeling of being 'stuck' with a sense of only minimal coping. Life is still an everyday battle with, seemingly, not much purpose or enjoyment. Resistance is common. This level of survival coping and well-being is less than before the adversity.

Reacting to adversity with different levels of resilience

The following case study highlights the different styles of coping that various individuals in one organisation might display.[5]

Different people — different reactions to adversity

A large and successful manufacturing company was recently experiencing tough times with consumers becoming more discerning, competition becoming fiercer and new competitors appearing in the marketplace, with stakeholders more demanding, skills shortages in critical areas and legal compliance more onerous. The overall impact was that margins were under pressure. In response, top leadership launched several new initiatives to meet the challenges.

The impact on the organisation was to make an already difficult and complex business environment even more pressured. Many people struggled to cope. Team members' close-knit relationships fragmented. Cliques formed. And productivity suffered. On the home front, loving relationships became strained, as employees spent more time at work and struggled to be 'present' when at home.

On the positive side however, there was a group of people who coped with the challenges, and some even seemed to relish meeting and overcoming them. This range of reactions was typified by four members of a team each managing regional sales and administration.

Stella was frequently overwhelmed and reacted in a passive-aggressive manner towards leaders, customers and the organisation. She complained that her job had become too much for her and her life, in general, had lost meaning. She seemed defeated by the demands of her job and home. She was known at work as the whiner and negatively affected her team's output. She drifted at work, was disengaged and uncommitted, only rousing to deal with

urgent issues. Her minimal level of work output only just prevented her losing her job. This type of coping can be labelled *Succumb* or dysfunctional.

Dennis coped sporadically better. His behaviour was characterised by enthusiastic beginnings but, typically, he soon ran out of steam when the going got tough. He blamed others for his problems and came to be regarded as an unreliable performer. His constant refrain was: 'They just don't understand!' He was often found in the coffee area, bemoaning his lot and complaining loudly about how management did not care about the staff. His team members frequently grumbled about his negative attitude and comments. This type of coping is *Disabled* or stuck.

Nona coped better and managed to avoid the high emotions that overwhelmed Stella and Dennis. She was able to curb her anxieties and focus on her job. She commented: "I can't influence the decisions the executives make or what will happen. I do my best and don't worry about the things I can't control. This approach has worked for me in the past, and I am sure it will work for me now". She effectively managed her difficult work-life balance and was generally able to sustain a constant level of performance, throughout the difficulties and changes in the company. Her coping method of tackling the challenges, dealing with issues and moving forward is called *Navigating*.

Thabo's coping was in an enviously different league. He was more than able to navigate the turbulent waters of change – he thrived, with inner strength and resourcefulness. This was reflected by his willingness to learn and his consequent growth and development. He thought that if the company was to survive and he was to keep his job, he had better contribute to enhancing productivity. Despite the pressures, he was able to maintain a sense of enthusiasm and realistic optimism. He had grit and mental toughness. His energy levels, both at work and home, were mostly unaffected. His 'can-do' attitude and contribution to his team were always valued. Through his efforts, the team's output improved and he became a top performer. Personal advancement inevitably followed. His coping is called *Thriving*.

These four different coping levels, together with the different reactions to adversity, are shown in the table below:

The different reactions to adversity	
Succumb: dysfunctional functioning	• Frequently overwhelmed • Passive aggressive • Has little purpose in life and work • Does minimum to keep job
Disabled: survival coping; stuck	• Copes sporadically • Eager beginnings but not sustained • Is quick to blame others • Unreliable performance
Navigating: moving forward; dealing with issues	• Copes under pressure • Has balanced outlook at work • Reconciles work-home balance • Stable performance
Thriving: enhanced resourcefulness and strength	• Growing and developing • Realistically optimistic and enthusiastic • High energy at work and home • Superior performance

Busting the myths about resilience

Despite resilience being a common but powerful ability everyone has, there are many misconceptions about it. Having covered what resilience is, it's important to understand what resilience isn't. These are the myths of resilience.

Myth 1: Resilience is a characteristic that shows up in extraordinary people. It is something you are either born with or not.

This myth probably arises from the press and electronic media publishing heroic examples of people who have risen, dramatically, above their circumstances. We often see on TV talk shows, the evening news or on the internet, examples of people who have been through the most remarkably difficult circumstances and have been able to cope and even thrive.

An example is the story of Callie and Monique Strydom, who were kidnapped in Malaysia by Al Quaeda rebels and who survived four months under the harshest conditions. They were threatened with death every day. They lived on an emotional rollercoaster, as their hopes of rescue were raised, only to be cruelly dashed, time after time. They eventually returned triumphantly to South Africa and established a trust in their names to assist disadvantaged people[6].

Callie and Monique are exceptional individuals who suffered greatly in captivity. It is easy to see how resilient they were over a long time period. When we think of what they went through and compare this with the problems we face, many of our problems pale into insignificance.

Examples of such courage and resilience can, ironically, lead us to despair if we feel we can never be as strong as they were. We can easily conclude that their resilience is a special gift, meant only for extraordinary people.

A wise man adapts himself to circumstances as water shapes itself to the vessel that contains it.

Chinese proverb

The good news is that this belief is totally incorrect. Resilience is a common attribute. Everyone has it. What we do need, however, are the tools and techniques to enhance our resilience, so that we can be resilient in times when we need it most.

Myth 2: Resilient people do not experience as much emotional pain or distress as others.

Everyone has huge wants. We want our loving relationships to be strong and endure. We hate the thought of the people we love aging, becoming infirm and ultimately dying. Parents want the very best for their children and, in particular, for them to grow up resisting the temptations of alcohol, drugs, lawlessness, devious behaviour and illicit sex. At work, we all want our jobs to be secure, to have a boss who treats us well and to be paid fairly. And we want all of this now, all of the time.

However, that's not how life works. Everyone experiences up and downs in life and no matter who you are, life is difficult at times. No matter how much we want something to happen, no matter how hard we work for a particular result, there will be times when we are disappointed, frustrated and let down. This happens to everyone – and resilient people are not exempt.

In addition, bad things happen to good people. Robberies, random violence, car accidents, rape and murder can happen at any time with terrible results and consequences for both victim and family. No matter how many precautions you take, you can't ensure that nothing bad ever happens to you.

When we experience tough times in our lives, when what we earnestly desire and wish for does not come about, it is natural to experience pain and distress. In getting through the pain and distress, resilient people choose to be positive and find joy and happiness in the face of the challenges. They feel the pain as much as anyone else, but their resilience enables them to let go of issues;

not allow negative emotions to leak into all the areas of their lives. They are better able to control their negative self-talk and self-recrimination.

Myth 3: Resilient people are more pessimistic. They have a far better grasp of reality than optimists.

Some people believe that to be resilient you should be pessimistic. In that way you won't be disappointed by what happens in your life.

The truth is that resilient people are more optimistic than pessimistic. They explain tough times and failures to themselves as things that happen to everyone and not just them. In addition, they are better able to compartmentalise their experience of adversity, so that the bad things that happen to them have a limited effect and don't negatively taint all aspects of their life.

Resilient people are realistically optimistic. Having false optimism or being over-optimistic is, of course, dangerous and sets you up to be disappointed. Either by luck of genes at birth or by their own choice, they find hope and look for positive aspects in the situations they face. Importantly, they keep their feet on the ground, with their positive outlook grounded in reality – it's not the 'pie in the sky' type of optimism that sets them up for later disappointment.

> A pessimist sees difficulty in every opportunity; an optimist sees the opportunity in every difficulty
>
> *Winston Churchill*

Now, if you are by nature more pessimistic than optimistic, you may feel disheartened. The good news is that optimism can be developed, and you can train yourself to be more optimistic than you are at present.

Myth 4: Resilient people stay resilient over the passage of time.

Some people think that, if you are resilient, you should be able to remain resilient over long periods of time. Unfortunately, this is not the case. Even resilient people experience down periods in their lives – they experience hardships, setbacks, betrayals and bereavements, just like anyone else. During difficult times, their resilience slips and they too experience the same negative feelings of fear, disappointment, frustration and anger as everyone else.

Resilience is not a magic potion that makes you immune to the problems of life. What sets resilient people apart and makes them resilient, is the way they react to and cope with adversity. Resilient people will say that you should persevere through the tough times, not giving up hope that things will get better. They will tell you that bad times don't last forever. They believe that there are ups as well as downs in life but that the downs come to an end.

Resilient people experience the same bad things and tough times as people who are less resilient. The difference is in the way resilient people cope, which enables them to experience less negative effect and to recover quicker.

Myth 5: Understanding, and developing, your character weaknesses is the key to being resilient.

This myth comes from the belief that a resilient person is 'balanced' and an 'all-rounder'. According to this myth, if you can understand you weaknesses and what's wrong with yourself, you can then work on those defects and make them strengths, and that will lead to resilience.

Talent is commonly developed at the expense of character.

Ralph Waldo Emerson

The myth has its origins in the school system and extends to business and almost all walks of life. The outcome of the myth is the belief that time and effort should be spent understanding and developing skills, knowledge and personality deficit areas in order to make them strengths. This common belief is deeply flawed. First, it's extremely difficult, if not impossible, to develop all one's skills, knowledge and character strengths to an equally high level. Second, when coping with adversity it is always a lot easier to use your natural character strengths, rather than trying to use your weaknesses.

Another way of understanding why this is a myth is to consider your life's purpose. Many people believe that they have been given a purpose in life, even though it's not always easy to fully understand or discover it. If that is true, then it follows that you must also have been provided with the wherewithal to achieve this purpose. It simply would not make sense to be given a life purpose but not be given the wherewithal to fulfil it. The tools you have for fulfilling your life's task, are in the form of your particular character strength combinations. Understanding and using your character strengths is the key to fulfilling your purpose in life, rather than understanding, trying to develop and using your weaknesses.

When we use our strengths we feel effortless, work is easy and enjoyable and time seems to stand still. We experience real fulfilment and upliftment. Using weaknesses, on the other hand, is a totally different experience. Work is heavy, difficult and tiresome and we are often left feeling tired and depressed.

Resilient people cope with adversity by using their natural character strengths. This enables them to recover, heal, grow, develop and move on with their lives.

Myth 6: Resilience is enhanced by rigorously thinking about your problems and difficulties.

This myth has as its origin the belief that, in order to solve a problem or deal with an unhappy situation, we need to thoroughly understand all aspects of it. In other words, the better we understand the problem, the better we are able to deal with it. While this is generally true in most situations, a specific myth about resilience has developed from it.

The myth arises in the belief that frequent rehashing and rethinking about the circumstances and events of what made you unhappy, and not resilient, will enable you to become happy and resilient. The problem is that this process leads to reliving the problem in your mind, which results in experiencing the negative emotions and helplessness all over again.

Rumination can lead to increasing the negative emotions and to negative, downward-spiralling thoughts and emotions.

This type of thinking pattern is called rumination. Rumination[7] is the constant reliving of unhappy events and conversations, feeling the associated negative emotions all over again. It dwells on the problem and feelings, rather than the solution.

Resilient people are able to break out of negative spirals of ruminative thinking. They do this by reframing the negative experience, then going on to what can be done to cope and deal with the adversity.

Resilience, grit and hardiness

Resilience has received increasing attention from researchers and scientists over the past few years. This has made it possible to differentiate the concept of resilience from that of grit and hardiness. Resilience is an adaptive process involving thoughts, feelings and actions in response to difficult or even life changing circumstances.

Both grit and hardiness are personality traits, and both are difficult to acquire.

This is different from grit, which is the ability to persevere with passion to reach long-term goals[8]. A related concept is that of hardiness. Hardiness concerns the courage and motivation to change significant challenges into successes[9].

What's important for us is that resilience is not a fixed personality trait. It involves a process that can be learnt. While everyone is resilient to some extent, most people would like to be more resilient. To get through difficult and challenging times quicker and easier.

You can do this by enhancing your resilience through applying the tools and techniques outlined in this book. In so doing, you may also improve your grit and hardiness.

Exercises

Here's an exercise to start enhancing your resilience. We all have to deal with ups and downs on our life's journey. You have, no doubt, been severely tested and, eventually, have triumphed. Spend some time undertaking the written exercise below, ensuring that you write out your answers in full.

Your diligence in completing this exercise will be rewarded by an appreciation of how resilience has already worked well for you in your life. You will find that you have been resilient in the past and the challenge, now, is to boost and reinforce your resilience capability to deal with day-to-day difficulties as well as with severe adversity.

Written exercise: Learning from an adversity you overcame

Think of the time when you overcame an adversity. Choose a fairly severe adversity from your life at work or at home, but which you overcame and triumphed. Write down your answers to the following questions in your workbook or journal:

1. What was the adversity?

2. What were you thinking and feeling at the time of the adversity?
3. What information did you have and what did you need?
4. What got you through the experience?

When you have completed this exercise, reflect on the answers that you have written down, and ask yourself the concluding question:

5. What did you learn from this adversity?

ENDNOTES

1 Adapted from: Warner, R.B. 2007. Staying the course: building personal resilience for successful organisational change. *Convergence,* 8(2):20–23.

2 Based on: Meichenbaum, D. 2005. Understanding resilience in children and adults: implications for prevention and interventions (paper delivered at the Melissa Institute Ninth Annual Conference on Resilience), and Patterson, J.L. & Kelleher, P. 2005. *Resilient School Leaders: Strategies for Turning Adversity into Achievement.* ASCD.

3 Reivich, K. & Shatte, A. 2002. *The Resilience Factor: 7 Essential Skills for Overcoming Life's Inevitable Obstacles.* New York: Broadway Books.

4 See reference 1.

5 Adapted from: Warner, R.B. 2009. Coping with resilience in tough times. *Management Today,* February.

6 Sourced from: http://www.strydomtrust.com. Accessed on 1 September 2011.

7 Nolen-Hoeksema, S., Wisco, B.E. & Lyubomirsky, S. 2008. Rethinking rumination. *Perspectives on psychological science,* 3:400–424.

8 Duckworth, A.L., Peterson, C., Matthews, M.D. & Kelly, D.R. 2007. Grit: Perseverance and passion for long-term goals. *Personality processes and individual differences,* 92(6):1087.

9 Maddi, S.R. 2006. Hardiness: The courage to grow from stresses. *Journal of positive psychology,* 1:160–168.

2

Building Resilience: blocks, principles and steps

In order to better understand the concept of resilience in adults, I did some research.

I was initially delighted with the amount of academic research that has, to date, been done in this field. There is a great deal of material about soldiers who return home with post-traumatic stress disorder and who experience difficulty in returning to civilian life and finding gainful employment.

There is lot of information about how immigrant ethnic groups struggle to cope with new cultural environments.

There is also an impressive number of publications concerning children coping with dismal schooling and poor housing environments in inner-city ghettos, and their challenges in not succumbing to gangsterism and drugs.

And there's a staggering amount of literature published about how people cope after having been diagnosed with mental disorders ranging from mild depression to other serious conditions.

The missing perspective on resilience

Unfortunately, all this research did not help me to find what I was seeking. I was specifically interested in adults rather than in children, and my particular focus was on adults coping with adversity at home and at work.

I was interested in adults who had suffered their normal share of life's troubles and traumas and who had sufficiently recovered from them to be able to function in a work environment. These adults were ordinary folk who were employed and were able to hold down jobs in spite of what they had encountered in their life journey.

What I had in mind was that if I could better understand the factors that helped ordinary people deal with organisational stresses, in addition to the life difficulties that everyone goes through, then, perhaps, I would find and develop tools and techniques to help them cope during really tough times, as well as during day-to-day hassles.

I did not want to focus my attention on how those who were not coping could be helped to return to their base-level coping before their troubles had started. Instead, I wanted to understand not only how resilience enables people to 'bounce back' but, in particular, how it enables people to 'bounce higher'. I was interested in how resilience enables people to grow and thrive in the face of adversity and live a life of joy and happiness despite the tough times that everyone has to go through[1].

Our greatest glory is not in never falling but in rising every time we fall.

Confucius

Researching resilience

To address this missing perspective on resilience, I carried out interviews with 76 people. The people interviewed were, with one exception, all employed, and were drawn from seven organisations. I used a technique called 'critical incident' interviewing, which lasted for two or three hours, as well as focus group sessions, lasting about an hour each.

The interviewing technique entailed asking people to tell me a story about when they had faced adversity, firstly outlining the background and the circumstances that led to the situation. I then asked what they did to deal with the adversity, including their thoughts and feelings. Finally, I asked for the outcome of their actions. Each of these stories, or critical incidents, was carefully recorded. In this way I obtained a total of 822 critical incident stories that fitted the criteria of having a clearly described background, action taken, and an outcome.

I rewrote each of the stories on a separate piece of paper, which I then sorted into piles on my study floor, grouping them by aspects they had in common. Initially I found about twenty groups – which was too many. Finally, I reduced the piles down to just seven groups, with clear conceptual boundaries between them. I then used focus groups to check the accuracy of the groups.

My next step was to systematically summarize the characteristics and elements of each group. This helped me see how the seven groups could be categorized into three major areas. In this way, I classified the 822 critical incidents into three major areas (Domains), seven categories (Constructs), with a total of 35 sub-categories (Elements).

At this point I was very excited. I felt that I'd had a breakthrough in my understanding of resilience.

I had distilled the elements of resilience from what people had experienced and told me, rather than what I thought resilience to be. Most important, this insight came from ordinary people who had coped with a range of adversities in their lives, from dealing with day-to-day hassles to extraordinary, heart-wrenching traumas. In essence, the identification of the elements of resilience was based on real experiences, rather than on theory.

The people I had interviewed confirmed what researchers had found[2]. Resilience is a *process* that you go through[3]. It's not a fixed personality trait[4]. The exciting implication was that resilience could be developed using the outcome of my research.

The building blocks of resilience

The code below refers to the information below the diagram.

Qualities as building blocks of personal resilience

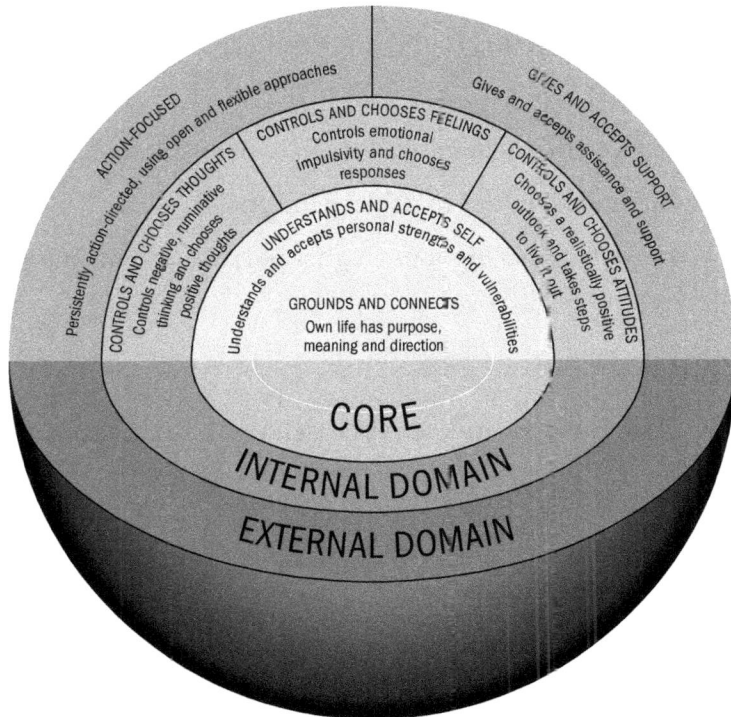

- ACTION-FOCUSED — Persistently action-directed, using open and flexible approaches
- CONTROLS AND CHOOSES THOUGHTS — Controls negative, ruminative thinking and chooses positive thoughts
- CONTROLS AND CHOOSES FEELINGS — Controls emotional impulsivity and chooses responses
- GIVES AND ACCEPTS SUPPORT — Gives and accepts assistance and support
- CONTROLS AND CHOOSES ATTITUDES — Chooses a realistically positive outlook and takes steps to live it out
- UNDERSTANDS AND ACCEPTS SELF — Understands and accepts personal strengths and vulnerabilities
- GROUNDS AND CONNECTS — Own life has purpose, meaning and direction
- CORE
- INTERNAL DOMAIN
- EXTERNAL DOMAIN

> ⊙ The *Core Domain* consists of connecting to one's life purpose and meaning, as well as understanding and accepting one's self.
>
> ▣ The *Internal Domain* refers to the internal world of thoughts, feelings and attitudes.
>
> ◈ The *External Domain* involves taking action and giving and accepting support.

The *Constructs* and their associated *Elements* are detailed on pages 26–29, where the elements refer to attributes associated with resilient individuals.

⊙ Grounds and connects

Definition: Own life has purpose, meaning and direction

ELEMENTS:

- Feels own life has meaning
- Has life goals
- Feels connected to significant issues, such as people; causes; faith
- Takes incremental activities to achieve life goals
- Reframes adversity as having some higher purpose and meaning.

⊙ Understands and accepts self

Definition: Understands and accepts personal strengths and vulnerabilities

ELEMENTS:

- Understands own strengths
- Understands own vulnerabilities
- Accepts own capabilities and limits
- Draws strength from having overcome previous adversities
- Accepts self.

▣ Controls and chooses thoughts

Definition: Controls negative, ruminative thinking and chooses positive thoughts

ELEMENTS:

- Is aware when persistent and strong negative thoughts occur
- Able to stop persistent and negative thinking when it occurs
- Redirects negative thinking to positive thinking

- Identifies and avoids the thinking which triggers persistent negative thoughts
- Strives to be in harmony with thoughts.

▣ Controls and chooses feelings

Definition: Controls emotional impulsivity and chooses responses

ELEMENTS:

- Quickly aware of own strong emotional feelings when they are experienced
- Controls own strong emotional feelings
- Expresses strong emotional feelings in ways that others understand and accept
- When experiencing strong emotional feelings, is able to choose actions and behaviours rationally, rather than being driven by emotions
- When experiences strong emotional feelings, takes action to deal with the issue/s.

▣ Controls and chooses attitudes

Definition: Chooses a realistically positive outlook and takes steps to live it out

ELEMENTS:

- Believes can influence own life's direction
- Believes own personal problems can be solved
- Chooses to be positive rather than negative
- Chooses to be realistically optimistic
- Engages in enjoyable, relaxing and recharging activities.

◈ Action–focused

Definition: Persistently action-directed, using open and flexible approaches

ELEMENTS:

- Determined to deal with issues and solve problems
- Persistently seeks solutions
- Tries out different approaches to solving problems
- Listens to people with different views when problem solving.
- Takes considered risks.

◈ Gives and accepts support

Definition: Gives and accepts assistance and support

ELEMENTS:

- Shares own emotional state with trusted others
- Easily accepts assistance and support
- Sensitive to the feelings, needs and motivations of others
- Responds sensitively to the feelings of others, by acknowledging and showing understanding
- Easily gives assistance and support.

A potential criticism of this research method is that it focused only on what I was told by the people I interviewed. It dealt exclusively with their behavioural response to the adversity. The critical incident method did not allow for speculation on, for example, the influence of childhood encouragement, or deprivations, on the development of their resilience.

Rather than being a weakness, I regarded it as ideal for my purposes. It allowed me to identify the behaviours people use in the face of adversity. Behaviours are, fortunately, almost always able to be developed by training and practice, and thus can be taught to people wanting to enhance their resilience.

Development of the Building Resilience workshop

Having created a new understanding of the behavioural building blocks, or competencies, of resilience, I then researched and developed a range of tools and techniques to train people in each of the constructs. I presented these in the form of a training workshop, called Building Resilience. I conducted the workshop for organisations that had people who wanted to be able to deal with adversity more effectively and who also wanted to thrive in the face of organisational and life pressures.

The workshops were extremely well received. On asking delegates whether the tools and techniques taught could be applied immediately in their home and work lives, every single delegate, without exception, replied in the affirmative. I asked delegates to rate their experience of the workshop on the scale of one (low) to five (high). The ratings averaged 4.8.

Some even commented that the experience of the workshop was so profound that it would change the way they lived their lives.

But I was concerned that, although the participants left the workshop very motivated, their enthusiasm might wane over the subsequent weeks and months. I then conducted a follow-up with randomly chosen delegates three months after the workshop to see whether the effect of what they had learned still persisted. I was very happy to find a significant enhancement in how they rated themselves against the constructs, three months after the workshop, compared to before the workshop.

Development of the Building Resilience principles and steps

While running the resilience workshops, I asked for and received much feedback on how they could be improved. This led to many incremental improvements for which I am extremely grateful.

One common thread of feedback was that the Domains, Constructs and Elements were perceived as academic and not very intuitive. Delegates said that they were not really interested in the academic aspects of resilience, but were much more interested in practical ways they could improve their own resilience.

The relevance of the Building Resilience principles and steps is that they can assist you to cope with the turbulence created by significant difficulty and change, and foster your ability to recover.

I realised I needed to make the terms more approachable and applicable to everyday life. And so I created principles from the constructs. These principles are the enduring *behavioural attributes* needed to be resilient. I also identified four steps to being resilient, which refer to the *behavioural process* of being resilient in the moment.

The principles and steps together serve as the framework for developing and applying resilience in times of adversity.

In addition, the principles and steps help to build buffering capacity during good times and which can be called on in tough times.

What follows is an overview of the Building Resilience principles, followed by a description of the Building Resilience steps.

Building Resilience principles

Personal resilience building blocks

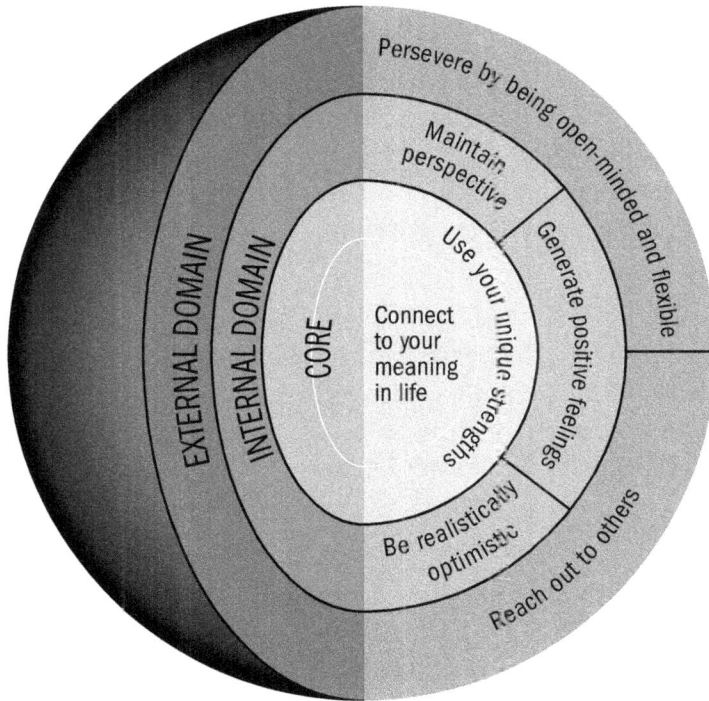

1. Connect to your meaning in life

We have all wrestled with the question of what gives meaning and purpose to our lives and, for many, this search continues throughout their lives. The humdrum issues of paying bills, resolving work problems, completing chores around the home, and so on, easily distract us from the focus of living an authentic life. In times of adversity, this connection to your meaning in life comes into sharp focus as it directly relates to the issue of what drives you to persevere, rather than to just give up.

Building Resilience principles	
1.	Connect to your meaning in life.
2.	Use your unique strengths.
3.	Maintain perspective.
4.	Generate positive feelings.
5.	Be realistically optimistic.
6.	Persevere by being open-minded and flexible.
7.	Reach out to others.

My research on resilience established that meaning is typically found in one or more of three categories of significance – people, causes and faith.

A strong sense of meaning is the bedrock from which coping, healing, and renewal after adversity is made possible.

SIGNIFICANT PEOPLE

These were most often children and partners, for whom there was deep caring and love, and which was expressed in the desire to show them love; to provide for them; to live up to their expectations and to set an example; or simply not let them down.

SIGNIFICANT CAUSES

These were diverse. The examples given by people I interviewed included de-oiling penguins; raising funds to sustain a shelter for homeless people; adopting an AIDS orphan, and preserving indigenous fynbos in the Western Cape.

SIGNIFICANT FAITH

This was frequently cited and examples ranged from formal religion, with a powerfully felt, deep personal relationship with their Creator, to a less formal feeling of connection to the Universe and the interrelatedness of life, which also gave strong feelings of meaning to life.

In the face of adversity, the personal meaning assigned to living sustains and provides the motivation to persevere. This connection and personal belief system was sometimes expressed as knowing the adversity had a higher purpose or meaning, even if that purpose was not clear at the time. For example, on the death of his child, a young father said: 'I don't know why this happened, but I do know that there is a reason for everything. So I have to accept it and carry on.'

This principle of resilience, *Connect to your meaning in life*, also incorporates the belief that, by persevering through the adversity and tough times, you will emerge stronger, more resourceful and better for the experience. For example, 'special children have special parents' was the mantra-like, encouraging phrase used by a family for coping with severe financial and emotional demands in rearing children with learning difficulties.

Developing life goals related to one's meaning is also an important strategy to strengthen this principle in one's life.

2. Use your unique strengths

Self-knowledge emerged as an important component of resilience in the interviews I conducted.

Character strengths are different, compared to job strengths: the former are life-long whereas job strengths are specific and change with circumstances. Unfounded beliefs about character strengths and vulnerabilities can potentially hinder or even derail action to recover from adversity.

> Realistic self-insight into one's own character strengths and vulnerabilities is the basis for understanding one's capabilities and limits when dealing with adversity.

People describe doing things that draw on their strengths as being light, easy, fun and obvious. Using our natural character strengths to solve problems, devise creative solutions and reach out to others during adversity comes easily to us, and may even be experienced as joyful.

People attending the Building Resilience training workshops often struggle to identify their strengths, whereas they can easily reel off a list of their weaknesses or 'development areas'. Ironically, they frequently report having tried to improve their weaknesses for many years, often with slow or even no

> Realistic self-insight into one's own character strengths and vulnerabilities is the basis for understanding one's capabilities and limits when dealing with adversity.

progress. They frequently downplay their character strengths, on the other hand, explaining that acknowledging and deliberately focusing on them feels like boasting. This lack of balance is unfortunate because, logically, there should be greater success using natural strengths (rather than weaknesses) in coping with adversity.

Developing awareness of and correcting one's weaknesses to a minimum level of competence will, at best, prevent failure. Developing and using character strengths, on the other hand, has the potential to create personal excellence. Using character strengths is uplifting and forms part of the foundation for living a fulfilling and joyful life.

3. Maintain perspective

Abigail described her ruminating negative thought pattern as being 'like in a washing machine … going round and round … then pausing …. and then going round and round again, on and on'.

Maintaining perspective concerns the inner world of your thoughts. It is particularly important because, as a species, we are programmed from our past to be more alert for negative than positive environments. This negative focus was very useful in providing narrow focus when confronted by a sabre-toothed lion or marauding tribes on the veld of ancient Africa. But it is less helpful in finding creative solutions to modern adversities, which require open, creative and flexible thinking. In today's world, this ancient negative bias sometimes intrudes into our lives as unwelcome, strong and persistent negative thoughts.

To build resilience, negative thinking and persistent negative self-talk need to be reframed. This can be done by finding alternative ways of thinking about the problem or event, such as how you can learn from it, or how you can accept it. Other ways of reframing are to choose milder and less calamitous ways of expressing the adversity. Or, to change the statements that run through your mind into questions, and then to focus your thoughts on finding answers to the questions.

Some people find that changing their behaviour changes their negative thought bias and thinking patterns. Examples include exercising; talking with supportive friends; eating a favourite food such as chocolate or ice-cream; shopping; going to movies; reading a novel; partying. Not all these activities will reduce everyone's negative thinking: the challenge is to find what works for you. The outcome should be distraction from the stress of the adversity, recharging energy and then returning with renewed vigour to deal with the stress and difficulties.

It is also useful, where possible, to avoid or minimise situations which trigger persistent negative thoughts. Examples I have been given include particular events: a stressful monthly family get-together; interactions with certain people (negative colleagues or difficult clients) and avoiding negative physical conditions (tiredness and being hungry). Alternatively, challenging negativism in others, such as negative statements or opinions that are unfounded, biased, or open to interpretation, may also be a useful way of controlling one's own negative thoughts in order to maintain perspective.

People who have been trained in mindfulness techniques say the process is very useful in coping with their negative thoughts. They say that they are more accepting and in harmony with their thinking, when they practise observing their thoughts in a non-judgemental way and not reacting to them.

4. Generate positive feelings

Adversity typically involves strong negative emotions, which have the potential to hijack rational thought and so reduce resilience. Fear, anger, guilt and grief are commonly experienced during the dark night of significant adversity. These negative emotions are associated with surges in adrenaline and cortisol (the stress hormone) which prepare the body for the life-preserving fight, flight or freeze responses. In modern times, however, the associated physical reactions are seldom useful and if experienced over a prolonged period, can be harmful.

Negative feelings are, in themselves, not 'bad' as they convey important messages about the severity of the adversity. In excess, however, they can lead to substantially reduced mental and even physical functioning and the ability to deal with the adversity: thinking and decision-making become impaired; sleeping, eating and relaxing become difficult.

Some simple strategies to deal with strong, personal, negative emotions include deep breathing, taking time out, positive self-talk and meditation.

Controlling negative feelings is the first step; generating positive feelings, needed for resilience in order to bounce back, is the next.

Resilience in the face of gangsterism

The need to keep perspective and to control strong negative feelings was highlighted by a single parent, the mother of a ten-year-old son, who was living in a gang-infested part of the Cape Flats area of Cape Town. She described her son as having been an ideal child, doing well at school, having good friends, attending church with her and helping out in their small apartment.

Then, with a sinking heart, she one day realized that her son's behaviour had changed. He was missing school and mixing with a different group of friends. She discovered he was a runner in the sale of drugs. She was both furious and terrified.

She first tried screaming and punishing the boy. That didn't work. Then she tried shaming him. That also didn't work.

Finally, when she had mastered her emotions to the point that she could deal with the situation rationally, she sought help from his school officials. With their help, she eventually managed to get him back into school where she and the teachers now kept a close watch on his daily activities.

5. Be realistically optimistic

The principle of being realistically optimistic to build personal resilience concerns choosing to live with a positive attitude. This positive attitude should be realistic, however, as being over-optimistic, or having optimism that is not based in reality, usually results in unrealistic expectations that, ultimately, result in disappointment when they are not fulfilled.

At the heart of this principle is the strong belief that you can, to a large extent, influence the direction of your life and that the inevitable problems encountered along life's journey can be solved. This construct echoes Viktor Frankl's thoughts and logotherapy concepts: '...everything can be taken from a man but one thing – the last of the human freedoms – to choose one's attitude in any given set of circumstances, to choose one's own way'[5]. Resilience thus entails choosing to be positive rather than negative.

> '...everything can be taken from a man but one thing – the last of the human freedoms – to choose one's attitude in any given set of circumstances, to choose one's own way'

We all tell ourselves stories about ourselves to make sense of our experiences of life. Researchers call this our 'explanatory style'[6]. These stories have the power to mould and ultimately define who we are. The stories we tell ourselves create ourselves. Optimists view the good things they experience as permanent and affecting everything, whereas the bad things they experience are perceived as temporary and having limited effect on their overall lives.

Some people are born more optimistic than others, but the good news is that realistic optimism can be enhanced, and so you do not need to be stuck in the mind-set of persistently seeing doom and gloom.

6. Persevere by being open-minded and flexible

Dealing with adversity inevitably requires some action, or some change, to cope with and address difficult circumstances. Perseverance is the key.

Resilience in dealing with adversity requires open-mindedness and a flexible, problem-solving approach, allowing for listening, consideration of differing views and being open to a change of tactics or even strategy.

Perseverance is, however, a double-edged sword. On one hand, too little perseverance means we succumb to, or become disabled by, adversity. We have all experienced how easy, and even tempting, it is, during really tough times, to surrender to inactivity, stupor and defeat and even give up entirely.

An excess of perseverance, on the other hand, can result in a blinkered and bull-headed approach, characterised by a fixed mind-set, minimal listening, tunnel vision and using brute force to deal with adversity. In such cases, it is often 'action taken for the sake of action'. There is little or no time for creative thinking or reflection. In this way, both too much and too little perseverance can lead to poor decisions, which create their own unintended negative consequences.

7. Reach out to others

'Other people matter' is the pithy finding of noted psychology researchers Christopher Peterson, Jane Dutton, Kim Cameron and others.[7] [8] This concept especially applies to dealing with adversity. So the seventh and last principle in building resilience is: Reach out to others.

This principle has two components – reaching out to others *to ask* for help, and reaching out to others *to offer* help.

Asking for help is often difficult to do. For people who have a socialised 'cowboys-don't-cry' attitude, even the idea of admitting to having a problem can be very threatening, never mind actually asking for help.

Males, in general, seem to have more difficulty than females when it comes to asking for help. In addition, and again as a generalisation, the more senior a person is in the organisational hierarchy, the more difficult it is to ask for help. This may be because asking for and accepting assistance may be perceived as a weakness or demonstration of not being up to the task and a sign of not coping.

As a consequence of these fears, we may err on the side of delay in asking for help thereby, possibly, allowing the problem to get worse. Like most difficult conversations, however, it is better to have the conversation sooner rather than later.

On the other hand, offering and giving support and assistance to others is usually an easier conversation than asking for help. This is particularly the case in a work context, if one's role requires mentoring and coaching. There is a payoff for the person giving the support, as assisting others in need boosts the giver's resilience, even in cases when the giver is experiencing adversity themselves.

Building Resilience steps

As has been outlined, the Building Resilience principles are the enduring *attributes* you need to be resilient in the face of adversity. By contrast, the four Building Resilience steps are the *questions* that need to be asked and answered, in the heat of the moment, when your emotional and physical well-being is threatened by adversity. The steps are interrelated and are as applicable when persistent everyday hassles threaten to overwhelm as when significant adversity occurs.

The steps apply to dealing, in the moment, with a specific challenge such as when a taxi in front of you stops in the middle of a busy intersection for passengers to disembark, or when the bank calls to tell you that yet another of your applications for a housing loan has been turned down.

The steps also apply to dealing with more pervasive challenges, such as those potentially life-changing conversations. For example, when your partner says: 'I need more freedom in our relationship ...' or when one of your offspring says: 'I have decided to stop studying and tour overseas in a band ...' or when your employer says: 'Thanks for the long service that you have given the company over the past years, but ...'.

Building Resilience steps
1. What do I really, really want?
2. What thoughts and feelings will assist me?
3. How can I keep perspective?
4. How can I persevere and reach out?

Step 1: What do I really, *really* want?

The first thing to do when encountering a situation which makes your heart hammer and your eyes grow large is to pause. Not to react immediately. Except in the face of a physical threat, such as encountering a bush fire, a quick response is frequently one you will later regret. This is because a quick response is often an automatic response, coming from deep within that part of the brain which deals with the threats that our species faced, such as encountering animals looking for an easy meal. In those situations, where a quick physical reaction was vital for survival, the amygdalia in our brain determined our physical reaction: fight, flight or freeze. Powerful chemicals, such as the hormones adrenaline and cortisol, instantly flooded our bloodstreams to give our muscles the strength we needed to save ourselves from the physical threat.

Do not react immediately.

The physical and mental changes created by threat, that we are hard-wired to experience, are not particularly useful today.

Unfortunately, this hormonal flooding still occurs in our modern world and it comes at a cost. If the hormones are not used up in physical action, they remain in the bloodstream and create wear and tear on organs in our bodies. They create high physical alertness which depletes energy and leaves you trembling and exhausted. After a shock, for example, hand tremor, shortness of breath, and raised level of alertness are commonly experienced, together with elevated blood pressure and an enhanced risk of stroke.

Associated with this physical survival response, in the face of a threat, is a mental survival response. This narrows your focus. In the face of suddenly encountering a threat such as a fire or a mugger, a narrowed focus cuts out extraneous things and enables you to see only the physical threat and to give it your undivided attention. Awareness of the minor details in the environment is sacrificed for the life-saving, intense and narrow focus on the threat and personal safety[9].

Like the state of elevated physical alertness, this narrow focus is frequently inappropriate in modern business and in personal life crisis situations, which call for cognitive solutions typically requiring lateral thinking, creativity and innovation.

So how can you be resilient and deal with the hard-wiring in your brain that drives you to respond in this powerfully primitive manner?

ASK THESE QUESTIONS

- The first step is to ask: 'What do I really, *really* want to achieve from this situation?'
- At a deeper level, ask: 'How can this situation help me reach my life goals?' This question echoes back to the Building Resilience principles: *Connect to your meaning in life* and *Use your unique strengths.*

Simply asking yourself the primary question will have the effect of creating a pause or space, so that the immediate response that comes to mind can be checked, to see if it is, indeed, the response that you wish to make. Trying to identify what it is that you *really* want takes you back to your values and what is important to you from a long-term perspective. In an argument with a loving partner, for example, do you want to win, or do you want to deepen your relationship? In conflicts with your offspring, do you want to prove you are right, or have your children take responsibility for their actions?

Asking what you really, *really* want is thus the first step in breaking the quick response cycle of escalating argument and hostility. Answering this question gets to the core of what is important to you and helps identify your real objective. It also breaks the focus on what is wrong and shifts it to the goals you would like to achieve.

Step 2: How can I keep perspective?

This step is related to the Building Resilience principle: *Maintain perspective*. In stressful situations, negative thoughts and narrow thinking are associated with a reduction in positive feelings, which are literally squeezed out by the more powerful negative feelings.

The world becomes bleak. It's easy to slip into a downward spiral of negative thinking. This is humorously portrayed on a plaque, half-way up the long and arduous trail of the Hex mountain range, before the starting overnight hut on the Wit Els kloofing trail:

The way is long and getting longer
The road goes uphill all the way,
and even farther.
I wish you luck. You will need it.
The way is dark and getting darker
The hut is high, and even higher
I wish you luck
There is none.

Adapted from *The 13 Clocks* by James Thurber

Experiencing fear, anxiety and strong negative thoughts is a common reaction to being confronted by a significantly stressful situation. The problem with negative thoughts, and the associated narrow thinking, is that it shuts out and excludes the type of broad thinking required for flexibility and the exploration of alternatives.

Our perspective is the result of a choice we make and can thus be changed.

BENEFITS OF POSITIVE THOUGHTS

Positive thoughts and feelings have many benefits[10]. We become

- more open to possibilities

- more creative

- more expansive in our thinking

- better at learning new skills

- better at building personal networks.

This, in turn, initiates upward spiralling patterns of positive achievement followed by good feelings, which further enables growth and development.

Step 3: What feelings and attitudes will assist me?

This step is related to the Building Resilience principles: *Generate positive feelings* and *Be realistically optimistic*.

We can't choose the emotions we experience, but we can choose how we respond to them. In particular, we can choose not to allow ourselves to feed into our negative feelings This prevents spirals of increasing negative emotion.

When it is dark enough, you can see the stars.
Ralph Waldo Emerson

Positive emotions, on the other hand, have a welcome physiological effect. They actually change body chemistry, which enables the upward spiralling thought patterns. This biological impact extends even to enabling positive thinkers to live longer[11].

Optimists view the good things they experience as permanent and affecting everything, whereas the bad things they experience are perceived as temporary and having limited effect on their overall lives.

Some people are born more optimistic than others but, fortunately, realistic optimism can be developed. So you do not need to be stuck with the mind-set of persistently seeing doom and gloom. One of the ways of enhancing optimism is to reframe the adversity to find what can be learned from it or what you will do differently next time.

We tell ourselves stories about ourselves to make sense of our experiences of life. These stories mould and ultimately define who we are and, in this way, the stories we tell ourselves continually create and recreate ourselves. Changing the story you tell yourself, enables you to choose a more balanced and positive outlook on life. Negative thinking becomes more balanced which, in turn, leads to feeling more positive. Ultimately your outlook will become more optimistic. It even works for people who are naturally inclined to be pessimistic.

Changing the story you tell yourself, enables you to choose a more balanced and positive outlook on life

Adopting and maintaining a realistic and optimistic perspective is both a strong way of thinking and an attitude. Both of these can be learned. The benefits of deliberately maintaining a positive and optimistic outlook are profound. People who regularly practise balancing perspective exercises report enhanced optimism, positivity, energy and connectedness[12].

Step 4: How can I persevere and reach out?

Having dealt with the issues of the heart and head, and maintaining an appropriate perspective when confronted with challenging times, we can now turn to dealing with the actual adversity. This involves perseverance and reaching out to others. This step has its origins in Building Resilience principles: *Persevere by being open-minded and flexible* and *Reach out to others.*

Perseverance is necessary to deal with changed circumstances and tough times. Logically, resilience seems to imply you need to guard against giving up too soon, or being overwhelmed in the face of great difficulties. The reality, however, is somewhat more subtle. A special kind of perseverance is needed, which is characterised by open-mindedness and flexibility. This is different from the type of bull-headed, 'full speed ahead and damn the torpedoes' persistence, which involves resolute drive, power and tenacity.

To be open-minded and yet have perseverance almost sounds like a contradiction. The following paragraphs explain my point.

To be resilient, you must

- be open to new ways of doing things
- embrace different ways of dealing with problems
- employ active listening
- seek differing views and be open to a change of tactics or even strategy.

The other part of this step is that of reaching out to others. This has two aspects to it:

- Reaching out to *ask for help*
- Reaching out to *offer help.*

The problem people often face, when asking for help, is that of their pride and being uncomfortable with 'owing favours'. This difficulty is often felt more strongly the higher up the person is in the organisational hierarchy. Yet most people say that when they finally pluck up the courage to ask for help, they are overwhelmed by the generosity of the responses they receive.

Offering help is often easier, particularly in an organisational context, where work roles require giving help. In these cases, managers of staff may find it easier to counsel and mentor others than to ask for help themselves.

Perseverance and reaching out both require a shift in focus away from the adversity itself to the changed circumstances it creates and the action that is required. This, inevitably, necessitates staying focused on your goals and solutions. It calls for risk-taking, action orientation and taking incremental steps towards your goal.

Thriving in the face of life's challenges

While no-one chooses to experience tough times and adversity, dealing with them 'successfully' does have an upside. Personal growth and development occurs most when one is in unfamiliar territory, when comfort levels are breached, when one is out of one's depth and struggling. Adversity creates such an environment and a resilient response enables growth, development and even life-enhancing change to take place.

In this context, resilience is the life-force by which we can overcome adversity, and strive towards being the best we can be.

The principles and steps will help you to build resilience in order to deal with the tough times and changes we all face. They are as applicable for dealing with a stressful situation in the moment as they are for dealing with prolonged adversity. The principles and steps will assist you to build inner resources and buffering capacity during the good times, which can be called on in times of stress and challenge.

The personal benefit for us in being resilient is that we have the inner strength and resourcefulness to absorb 'the slings and arrows of outrageous fortune' and live a joyful life.

But can I improve my resilience – really?

The answer is a resounding *yes*. My research, as well as the research of others, has conclusively demonstrated that the innate skills relating to each of the seven building resilience principles can be developed and enhanced by using the resilience-building tools described in this book. These tools have been used successfully by individuals, by teams at work, by partners in loving relationships as well as by parents with their children.

The next chapter contains a questionnaire to help you assess your personal resilience. Complete the questionnaire before reading about the principles and embarking on the exercises to enhance them. Once you have this benchmark, you will be able to return to it at the end of the handbook and to compare your new level of resilience to what it is now. You will be delighted with the increase in your resilience.

ENDNOTES

1 Strumpfer, D.J.W. 2003. Resilience and burn out: A stitch that could save nine. *South African journal of psychology,* 33(2):69–79.

2 Masten, A.S. 2009. Ordinary Magic: Lessons from research on resilience in human development. *Education Canada,* 49(3):28–32.

3 Rutter, M. 2008. Developing concepts in developmental psychopathology. *In* J.J. Hudziak (ed.). Developmental psychopathology and wellness: Genetic and environmental influences (p. 3–22). Washington, DC: American Psychiatric Publishing.

4 Luthar, S.S., Cicchetti, D. & Becker, B. 2000. The construct of resilience: A critical evaluation and guidelines for future work. *Child development,* 71(3):543–562.

5 Frankl, V.E. 1982. *Man's search for meaning.* Washington: Square Press.

6 Seligman, M. 2006. *Learned optimism: How to change your mind and your life.* New York City: Random House.

7 Peterson, C. 2004. Positive social science. *Annals of the American Academy of Political and Social Science.* 591:186–201.

8 Park, N. & Peterson, C. 2009. Achieving and sustaining a good life. *Perspectives on psychological science,* 4:422–428.

9 Fredrickson, B. 2009. *Positivity: Groundbreaking research reveals how to embrace the hidden strength of positive emotions, overcome negativity, and thrive.* New York: Crown Books.

10 Fredrickson, B. 2001. The role of positive emotions in positive psychology: The broaden-and-build theory of positive emotions. *American psychologist,* 56:218–226.

11 Fredrickson, B. 2003. The value of positive emotions: The emerging science of positive psychology is coming to understand why it's good to feel good. *American scientist,* 91:330–335.

12 See reference 3.

3

Personal resilience questionnaire

Before you delve any further into the contents of this book, I suggest you assess your level of personal resilience so you know your present level of resilience. When you reach the end of the book, you can take the questionnaire again to re-assess your personal development.

Completing the questionnaire will also help you identify those components of resilience where you are naturally strong and which are helpful to you in times of adversity. It will also give you an indication of areas where you have potential vulnerabilities or weaknesses, and where it will be useful to focus in order to build your resilience capability.

A fun instrument

Please note: this questionnaire is *not* a psychometric test and has not been validated against norms. It is designed as a fun instrument to give you some insight into your resilience by

- understanding the elements which make up the seven principles of resilience

- identifying the areas of resilience which are your potential strengths and also those which are potential vulnerabilities.

The interpretation of the questionnaire will give you insight into those chapters you should concentrate on in order to enhance your resilience.

How to complete the Personal Resilience Questionnaire

Read each statement. Use the scale below to rate *how much you agree or disagree* and write that number in the rating box.

1 = Strongly disagree	2 = Disagree	3 = Agree and disagree	4 = Agree	5 = Strongly agree

No	Statements	Rating
1	I feel my life has meaning.	
2	I know my personal strengths.	
3	I am quickly aware of having unwelcome, persistent, negative thoughts when I experience them.	
4	I am quickly aware of my own intense emotions when they occur.	
5	I believe I can influence the direction of my life.	
6	During tough times, I am determined to deal with issues and solve problems.	
7	During tough times, I share my feelings and concerns with people I trust.	
8	I have clear life goals.	
9	I know my personal vulnerabilities or weaknesses.	
10	When I experience unwelcome recurring negative thinking, I stop it.	
11	During tough times I control my own strong feelings.	
12	I believe I can solve the personal difficulties I experience in my life.	
13	During tough times, I persistently seek solutions.	

No	Statements	Rating
14	I find it easy to ask for and accept assistance and support from others during tough times.	
15	There are significant people, causes and faith in my life.	
16	I accept my own capabilities and limits.	
17	When I find myself dwelling on negative thoughts, I deliberately change my thinking to positive thoughts.	
18	During tough times I express my own strong emotions in ways that others can understand and accept.	
19	In my life I choose to be positive rather than negative.	
20	When dealing with problems during tough times, I try out different approaches to solving the problems or issues.	
21	During tough times, I am sensitive to the feelings, needs and motivations of others.	
22	I am taking steps to achieve my life goals.	
23	I draw strength from having overcome previous difficulties and tough times.	
24	I avoid getting into persistent negative thinking patterns.	
25	When I experience intense feelings during tough times, I rationally choose my actions and behaviours, rather than being driven by my emotions.	
26	During tough times I choose to be realistically optimistic.	
27	When problem-solving during tough times, I listen to people with views different from mine.	
28	I respond sensitively to the feelings of others during tough times, by acknowledging them and showing understanding.	
29	I view experiencing tough times in my life as having some higher purpose and meaning.	
30	I accept myself for who I am.	
31	During tough times I strive to be in harmony with my thoughts.	
32	When I experience powerful negative emotions during tough times, I take action to deal with the issue/s causing them.	
33	When experiencing tough times I create balance in my life by doing things that are enjoyable, relaxing and recharging.	
34	I take considered risks to deal with problems during tough times.	
35	I easily give assistance and support to others during tough times.	

Scoring the Personal Resilience Questionnaire

Transfer the scores you gave each item on the Personal Resilience Questionnaire to the appropriate box below. Then add the scores for each row to calculate the scores for each one of the Building Resilience principles. Write this score in the box at the end of the row. Then finally add the scores for each of the seven principles to give the total score of your resilience.

Building Resilience principles	Item no.	Your score	Item no.	Your score	Item no.	Your score	Item no.	Your score	Item no.	Your score	Totals for principles
Connect to your meaning in life	1		8		15		22		29		
Use your unique strengths	2		9		16		23		30		
Maintain perspective	3		10		17		24		31		
Generate positive feelings	4		11		18		25		32		
Be realistically optimistic	5		12		19		26		33		
Persevere by being open minded and flexible	6		13		20		27		34		
Reach out to others	7		14		21		28		35		

TOTAL RESILIENCE SCORE

Interpreting the scores

The maximum total resilience score is 175. The lowest possible score is 35. For each of the individual Building Resilience principles, the lowest score is 5 and the highest is 35.

Locate your overall resilience score in the range of values below.

SCORE RANGE 169 TO 175
Very resilient

You are consistently able to deal with challenges, tough times and change. You find fun and enjoyment in change. You have meaning in your life and know yourself well. You are aware of and able to control and choose your thoughts, feelings and attitudes, and deal with change and difficulties effectively. You enjoy life and thrive. Sustain your high levels of resilience by being aware of the principles of resilience which are outlined in Part 2 of the book and use them in your everyday life.

SCORE RANGE 145 TO 168
Resilient

Most of the time, you are able to cope and deal positively with tough times, challenges and change. You have strategies to cope which enable you to experience joy and fulfilment in your life from time to time. In order to be able to bounce back from adversity quicker, with less difficulty, and also to live your life filled with more joy and fulfilment, consider developing your resilience in your lower-rated principles of resilience. The exercises in Part 2 will give you useful guidelines and pointers on how to achieve this.

SCORE RANGE 101 TO 144
Somewhat resilient

You have some strategies which you use to deal with change and tough times. These strategies, however, do not enable you to consistently and effectively cope and thrive in demanding and stressful circumstances. You will benefit from working through

Part 2, paying particular attention to those areas of resilience where you need to enhance your capacity. The exercises will help you to do this.

SCORE RANGE 35 TO 100
Not very resilient

Change, adversity and tough times often seem to upset your equilibrium; you struggle to cope with the uncertainty and lack of stability they bring. At times like this, you do not experience much joy and vigour, and you often struggle to get through the day. In order to cope and bring realistic perspective, fun and enjoyment back into your life, start by carefully reading each of the seven chapters in Part 2. Pay particular attention to the exercises and complete all of them.

I highly recommend that you take the resilience questionnaire again, after you have completed reading the book and have completed the exercises at the end of each chapter in Part 2. This will enable you to see the improvement that you have achieved in your resilience over time.

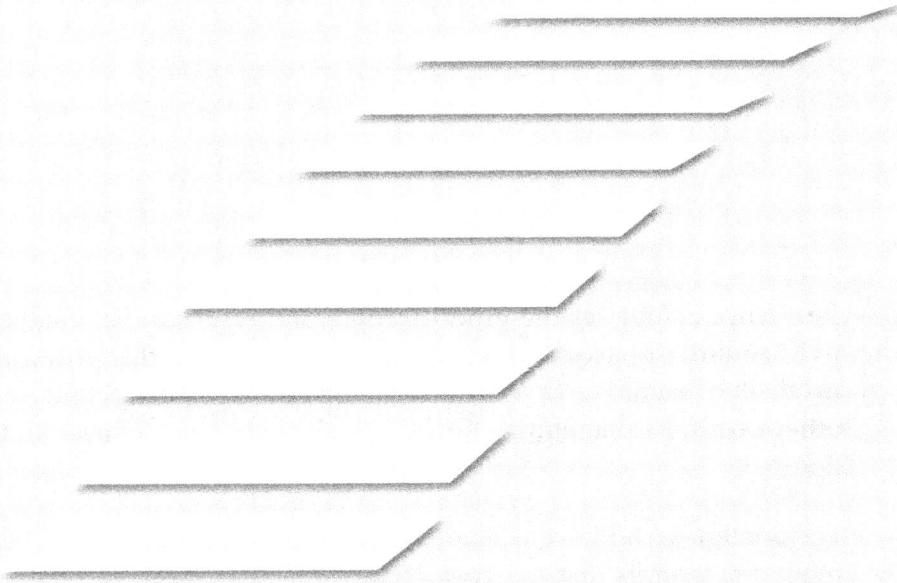

PART TWO

4

Connect to your meaning in life

Connect to your meaning in life	
Use your unique strengths	Maintain perspective
Generate positive feelings	Be realistically optimistic
Persevere by being open-minded and flexible	Reach out to others

Resilience comprises the inner strength and reserves that enable us to endure the stress of tough times. But more than that, it is the magic that enables us to recover, heal and become better people. In other words, it's that human quality which enables us to thrive and flourish.

Fortunately we all have resilience. That's the good news. The bad news, however, is that for most people it feels as if our resilience fluctuates and often when we need it most, it's just not there.

So how do we hold on to it? What can we do to build our resilience to cope with the stress of tough times?

My research on resilience with South African adults found that a core component of resilience is a strong sense of personal meaning and a deep understanding of oneself.

The people I studied reported that when they experience really bad times and stress becomes almost unbearable, the question inevitably arises: 'Why carry on? Why not just give up?' Our national weekend papers frequently carry distressing stories of people who have just given up, and are often associated with tragic loss of life.

The first Building Resilience principle – Connect to your meaning in life – gives you a reason to persevere when times become really difficult, when a feeling of desperation makes giving up seem the easiest way out.

Meaning to be found in people, causes and faith

It is crucial to have clear meaning, connection and purpose in your life in order to be resilient. There are three categories of meaning – people, causes and faith. This trilogy of significance is what make us human and gives us joy and the strength to persevere when times are tough.

Significant people

The people I studied most often referred to family, such as parents and siblings and children, as the significant people in their lives. In addition, some people have a deep connection with others outside their immediate family who have had a marked impact on them as they grew up. Typically, there would have been an influential adult who had been a role model and influenced the person by giving advice, coaching and mentoring.

People become significant to us because of the loving attachments and emotional bonds we have with them. We construct our identity – who we are – in terms of what is important to us, and significant loving relationships are usually a core component.

When facing tough times, thinking about and reminding ourselves of these loving relationships is a source of great strength. It distracts us from the negativity of the situation and replaces our fear with positive feelings of love and respect. As we reconnect with these deep, positive feelings, it becomes clear that we can't give up or lose courage. We can't let them down or allow them to be disappointed in us. We must persist and persevere.

In this way, the relationships with the people we love and respect are profoundly important to our lives. Our reciprocal love helps build the internal resources we need to deal with adversity. The connection to significant people, and the feeling of powerful love for and from them, gives us the strength to continue when times are really tough.

Facing a parent's worst fears

Fatima counted herself fortunate to live in a rent-subsidised apartment, provided by the City Council. It was a compact two-bedroom unit in a large housing block, but situated in an area notorious for gang warfare and high unemployment. Despite its location, she prided herself on raising her only son on her own. He regularly attended church with her and was doing well at school. She always looked forward to preparing the evening meal together and chatting about the events of the day.

Then, seemingly out of the blue, Fatima's life changed. Her son started hanging out with a different bunch of kids after school and his behaviour changed dramatically. On investigation, she found he had been skipping school, and some cash and some valuables from their home were missing. Her worst fears were confirmed: he was smoking tik (a highly addictive amphetamine drug) and was working for the local gang.

Fatima was devastated. She lived for the boy and her hopes and dreams were focused on bringing him up as a proud member of society. She knew that if he continued smoking tik and became initiated into the gang, the very least he could look forward to would be a life of crime and jail, and, at worst, a gruesome death at a very young age. She felt she was on an emotional rollercoaster, alternating between feeling rage and

fear, then disappointment, guilt and depression. She felt she was losing her mind.

Fortunately, she was able to use the services of her employer's Wellness Department counsellors for assistance. They helped her deal with her own feelings and helped her recognise that bringing up her son to be a responsible adult was still the most important thing in her life. She still loved him deeply and would use this huge challenge as a way of expressing her love.

With the coaching of the Wellness Department counsellors, she embarked on a strategy of 'tough love', which culminated in getting him into rehabilitation.

His first stay in a rehab centre did not work, but he emerged from a longer stay, in a different centre, determined to remain drug-free.

Now a year and a half later, Fatima still keeps a careful watch on her son, who has now reached high school. Despite some scares about falling back into his old ways, he remains clean and has managed to avoid the gangs. She has great hopes that he will matriculate, with good enough grades to be accepted to study at the local technikon or even at university.

Significant causes

The second in the trilogy of significance associated with meaning is that of significant causes, which give meaning by satisfying a deep human need we all have. Time and energy are typically given willingly to satisfy this powerful need for purpose and meaning beyond oneself.

Significant causes are absorbing obsessions, which can become all-important and all-consuming in a person's life.

A colleague of mine who was deeply committed to the environment and very sensitive to alleviating pain and suffering was very distressed by newspaper articles about penguins being washed up on local beaches with feathers fouled by bunker oil, discharged by a tanker off Cape Point. They were dying in their thousands.

For eight weeks, her life centred on saving penguins. Managing a demanding job during the day, she worked tirelessly in the evenings and over weekends to clean and rehabilitate the birds. Despite being exhausted most of the time, she loved every minute of it.

When it was all over, she laughingly described her involvement as her 'magnificent obsession'.

We are all in the gutter, but some of us are looking at the stars.
Oscar Wilde

Often what is called 'flow' is experienced in situations like this. Flow is that condition in which time seems to stand still or becomes unimportant. The work or task becomes effortless. One spontaneously follows instinct and there is a feeling of lightness, joy and connection[1].

Michelangelo may have painted the ceiling of the Sistine Chapel in the Vatican in a state of flow. He is reputed to have worked on many areas of the ceiling totally absorbed, ignoring food and sleep to the point of exhaustion.

Examples of significant causes which are not so intensely demanding, but nevertheless give great meaning, are active participation in clubs and societies; participating in demanding leisure activities; sports and hobbies; working with street children; building homes for destitute people and volunteering at the local library.

These activities provide more than just a break from normal routine, or variety and interest. Significance is attained when there is meaning, beyond the activities themselves, that fuels passion and connection in life.

My greatest achievement

Frans considered himself extremely lucky to have worked as a botanist, and obtained his doctorate in the biodiversity of the Cape Floral Kingdom. This area of the Western Cape contains over 9 000 species of plants, of which about 6 200 occur nowhere else in the world. It is the smallest and richest of the world's floral kingdoms.

Through his studies, he was keenly aware of how fragile this area was, with threats such as climate change and pressures for the land to be used for residential, farming and commercial purposes. Frans contributed to environmental impact study assessments, participated in radio and television programs and regularly gave talks about the role, history, preservation and use of the indigenous fynbos plants. Over many years, he became regarded as an expert in this field and received local and international recognition.

At his retirement function, he was asked to address a large gathering of colleagues, reflecting on the extensive role he had played in conservation. In his speech he said that he believed his single greatest achievement was saving from extinction a single species of fynbos that occurred only in a very small area. A large commercial development had controversially been given the go-ahead to begin building operations, but he had managed to get a court injunction to stop the development, long enough for him to find and remove that particular species. It was subsequently cultivated in various nurseries and now, several years later, is no longer as endangered as it was.

Frans told his colleagues that whenever he felt down, whenever he felt he was not making progress and questioned his life's work, he reminded himself of this achievement. If not for his intervention and persistence, this species of fynbos might well be extinct today. He had preserved it for his children and his children's children.

When he reflected on his most important contribution to conservation, t was saving that plant species that had given him the deepest satisfaction in his life.

Significant faith

For many people, faith is an important part of their lives and they attend religious services on a regular basis. Their faith comes from religions of the world such as Christianity, Judaism, Islam, Hinduism, Buddhism and others.

These people incorporate the beliefs and practices of faith into their lives and strive to live their lives in alignment with the challenges and commitments outlined by their religion's doctrines.

People with strong formal faith beliefs usually find it quite easy, during tough times, to fall back on their faith-based belief systems.

A commonly repeated refrain, heard from people with faith-based values, is: 'I will not be tested more than the ability I have been given.' One humorist wryly added that she sometimes just wished that her Creator did not trust her so much!

Others profess less formal and structured faith systems, referring to themselves as spiritual rather than religious. They describe their beliefs as a 'connectedness with the universe', or seeking the experience of a 'loving universe'.

There are people who do not believe in a deity, feeling that religion is nonsensical or, at least, unprovable. Even for them, however, finding meaning and purpose in life is just as important as for religious people. They also need to live their lives in a manner cohesive and congruent with their values. Their aims may be secular rather than religious, but what is common to everyone is the need to harmonise and direct our lives towards satisfying our need for meaning.

In this way, whether people find purpose from a formal faith or create their own sense of purpose, we all need to believe in something beyond and larger than ourselves for life to make sense.

From the perspective of resilience, the nature and type of faith is less important than actually having some belief in the purpose and meaning in life. A feeling of deep connection beyond oneself gives and enhances the meaning and experience of our lives.

Keeping the dream real

Ragnesh worked for many years for a multinational manufacturing company, rising to a senior human resources position. He became increasingly frustrated with organisational politics and his role, which had become more strategic, though he preferred the operational aspects. After lengthy deliberation, he resigned and started his own human resources consultancy, working out of his garage, which he extended and converted into open-plan offices. He employed several of his friends in specialist roles and they launched their consultancy, offering work in all of the human resource disciplines.

Ragnesh committed himself to finance a temple for worship with the profits from the business. He had already identified a site, with an option to purchase, and had preliminary sketches drawn up by architects. He was committed to leaving this temple as his legacy.

The start-up of the business was a very exciting time for Ragnesh and his colleagues. They worked until they were too tired to continue at night. Every day brought new ideas about how they could make their services different, unusual and attractive. Involvement, commitment and creativity swept-up the friends and they produced amazing products.

They soon signed up a large-scale and lengthy government contract. Personal dedication and camaraderie helped sustain hundred-hour work weeks until delivery was complete. By the time the contract came to an end, Ragnesh and the friends were exhausted and all took a long break.

On reconvening, they found that the business environment had changed significantly from the time they had started. The economy was going through a steep decline, precipitated by the sub-prime banking crisis in America and, in response, their potential clients had put many of their contracts on hold and were not issuing new tenders. Work for Ragnesh and his colleagues dried up and almost disappeared.

During the tough months that followed, Ragnesh put his own capital into the business while they desperately tried to market their products and services. The few small assignments they managed to secure did not cover the running costs of the firm and both Ragnesh and his organisation slipped into debt.

The atmosphere in the office slowly changed from unbridled optimism to clench-jawed desperation. Tempers frayed and creativity dropped. Arguments about organisational priorities and direction became commonplace. Work was no longer a joyous obsession. One by one, each of the friends resigned and left until only Ragnesh was left.

During the tough times, Ragnesh frequently spoke about his dreams of building the temple. He would describe what it would look like, about the furnishings and the worshippers. He even started to plan the parking and the access for worshippers from their cars to the temple. This calmed and composed Ragnesh. By the end of these 'dreaming sessions', as he called them, he was back to being his old determined self again and able to continue fighting to keep the business out of bankruptcy.

In summary, my research showed that significant people, causes and faith are important in providing the foundation for the inner resources and strength needed to deal with adversity. Connection to meaning in life underpins resilience. Everyone should strive to keep these connections strong in good times as well as during tough times.

How strong is your connection?

To assist you to learn more about meaning, and to help you to find or strengthen meaning in life, several exercises follow that will help you to achieve this.

Finding joy in troubled times

At a period in my life when I was experiencing deep adversity, when it felt like I was walking through a dark night of despair with no hope in sight, I sought advice from my wise friend Randall Falkenberg. I poured out my troubles to him, explaining in detail everything that had gone wrong, the problems I was facing and the huge negative implications for my future.

At the end of an hour's litany of my woes, I finally said that I'd come to him because I knew he would give me advice on how to cope and deal with all these problems.

He took a minute or so to think, while I waited expectantly for his sage advice. He looked me in the eye and said I should make a list of the things that brought me joy in my life.

What? I could not believe my ears. Was that all? Here I was, at the end of my tether, in a desperate situation, asking for practical help and all he could tell me was to list the things that brought me joy. The man had obviously become senile and stupid.

He calmly persisted. I should go home and immediately write an essay, describing all the joyful things in my life. I was disappointed, and more than a little annoyed. But that evening, with nothing better to do, I reluctantly opened a new writing pad and started on my essay.

Several hours later I had written seven pages of the joy my life holds. I experience great joy from people that love me, that depend on me and whom I can't let down. I love being in the zone, during long-distance road and trail running. I experience peace when camping and hiking in wilderness areas. I experience great satisfaction when designing creative interventions to help people improve their performance at work. I am thrilled when I work with groups of people to help them make changes to their attitudes and behaviour.

The pages were damp with my tears. I felt profound meaning and happiness in writing all the things that brought me joy. I was no longer experiencing the fear and anxiety which had incapacitated me. I had reconnected with what was really important for me and with those reasons to persist and not give up.

The feeling of happiness had another effect. I started to feel positive and optimistic about my future. My body felt less heavy, as though the physical burdens of my troubles weren't as weighty and didn't press me down as before. I had a different perspective. I felt more positive and optimistic. Perhaps my problems could be solved after all. It was as though my vision and thinking had cleared.

I have so much joy in my life that, when I focused on it, it crowded out the terror of my predicament. Of course, the problems that I faced remained. But what had changed was the way I felt about myself and how I viewed the problems. I had found my joy in life again. I had a new perspective and for the first time in a long while, I had hope.

> Find a place inside where there is joy, and the joy will burn out the pain.
>
> *Joseph Campbell*

Now try the same exercise for yourself. This will help you clearly identify those things that make you happy and uplift you, that have meaning for you. You will find that completing the exercise will evoke positivity and re-establish the important connections and meaning in your life.

Written exercise: Finding your joy

Write out all those things in your life that bring you joy, happiness and meaning. Explain, in an essay, what you do in those important areas and how this makes you feel. Give examples and explain in detail. (Omit sex and food unless you want to spend time in those industries!)

It is best if you tackle this exercise when there is no time pressure on you. And be prepared to spend an hour or two on it.

Approach the exercise as if you are writing a letter to yourself explaining all those areas of your life that bring you joy, happiness and meaning.

Finding meaning in your life

Now let's turn to clarifying your meaning in life. For some people, identifying what is their meaning in life is quite easy. They have a clear idea of what they want to do and get on doing it. For others, it's not so clear nor so easy. Ironically, it's often difficult for those people who have many talents, which makes it difficult for them to know which particular path to choose. It can also be difficult for people who are curious and love exploring alternatives, finding it hard to settle on particular aspects that give meaning.

If you find yourself not sure of your purpose and meaning in life, the following exercise will help you. The exercise has its roots in the quality improvement movement and has also been proven to be useful in a wide variety of problem-solving situations.

Written exercise: The Five Whys

Write a one-sentence answer to the following question: Why do you go to work?

Having written the answer to that question, ask yourself: Why do you want to do that? Write a one sentence answer to that question. That is the first of the whys.

Using the new sentence you have written, ask yourself: Why do you want do that? Again restrict your answer to a single sentence. That is the second of the whys.

Continue asking the question 'why do you want to do that?' until you have a statement to which further asking the question 'why?' does not elicit an answer. At this point, you will have the answer to your mission and purpose in life.

For most people, this exercise takes between four to six repeats of the question, from which the exercise derives its name.

To give you an example, let me show you my answers to these questions. The exercise helped me clarify what I believe is my purpose in life.

Question 1: Why do you go to work?

Answer: In order to earn money and enjoy myself at work.

Question 2: Why do you want to do that?

Answer: I need to provide for my family and I get a real kick out of working with groups of people and giving them ways of dealing with issues in their lives.

Question 3: Why do you want to do that?

Answer: It's really satisfying to design new tools and techniques, to help people learn how to be more resilient.

Question 4: Why do you want to do that?

Answer: Helping people build their resilience and cope with the stress of normal living brings me deep satisfaction and also helps make me a better person.

Question 5: Why do you want to do that?

Answer: It feels that the deeply satisfying work I am meant to do is to help people build their inner resources and be more resilient, which, in turn, enables them to live the lives they are meant to lead.

Creating meaning at work and at home

Creating engagement at work is the holy grail of modern leadership. Too often, employees are disengaged, only doing the minimum to get by. The results are poor customer relations, reduced productivity and a negative, downward spiral of morale, with employees not caring about the goals of the organisation and the organisation not caring about its people.

Engagement at work is substantially dependent upon meaning. Meaning is found in the work itself (*meaning in work*) as well as created by playing a significant role in a workgroup *(meaning at work)*[2].

MEANING IN WORK

Meaning in work can be enhanced by

- ensuring people understand the mission, vision and values of the organisation
- telling stories about how the values of the organisation have been used when making tough decisions
- regularly pointing out the inherent value of the organisation's products and services
- highlighting the organisation's involvement in community and charity activities
- encouraging employee participation in the organisation's social investment activities
- telling stories about what ordinary employees did to help customers.

MEANING AT WORK

Meaning at work is created and enhanced when people feel they are part of a work group and play a meaningful role, as well as helping others in the work group play a meaningful role. This can be achieved by

- creating formal and informal mentorship programmes
- structuring work to create more 'whole-work' by reducing the fragmentation of tasks
- creating a group or team incentive for meeting performance objectives
- having regular social get-togethers
- using social settings to recognise the importance of the role played by various people.

Creating meaning in tedious jobs

Management of an insurance company was concerned about the high potential for fraud in payment of death claims. The claims procedure was consequently changed by instituting a series of lengthy checks before a claim could be paid.

Staff complained that the new procedures would delay payouts to customers. They also said the new procedures were bureaucratic and reduced their decision-making discretion.

Claimants found the new procedures complicated and onerous, and complained that the staff members they dealt with were often dismissive and uninterested in their problems.

The result was a negative spiral of unhappy clients, dealing with frustrated staff, which rubbed off on the clients, creating more frustration for them. Within a short space of time, the reputation of the organisation had suffered and employee morale sunk to an all-time low.

To address this problem, a well-known consumer activist was engaged to produce a series of real-life video case studies on the experiences of clients. In one such case, she followed the claims experience of a father whose son, together with his girlfriend, had been killed in a motor accident. The twenty-minute video recreated the father's experience from being woken by the police early on a Sunday morning, identifying his son's body, and approaching the insurance company with a claim to be used to pay the funeral costs. The gritty narration by the father graphically captured his devastation and the insensitive treatment he received at the hands of the claims clerks.

This video, together with other similar videos, was shown to claims clerks and process design staff. There was scarcely a dry eye in the room. The outcome was a deeper understanding of the importance of the work done by the claims clerks and how important their interactions with claimants were. Several months later, a revised claims procedure was instituted and employee engagement and morale increased. And perhaps, most importantly, measurements of the experience of claimants also showed a marked increase in satisfaction.

Creating family rituals to enhance meaning

We all want deep and satisfying relationships with our loved ones, expressing our love and being loved in return. Family rituals enhance these relationships by creating shared meaning. Here are some ideas to achieve this:

FRIDAY NIGHT SUPPERS TOGETHER

Regular family meals are a wonderful way of keeping the family together and ensuring the family stays together. As children grow up, it is often very difficult to eat together every night. This is worsened if one or both parents regularly travel for their work. A solution is to set aside one evening a week for a meal for all family members. Jewish, Muslim and Italian families are often good examples of how this can be made to work.

FAMILY HOLIDAYS TOGETHER

Our neighbour comes from a family of five siblings. Every year the five siblings get together for a long weekend to catch up, celebrate and commiserate.

CHRISTMAS TREE DECORATION

For families who decorate Christmas trees, specific decorations can be made to commemorate important events, for example the birth of a baby, a graduation, or building a night shelter. Putting up these decorations every year, and explaining them to children and others, creates tradition and reinforces family values.

SCRAPBOOKS AND PHOTO ALBUMS

Making these encourages remembering good times and important relationships. It has the added advantage of having something tangible to show and explain to significant others.

WORSHIPPING

People and families who worship together reinforce their bond and common values. It is said 'families that pray together stay together.'

Identifying goals to achieve your meaning in life

Having identified what gives you meaning in your life, we can now move on to identifying goals which will help you achieve your meaning.

The importance of measures and timing

After completing my university studies, I was appointed as a high school teacher. The salary was abysmal, which meant I had to manage my budget very carefully.

After a long search for suitable accommodation, I found a delightful garden flat in the grounds of a large Victorian house, within walking distance of the school. It was more expensive than I could afford, and so I agreed with the dear old lady who owned and lived in the house that I would do odd handyman maintenance jobs in return for a reduction in the rent.

I moved into my new accommodation and eagerly began life as a teacher. By the end of the first week I was dazed and exhausted. It had been a whirlwind of lesson preparation and dealing with very boisterous kids. I was looking forward to catching up on lost sleep and chilling over the weekend.

It was not to be. Early on Saturday morning I was roused from my deep sleep by banging on my window. Through bleary eyes I could just make out my landlady with sandpaper, paint and brushes. She said I'd better get busy sanding and painting the window frames if I had any hope of finishing them by nightfall.

I did not finish the task she had set by the end of the day, nor even by the end of the weekend. It took several weekends to complete the sanding and then painting under-coats and top-coats on the depressingly large number of window frames.

> In the absence of clearly defined goals, we become strangely loyal to performing daily acts of trivia.
>
> *Author unknown*

This gave me lots of time to ruefully reflect on how I had landed in this predicament, and what I could do to rectify it. It was clear that I needed to be much more specific about what I agreed to do. I needed to specify exactly *what* I would do, the *standard* to which it would be done and by *when* it would be completed.

Armed with these insights, I renegotiated our deal to meet her needs as well as mine. I made sure that in future all goals I set were specific, measurable and had times and dates for completion.

Setting meaningful goals

The way to influence and create the future is to set goals for yourself. Goals that are aimed at enhancing your meaning will assist you to create a positive and desirable future for yourself.

> Our plans miscarry because they have no aim. When a man does not know what harbour he is making for, no wind is the right one.
>
> *Seneca*

One of the obstacles to goal-setting, however, is getting caught up in the disappointments and heartaches of the past and all the things that 'could have been'. This can create an undertow, which drags us back and prevents us from moving forward.

On an ocean beach, the best way to avoid drowning is not to fight the undertow, but rather to wait until you reach calm waters, then strike out in the direction of safety. In the same way, rather than fight the negativity of the past, focus on what you desire, the changes you want to achieve and the steps needed to achieve them. The more you think about this engaging future, where you are connected with purpose and meaning, the more exciting it becomes and the more possible it seems that the goals will be achieved. This creates hope, energy and excitement. In this way, the goals that you set will themselves create the energy and enthusiasm you need to achieve them.

The most effective approach to goal-setting is to write them out. Written articulation helps to crystallise your thoughts, leading to focus and clarity. The goals you set should not only focus on what is important, but also provide direction or steps to get there, as well as specifying by when they should be achieved.

Here are some tips that will assist you to set powerful goals which are attainable and motivating.[3]

SET POSITIVE GOALS RATHER THAN AVOIDANT GOALS

Goals which stipulate positive outcomes are motivating. Examples include going away on a camping trip with the family every three months; enrolling in the local university summer school to learn more about astrology; reading bedtime stories to the children every night.

Avoidant goals deal with negative outcomes or things to avoid. These might include losing weight, drinking less alcohol or not allowing the boss to steamroll you so much. The problem with goals such as these, which are focused on trying to prevent something from happening, is that they lead to enhanced awareness of what is wrong. A negative focus and dwelling on the negative can lead to increased anxiety, as well as decreased levels of happiness and satisfaction.

Thus, ensure your goals are stated with the positive outcomes you wish to achieve.

SET INTRINSIC GOALS RATHER THAN ONLY EXTRINSIC GOALS

Intrinsic goals are aimed at satisfying an internal need that we have and are inherently satisfying. Any goal you set for yourself in the categories of significant people, causes and faith will inevitably be intrinsically satisfying.

Intrinsically motivated goals are associated with increasing happiness. This is because they produce a highly-valued outcome, are personally rewarding or are associated with personal growth and development.

Extrinsic goals, on the other hand, are aimed at achieving an external goal or reward. External motivators, such as wealth, power, popularity, physical attractiveness and fame, become problematic when they become the major focus in life. If that happens, they inevitably bring with them an unhealthy degree of anxiety, interpersonal problems and stress.

Now, of course it is necessary to have some external goals, relating to earning money, having a certain standard of living and providing wealth for retirement. But what's important when setting extrinsic goals is not to see them as the desired end in themselves. Rather, see them as 'enabling goals'. These are things that allow for the achievement of other important goals and aims in life. This will assist you in keeping the external goals in perspective.

ACCEPT THAT SOME GOALS MAY CAUSE GOAL CONFLICT

Goals are rooted in one's value system. Where goals reflect different values, there is the potential for conflict between them. For example, what is more important? Spending time with the family or taking time out for your sporting activities? Spending your free time with your partner on a home improvement project or participating in faith-based outreach programme?

Working mothers very often experience goal conflict with how they spend their precious after-work time, balancing the demands of the family with the need to take time out for themselves. From a personality point of view, some people are naturally curious, enjoy creating alternatives and exploring different avenues. This may lead to them struggling to settle on a limited number of goals. If this is you, it is probably wise to accept some goal conflict as a necessary part of choosing which of your goals to pursue. But try to avoid excessive goal conflict, as it can result in anxiety, unhappiness and even illness.

The solution is to identify your most important goals rather than dwell on the problems where your goals conflict. Action to implement the most important goals begins a process whereby the prioritisation of the goals often resolves itself. This may seem counter-intuitive, but it has helped many people who experience goal conflict.

In summary, don't allow yourself to become caught in a repeating cycle of analysing and rethinking the problem. Should you feel stuck, the best way to deal with goal conflict is to choose the goals that are absolute 'must haves'. Make a choice and stick to those goals for six to twelve months, after which you can review and change them if it's necessary.

Exercises

Here is an exercise to help you identify and set goals to enhance and achieve meaning in your life. The questions which follow may look rather morbid, but people who have done this exercise say that they find it useful, because it focuses their attention on what's important. So don't be put off by the questions. Just answer them at face value.

Written exercise: Identifying goals to achieve your meaning

Write your answers quickly for each of the following three questions, using a brainstorming approach. This means you should concentrate more on quality than quantity, and not evaluate your ideas:

1. If you knew you were going to die in five years, how would you live until then?
2. If you knew you were going to die in six months, how would you live until then?
3. If you found out you were going to die in 24 hours, what would you regret not having done?

On completing this exercise, most people find that there is a marked gap between, on one hand what they have identified as important ways of living, together with the things they would like to achieve in their lives and, on the other, how they are living their life at present.

This gap represents the opportunity for you to change the focus of your life.

So don't be discouraged if the gap is large. Rather see it as a great opportunity to make changes in your life to achieve what is really important and meaningful.

Written exercises: Establishing your goal priorities

1. In order to establish priorities, go back over your answers to the three questions and decide on the three most important things in each list. You will now have nine goals.

2. Now reduce those nine goals to the three that are most important to you, and will bring you closer to what gives you joy and to achieving your meaning in life.

3. For each of these three goals, brainstorm the activities that are needed to achieve them. As you have done with the previous brainstorming activity, concentrate on creating a long list of all the activities that will bring you closer to achieving your goal. Don't evaluate the list at this stage.

4. Now switch from being expansive and creative, to being discerning and practical. For each of these goals, select only the activities to which you can commit to spending time and effort. Ignore the activities you have not selected.

5. Write down the amount of time that you will commit to spending on the activities selected for each of the goals.

6. Specify an end date, by which the goal will be achieved, or at least a significant milestone towards achieving the goal.

You now have created three goals, with activities, and committed time and an end date to each of them. This will help close the gap between where you are and where you would like to be, to live your life with meaning and connection.

It is really important to plan how you will spend your time, not only accomplishing the day-to-day activities, but also the longer-term steps you need to meet the goals you have set. This will help keep your ideal of living a life with meaning at the top of your mind. Most important, it will help you to get closer to achieving them, step by step. In addition, the process of setting goals creates and sustains happiness and well-being.[4]

The final exercise in this section of connecting to your meaning in life is designed to consolidate the various sections of this chapter and to tie up any loose ends. Choose to answer one or more questions from the list below, to consolidate and apply your learning about connecting to your meaning.

Written exercises

1. Reflect on the exercise in Chapter 1, where you described an adversity that you have overcome. To what extent did the clarity of your meaning and purpose in life assist in dealing with the adversity?

2. How can you use your connection and purpose in times of future adversity?

3. What can you do to strengthen your connection to your life purpose, to what really matters and which brings you joy? It may help to answer this question using the headings of significant people, issues and faith.

ENDNOTES

1 Csikszentmihalyi, M., Abuhamdeh, S. & Nakamura, J. 2005. Flow. *In* Elliot, A., *Handbook of Competence and Motivation* (p. 598–698). New York: The Guilford Press.

2 Pratt, M.G. & Ashforth, B.E. 2003. Fostering meaningfulness in working and at work. *In* Cameron, K., Dutton, J. & Quinn, R. (eds.). *Positive organizational scholarship: Foundations of a new discipline* (p. 309–327). San Francisco: Berrett-Kohler.

3 Biswas-Diener, R. & Dean, B. 2007. *Positive psychology coaching: putting the science of happiness to work for your clients*. New Jersey: John Wiley & Sons, Inc.

4 King, L.A. & Hicks, J.A. 2007. Whatever happened to 'what might have been'? Regret, happiness, and maturity. *American psychologist*, 62:625-636.

5

Use your unique strengths

Use your unique strengths	
Maintain perspective	Generate positive feelings
Persevere by being open-minded and flexible	Be realistically optimistic
Reach out to others	Connect to your meaning in life

In the previous chapter you were encouraged to identify your meaning in life, to set goals to live out your higher purpose in the world.

If you believe that you are placed on Earth and given life for a purpose, you obviously need to be given the ability to achieve that purpose; otherwise having a purpose wouldn't make sense.

These gifts, your character strengths, are also the attributes that enable you to withstand life's harsh winds, and to recover and attain previous levels of functioning.

The second principle of Building Resilience concerns understanding your personal strengths and vulnerabilities and, in particular, using your unique character strengths. This is what we are going to explore in this chapter.

Understanding your personal strengths and vulnerabilities

We are all made up of strengths and vulnerabilities in different combinations. Because there are so many potential character strengths, as well as so many potential vulnerabilities, the particular combination that each of us possesses is highly unlikely, if not impossible, for another person to have in the exact same mix. Your particular combination is one of the things that make you unique.

> The foundation of your ability to fulfil your purpose in life is your character strengths – that particular combination of gifts that you have been given.

Realistic insight into your own strengths and vulnerabilities is the basis for understanding your capabilities and limits when dealing with adversity and building resilience. Unfounded or false hope about personal capabilities, on one hand, or vulnerabilities on the other, may provide momentary comfort, but ultimately leads to disappointment and disillusionment.

Overcoming previous adversities, particularly significant ones, can become a source of optimism and welcome, positive feelings. You no doubt experienced this when, in Chapter 1, you described the adversity that you had been through and triumphed.

An ultra-distance road runner once commented to me that training for and completing 24 Comrades Marathons (an 89 kilometre road race), had taught him to persevere and not to give up when things got tough. The training and race became a metaphor for his life, which he cited as: 'When the going gets tough, the tough get going.' He was clearly in touch with his character strengths.

We need to build our self-knowledge in order to become realistically optimistic about our capabilities. This includes understanding our own personal vulnerabilities or weaknesses. We need this balanced understanding for accurate insight, in order to create realistic recovery strategies from adversity. This was pithily expressed by a small business owner who, after describing an acrimonious divorce and having to sell and split the proceeds of his struggling business, said: 'I know who I am; what I can do and what I can't do. I have been through a lot of stuff in life and I have become an expert on myself.'

Use your character strengths to achieve your meaning in life

In order to fulfil your purpose and mission in life, and achieve your life goals, it is necessary to develop and use your character strengths to achieve your goals in the most effective way.

Our personal weaknesses can detract, and even derail, us from achieving our goals. So we should work on them, to bring them up to the minimum level of acceptability, so that they don't trip us up. But working on weakness and developing strengths is hard work. It feels heavy, difficult and almost everyone says it is not enjoyable. It also takes a huge amount of time and effort to overcome weakness and, anyway, it is highly unlikely a character weakness can ever become a strength.

Those of us who have been at the receiving end of performance appraisal reviews, where weaknesses have been identified, sometimes coyly referred to as 'development areas', will often have despaired over the same weakness being identified year after year. Despite personal development plans being drawn up to address the weakness, and diligent efforts being made to improve such, they often remain our Achilles heel. Unfortunately, experience attests that improving weaknesses is not only hard work but, in many cases, is unsuccessful. This is particularly the case if the weakness involves our personality.

In contrast to reversing weaknesses, developing strengths is experienced as light, exciting and joyful. As strengths are already at a high level of functioning and associated with insight, developing them even further is very often quick and easy.

Strengths, weaknesses and talents

Traditionally schools, families, universities and businesses have mostly tried to create excellence by attempting to overcome weakness rather than to capitalise on strengths. Identifying and rectifying areas of weakness is given a lot of attention, be it a child who is failing maths at school or a manager with problematic interpersonal skills. This deficit approach often involves huge corrective effort, such as providing counselling, extra training and opportunities for development to correct the areas of weakness.

The deficit approach is in marked contrast to the strengths approach. This identifies the child's strengths and how they can be used to address the problems experienced with maths; or the strengths the manager possesses, which can be effectively used in interpersonal situations.

Fortunately, a dramatic change in focus is sweeping through business, psychology, religion and education called the 'strengths' movement. This aims at correcting the negative bias we have traditionally experienced and to balance it with a positive or strengths focus. At its heart, the strengths approach is the deceptively simple idea that we should understand and develop our strengths to attain excellence, rather than focus on our weaknesses.

Although the idea is simple enough, the implications of the difference in approaches are profound. For example, understanding how alcoholics become addicted will provide useful insights into how the disease changes and destroys the mind and body. By contrast, understanding how alcoholics manage to break the cycle of addiction will give you fascinating insights into the ability of the mind and/or body to heal itself.

> Life only demands from you the strength you possess. Only one feat is possible – not to have run away.
>
> *Dag Hammarskjold*

> Although men are accused of not knowing their own weakness, yet perhaps few know their own strength. It is in men as in soils, where sometimes there is a vein of gold which the owner knows not of.
>
> *Jonathan Swift*

Also, studying and learning about dysfunctional teams at work, or families in their homes, will give you useful information on problematic group and interpersonal dynamics. But studying top performing teams and well adjusted families will give you completely different information on how to effectively deal with conflict, show respect to others and strive towards common goals.

Simply put, you can achieve more in life, be stronger and be happier, by understanding and using your strengths.

For this, as with all things in life, one needs balance. Just as it is very limiting to have only a weakness approach, it would be inappropriate to have only a strengths approach. Where we have deficits and weaknesses in our lives, we still need to address these areas. This is particularly important if the weak areas are crucial for our success. Thus, the child who needs maths for university entrance, must develop those skills, and the manager who is abrasive and wishes to continue to manage people, must become more socially adept.

Excellence is not the opposite of failure, and to understand and achieve excellence in your life you need to implement strategies for excellence, rather than strategies to overcome failure.

When these concepts are applied to resilience, the implication is that you should develop and use your strengths, rather than focus exclusively on developing and overcoming your weaknesses.

How to identify your strengths

Most people are able to identify that they're either 'good' at something, or 'bad' at it. For example, you may say that you are good at facilitating group discussions and getting seedlings to grow in the garden, but bad at handling conflict and understanding how the DVD player. But are these 'good' skills actually strengths?

The answer is that while these examples can indicate strengths, we need to be much more specific in defining strengths in order to make full use of them.

This is because ability or a skill is very often only situation-specific and may not reflect a real strength. For example, the ability or skill of facilitating group discussions may only be a strength in an organisational context. It may not apply to people who are in conflict, such as with stakeholder engagement over the site of a nuclear facility. Likewise, the ability or skill of understanding the accounting system at work may only apply to that particular software system, and may not apply to understanding all accounting principles.

A more useful understanding of what constitutes a strength is that of 'character strengths'. These are the gifts that we have been born with and last all our lives. They can be applied at any time and anywhere, rather than being only situation-specific.

> Few men during their lifetime come anywhere near exhausting the resources dwelling within them. There are deep wells of strength that are never used.
>
> *Richard E. Byrd*

Using character strengths feels great. We feel effortless. The work or task we are doing is easy. It's all so very obvious to us. And sometimes we get 'into the zone', a term athletes use to describe what they feel when everything comes together: time stands still and they have heightened awareness and power. When we use our character strengths, we almost always make a significant contribution.

When using character strengths we often see others struggling, who are not at our level of competence. When this happens, you may ask yourself why they can't do the things you do, that are so easy and so obvious. The answer is simply that they are easy and obvious for you, because of your character strengths. For other people it's not so easy or obvious, because they're not using their character strengths. Thus using character strength is not only associated with success, but also feeling great.

While using your strengths gives a feeling of power and competence, the feeling associated with doing things that use your weaknesses is completely different. That's when you struggle, have feelings of frustration and irritation and at the end are left feeling exhausted. Despite all the effort we put in, the results are usually mediocre at best. We seem hardwired to always have deficit areas in our lives.

Character strengths can be enhanced and developed in two ways:

BUILDING UP STRENGTHS

Building up strengths is the process of developing the gifts we already have. Very often this is a matter of enhancing insight and finding new ways to apply strengths. It is often associated with feelings of being powerful and competent, which give great satisfaction.

BUILDING UPON STRENGTHS

This involves learning to use our natural gifts that enable us to live our lives in alignment with our values. This is where we apply our strengths to increasingly wider areas of our lives, so that we live with authenticity. In this way, our strengths become the means by which we achieve our mission in life and do the work we believe we are meant to do.

Five ways to discover your character strengths

So how do you go about discovering or confirming character strengths? For some people this is more difficult than it may seem. Ironically, people are often very conscious of their weaknesses but not as aware of their strengths.

To exacerbate the situation, you may think that talking about and deliberately using your strengths feels too much like boasting. I once heard a young person say that she felt that if she used her strengths too much, she would become different from her friends and could even lose their friendship. In her case, the idea of identifying character strengths and using them may never make it out of the starting blocks.

The starting point is to understand one's strengths, and to use them in tough times to cope with adversity.

There are several ways of identifying character strengths. You can choose the method that suits you best, or choose to use several of the different methods, as a way of understanding and honing your understanding of your strengths.

VIA Survey of Character Strengths questionnaire

This questionnaire enables you to assess your character strengths against a list of 24 virtues or strengths. The questionnaire is free and can be completed at any time, as long as you have access to the Internet, because it is available from a website[1].

It was created by highly esteemed academic researchers Christopher Peterson and Martin Seligman and is backed up by their detailed explanation of character strengths and virtues.[2] Over a million people have completed the questionnaire and, although it takes about an hour, most people find it easy to understand.

To assess your character strengths, you will first need to register on the website and then from among several questionnaires, select the VIA survey of character strengths. At the end of answering the 240 questions you will be able to download a list of what they refer to as your signature strengths, starting at your most powerful and ending with the least powerful. The most powerful is your top strength, and what they refer to as the least powerful of your strengths is, in fact, your weakness.

VIA Signature Strengths[3]

Wisdom and knowledge	• Curiosity / Interest in the world
	• Love of learning
	• Judgement / Critical thinking / Open-mindedness
	• Ingenuity / Originality / Practical intelligence
	• Social intelligence / Personal intelligence / Emotional intelligence
	• Perspective
Courage	• Valour and bravery
	• Perseverance / Industry / Diligence
	• Integrity / Genuineness / Honesty
Humanity and love	• Kindness and generosity
	• Loving and allowing oneself to be loved
Justice	• Citizenship / Teamwork / Duty / Loyalty
	• Fairness and equity
	• Leadership
Temperance	• Self-control
	• Prudence / Discretion / Caution
	• Humility and modesty
Transcendence	• Appreciation of beauty and excellence
	• Gratitude
	• Hope / Optimism / Future-mindedness
	• Spirituality / Sense of purpose / Faith / Religiousness
	• Forgiveness and mercy
	• Humour and playfulness
	• Zest / Passion / Enthusiasm

The StrengthsFinder 2.0

The StrengthsFinder 2.0 is well researched and widely used in organisations. It is Internet-based, but you have to pay for it. It comes with a very easily readable book by Marcus Buckingham and Donald O. Clifton which explains and clarifies the 34 themes that they list as character strengths[4]. Their book is readily available from most booksellers and is particularly useful for people who would like to develop their strengths in an organisational context.

Realise 2 questionnaire

This questionnaire is also Internet-based and has a list of 60 character strengths against which you are assessed[5]. To use the test, you have to pay a fee, a portion of which is donated to charity. The report provided is really useful, as it places each of these 60 strengths in one of four categories:

- Strengths you use

- Those you don't use

- Those that you have learnt to do well but are draining

- Your weaknesses.

It also has a companion book to help you understand and further interpret the report, which is available from booksellers.[6]

Narrative Strengths Identification Process

This is an easy way of determining your character strengths and is surprisingly accurate. The only down side is that it does take more time. It simply involves spending time with people who know you well, asking the questions below and making notes of their answers. Ideally, you should do this with at least five people, although it will work with just three. A major advantage of this method is that names of the strengths and their descriptions will make sense to you. In addition, you don't have to go to the trouble of filling in questionnaires or buying books.

Set aside about 30 minutes for each conversation and follow the conversation sequence below:

1. Explain that the purpose of the conversation is your desire to better understand your character strengths. Using the strengths will help you fulfil your mission and purpose in life, which, in turn, will help you live in alignment with your values and be resilient. The other person's input will be invaluable to help you understand your strengths.

2. Ask the person to tell you a story of when they saw you at your best. This is a time that the other person remembers you made a significant contribution and impact. Take notes of what is said. At the end of that first story, ask for another and then another, until you have at least three stories.

3. When you have written down three stories, ask your friend to list the strengths that came out in the stories. As they name each strength, ask them to explain and tell you more about it. Listen carefully and write down what they tell you. Aim at identifying about five to eight strengths.

4. At the conclusion, show your friend the list and description of your strengths that they have made and check to see if you have recorded all the information from their perspective.

5. When you have completed all your interviews, compare the lists of strengths and their definitions and consolidate the information into a final list.

When all the comments are consolidated and integrated, particularly if they are from different aspects of your life, there is often an amazing congruence which leads to a deep understanding of how your strengths help you to live a powerful life in alignment with your values.

Narrative Strengths Identification Process using the VIA Signature Strengths

This method of determining your strengths is a variation of the previous one. It differs only in that you ask your friend to use the VIA Signature Strengths[7] categories and descriptions below when describing your strengths. All the steps for this method are the same as the previous method.

Set aside about 30 minutes for each conversation and follow the conversation sequence below:

1. Explain that the purpose of the conversation is your desire to better understand your character strengths. Using the strengths will help you fulfil your mission and purpose in life, which, in turn, will help you live in alignment with your values and be resilient. The other person's input will be invaluable in helping you understand your strengths.

2. Ask the person to tell you a story of when they saw you at your best. This is a time that the other person remembers you made a significant contribution and impact. Take notes of what is said. At the end of that first story, ask for another and then another, until you have at least three stories.

3. When you have written down three stories, show your friend the descriptions of the 24 strengths below, and ask them to use the descriptions to identify the strengths that came out in the stories. As they name each strength, ask them to explain why they chose it. Listen carefully and write down what they tell you. Aim to choose about five to eight strengths.

4. When you have completed all your interviews, compare all the lists of strengths and their definitions and consolidate the information into a final list.

When all the comments are consolidated and integrated, particularly if they are from different aspects of your life, there is often an amazing congruence which leads to a deep understanding of how your strengths help you to live a powerful life in alignment with your values.

Expanded VIA Signature Strengths

Wisdom and knowledge	
Curiosity: Curiosity/Interest in the world	Openness to new experiences, being flexible and tolerant of ambiguity. A desire to explore the new and novel.
Learning: Love of learning	Enthusiastically learning new skills and knowledge. Enjoying becoming the expert in subjects.
Open-mindedness: Judgement/Critical thinking/ Open-mindedness	Examining things from all sides, thinking things through and not jumping to conclusions. Basing decisions on solid evidence. Being open-minded to consider all evidence or views fairly.
Creativity: Ingenuity/Originality/Practical intelligence	Using ingenuity and creativity to solve problems and achieve goals. It involves going beyond the conventional way of thinking and is sometimes called 'practical intelligence' or 'street smarts'.
Social intelligence: Social intelligence/Personal intelligence/Emotional intelligence	Having a good understanding of yourself and others. Being aware of your own moods, and how to manage them. In addition, being aware of the moods and feelings of others and how to relate to them.
Perspective: Perspective	Being wise and an expert in the most important and difficult areas of life; looking at life in a sensible and practical way that is helpful to yourself and others.

Courage	
Bravery: Valour and bravery	Not shrinking from threat or pain. Overcoming your own fear and taking a stance or action based on principle or morality.
Perseverance: Perseverance/Industry/ Diligence	The mental strength to strive for and achieve goals; finishing what you start despite obstacles and setbacks.

Courage

Authenticity: Integrity/Genuineness/Honesty	Speaking the truth and living your life in a genuine and authentic manner. Being open and honest about own thoughts, feelings and responsibilities; careful not to mislead yourself or others.

Humanity and love

Kindness: Kindness and generosity	Doing favours and good deeds for other people without expecting personal gain. Finding joy in giving and helping other people.
Love: Loving and allowing oneself to be loved	Developing close and intimate relationships with others, allowing them to reciprocate. The outcome is deep trust in and from others.

Justice

Teamwork: Citizenship/Teamwork/Duty/ Loyalty	Being a team player, loyal and dedicated to your colleagues, working hard and making sacrifices for the success of the team.
Fairness: Fairness and equity	Treating everyone according to the universal ideals of equality and justice. Respecting moral guidelines and being compassionate and caring for all classes of other people.
Leadership: Leadership	Motivating, directing and coordinating people towards a goal. It also involves listening to the opinions and feelings of others so as to achieve goals in an efficient and amiable manner.

Temperance

Self-regulation: Self-control	Keeping your desires and impulses under control. Knowing and doing what's correct.
Prudence: Prudence/Discretion/Caution	Being practical and careful about choices without taking undue risks and being inappropriately short-term orientated. Understanding and anticipating consequences of actions.
Modesty: Humility and modesty	Not needing to be in the spotlight; being humble and open to feedback and allowing your strength and accomplishments to speak for themselves.

Transcendence	
Beauty: Appreciation of beauty and excellence	Appreciating beauty, excellence and skill in all areas of life. Having a sense of awe about the world around you.
Gratitude: Gratitude	Being aware of the good things that are happening and not taking things for granted. A sense of wonder, thankfulness and appreciation for life and the gifts you have.
Hope: Hope/Optimism/Future-mindedness	Expecting the best and that good things will happen in the future. Confident that your own efforts will create a positive future.
Religiousness: Spirituality/Sense of purpose/ Faith/Religiousness	Having a strong belief about the higher purpose and meaning and your place within the larger scheme of things. This awareness is of great comfort and shapes personal daily actions.
Forgiveness: Forgiveness and mercy	Forgiving when wronged. Always allowing people a second chance; guided and believing in mercy rather than vengeance.
Humour: Humour and playfulness	Enjoying laughing, friendly teasing and making others laugh and smile. Seeing the lighter side of life and enjoying playing.
Zest: Zest/Passion/Enthusiasm	Energetic, spirited and passionate. Living life wholeheartedly as an adventure. Being totally committed to whatever personal actions are undertaken.

Checking the accuracy of your strengths

When completing a strengths questionnaire for the first time, or defining your own strengths, you may not be sure if your strengths list is accurate.

There is an easy way of checking the accuracy. Simply ask people who know you well for their views of the list. Your partner, siblings or children will know you very well from a particular perspective. Your colleagues with whom you work; the people in your community; your neighbours and sporting colleagues – each know you from a different perspective. These different perspectives can provide useful insights into how you use your strengths in the different areas of your life.

Samson uses his character strengths

Samson worked as a project manager, was married and had three young children. He took the VIA Survey of Character Strengths which identified his top two strengths to be '**Perseverance**: Perseverance/Industry/Diligence' and '**Love**: Loving, allowing oneself to be loved'.

He felt bitterly disappointed when he read these strengths. He was hoping for strengths like leadership and perspective, which he felt were more appropriate to his work situation. He could see very little use in strengths like perseverance and love. He felt short-changed.

He decided to check the accuracy of the assessment. He asked two of his colleagues at work, his wife and a neighbour with whom he had worked on a community-based action group to describe times when they thought he was at his best and then identify his strengths.

There were many similarities in the stories that were told. Samson's perseverance came to the fore at work when he worked late into the night to ensure a project was delivered on time; at home, when painting and decorating, he worked without taking breaks; how he was regarded as the role model in the community for persisting and not giving up on their issues.

Samson's connection with people correlated to his strength of loving and allowing himself to be loved. He was highly valued in his role as project manager, where he showed a deep concern for the impact of the projects on staff who had to accept new ways of working. At home it was demonstrated by his care for his youngsters and assisting his wife with chores and home maintenance And in the community, his understanding and connection with people with different viewpoints enabled the action group to recruit more members.

To Samson, some of the instances in the stories were not particularly significant to him, and so it surprised him to see how significant they were to others. Hearing these stories changed Samson's understanding and appreciation of his strengths. He realised that the strengths enabled him to do things that he had regarded as obvious and commonplace, but were regarded by others as remarkable.

With these new insights, Samson extended the application of his character strengths and put them to good use in other areas of his life. As he did so, he experienced himself becoming more powerful in the way that he related to others and got work done.

If given the chance, he will now tell you that his strengths have grown and matured. They now define who he is.

Can character strengths be used anywhere in life?

To answer this question, let's take a strength and see if it can be used in various areas of life. Take the character strength of a *love of learning* and let's see how it can be used by a person who is an accountant, a mom and an active member of a political party.

In the role of accountant she can use this strength to keep up with legislative changes and best practice to see how they can be applied on the job. She could also look for opportunities to deepen her understanding of accounting principles. She may even initiate learning sessions with her colleagues in the accounting department to ensure they are kept up to date with accounting developments.

As a mom, she can apply the strength by continually looking for ways to be a more effective parent; by reading and researching contemporary literature on what makes for a cohesive family and intimate loving relationships. She can extend the strength to her family, encouraging her loved ones to be curious about the world around them and to use the Internet, the local library and wise friends to research and find out about topics that interest them.

Do not pray for easy lives. Pray to be stronger men! Do not pray for tasks equal to your powers. Pray for power equal to your tasks.

Phillips Brooks

As an active member of a political party, this strength can be used to research trends locally and internationally, to look for solutions and ways of getting them accepted by her party and by the national government. She might encourage like-minded people in the political party to adopt causes in which they are interested, and to find ways of advancing and applying the knowledge to local problems.

So the answer to the question posed earlier, is that character strengths can be applied to good effect in all situations. Using character strengths in achieving your life goals enhances the probability of your success and leads to greater feelings of satisfaction and well-being.[8] The outcome is not only better results and personal excellence, but a feeling of upliftment and joy.

Using strengths at home

The identification and use of strengths is very useful at home, with loved ones and balances any tendency to be overly focused on our loving partner's weaknesses and vulnerabilities. Helping your partner develop strengths not only benefits them but will deepen your relationship. Taking one of the strengths surveys is a useful way of creating a common language about strengths at home. The VIA Strengths Survey is available in both adult and child versions, which will enable you to create a common 'strength vocabulary' throughout your family[9].

A simple way of developing the strengths of your loved ones is to name them, together with the example of how they have been applied. Saying how you appreciate the use of their strength will reinforce its use. This works as well for adults as it does for children.

Another way of developing the strengths of a loving partner is to go on a 'strength date'. After you and your partner have identified your strengths, take time to deepen your understanding and appreciation of them in the other person's life. You can do this by chatting over a meal together or when walking in the park together. Each person names a strength of the other, and describes how the use of that strength impacts on them and how they appreciate it.

We all have ability. The difference is how we use it.

Stevie Wonder

Alternatively, on the 'strength date' you could talk about the strengths that originally attracted you to each other when you first started going out together. Those are the special qualities that you saw in the other person, and which were the starting point from which your love blossomed.

These conversations will enhance your understanding and use of character strengths, deepening your loving relationships.

Using strengths at work

Being able to use your strengths at work has really important payoffs for you. People who use their strengths every day at work are six times more likely to be engaged in their jobs than people who don't. People who use their strengths every day at work are three times more likely to report that they have an excellent quality of life[10].

If you are unlucky enough to find yourself in a job where you don't feel engaged, you could try to find ways of using your top strengths. Look for new and different ways of bringing your strengths into play as you do your work. This may mean you need to look beyond the confines of your immediate job and find ways of using the strengths to do more to meet customer needs or to help others.

Johannes makes use of strengths at work

Johannes worked as a driver of a minivan for a national chain of motor vehicle servicing agents. For many years he did the same job: dropping off customers at their workplaces when they brought in their vehicles to be serviced, collecting spare-parts during the day and, at the end of the day, bringing customers back to the workshop to collect their vehicles.

Johannes' top two strengths on the VIA Signature Strengths were rated as '**Curiosity/** Interest in the world' and '**Humour** and playfulness'. Now you may ask: how can a person who has such a narrowly defined job use these strengths at work?

For Johannes the answer was simple. His strength of curiosity led him to be naturally interested in the customers he transported – the jobs they held, their families and sporting interests. Repeat customers appreciated his remembering their names and personal details. They also enjoyed having a relaxed conversation with someone who took a personal interest in them.

Combined with his other strength (humour), the customers enjoyed Johannes' amusing anecdotes from his and his other customers' lives.

His employers very soon took advantage of his strengths and asked him to informally but regularly assess the customers' experience of having their vehicles serviced by the agency. His informal feedback enabled management to take quick action in areas of customer dissatisfaction and, in one case, even prevented the potential for fraud by one of the customers.

Johannes was a regular winner of the agency's Best Employee of the Month awards, although he always claimed his real satisfaction was putting a smile on the faces of 'his' customers.

Using his top strengths in creative ways enabled him to transform his job and to create deep satisfaction and meaning.

Deepening understanding of your character strengths

Everyone has character strengths, but what differs from person to person is the combination of strengths each has. Because there are so many potential character strength combinations, it is highly unlikely that anyone else has quite the same combination as you do. This means that there is no common formula or template that can be applied to everyone regarding use of their character strengths. Rather, it's up to you to understand how your unique combination of strengths interacts and reinforces the other, and how they can assist you achieve excellence in your life.

Other people can give you advice, but ultimately it's up to you to use and apply your unique character strengths to fulfil your purpose and mission in life.

So how can you develop a deep understanding and appreciation of your particular combination of character strengths? Here are two simple reflection exercises which you can use to play with the concepts of your strengths, in your mind, and by so doing, deepen your insight and understanding of them:

Deepening understanding of your character strengths: reflection exercise 1

1. Write down your top five character strengths.
2. Choose the top strength that you believe defines you, that makes you powerful and that you use most effortlessly. Incidentally, it may not be the one on top of your list.
3. Think of times when you have used this top strength to achieve greatness. Reflect on a specific example at work and also at home of how you've used your top strength and write down the specific results you achieved.
4. Make plans to find how you can use your top strength in other areas of your life – at work, at home, in the community and so on.

Deepening understanding of your character strengths: reflection exercise 2

1. Write each of your top five strengths on a separate card, one strength to a card. (An A4 sheet cut into four works just as well.)
2. Choose the top strength that you believe defines you, makes you feel powerful and that you use most effortlessly. Write down how you have used that strength recently.
3. Take a second strength and reflect on how this strength relates to your top strength and how it supports and interacts with it. It could work to amplify it by increasing its effectiveness, or work to modify it by moderating and tempering its influence. Write down your thoughts.
4. Take each of the remaining strengths in turn and reflect how that strength interacts with the top and the other strengths. Think of specific examples of when this occurred.
5. Move the cards around to physically demonstrate the patterns of how they interact and connect with each other. Some strengths might 'drive', whereas other strengths might 'harmonise'.

All courses of action are risky, so prudence is not in avoiding danger (it's possible), but calculating risk and acting decisively. Make mistakes of ambition and not mistakes of sloth. Develop the strength to do bold things, not the strength to suffer.

Niccolo Machiavelli

Some cautionary comments about using strengths

Using your character strengths has the potential to make you stronger, to enhance the impact of your contribution and build your resilience. Using your strengths will make what you are doing seem easy, logical and natural. You may be surprised that what is obvious to you is not obvious to others. These are the hallmarks of using your strengths in appropriate ways.

Used inappropriately, however, they can cause problems. Consider the case studies below.

When a strength becomes a weakness: 1

Vitore's top strength was **'Bravery:** Valour and bravery'. If Vitore believed that something was wrong, he would say so. In situations where other people would hold their tongues, he often fearlessly spoke up for what he believed was right.

His colleagues at work praised his courage and the fact he was prepared to say unpopular things when they weren't. They also praised him for sticking to his principles and speaking his mind. With time Vitore gained a reputation with his co-workers for courageous forthrightness.

There was another side to this reputation however. His courageous contributions were sometimes perceived by others as inopportune and disruptive. He also developed the reputation as a 'wild card' who 'shot from the hip without thinking'. Gradually, his reputation for having the courage to speak the truth was tainted by his making comments without regard for time and place.

Thus the impact of using 'Valour and bravery' was undermined by not considering that the *timing* of his contribution and the impact on others.

When a strength becomes a weakness: 2

Hanna's top strength was '**Hope**: Hope/Optimism/Future-mindedness'. She always saw the bright side of situations. She was loved and respected as a person with a sunny disposition, who could be counted on to see options and possibilities, even in difficult situations. Her optimism was contagious and people appreciated her positive approach to life.

Her use of this strength, however, did have a downside. This occurred at work where she was a team leader but failed to recognise negative trends in her department that required firm corrective actions to be taken.

She preferred to use her top strength to encourage her colleagues and subordinates to be positive and optimistic. The worse the situation became, the more she responded by using this strength to find reasons to be optimistic and hoping things would change by themselves. The result was that she delayed taking action and the situation worsened.

Finally it came to a head, when the workforce threatened to strike. Only then did Hanna realise that she had responded to the problem by increasing the *intensity* of her strength and did not appreciate the negative impact it had on the situation.

Both Vitore and Hanna had overused a single character strength, to the exclusion of others, ignoring the impact it had on other people. Their strengths became weaknesses.

To prevent this happening to you, imagine your strengths having both an on-off switch and a volume control knob. Use the on-off switch to remember there are times when it's appropriate to apply your strengths and others when it's not. Use the volume control knob to raise or lower the intensity of the strengths that you are using.

Exercises

Choose one or more questions from the list below to consolidate and apply your learning.

Written exercises

1. Reflect on the adversity over which you have triumphed, which you described in Chapter 1. How did you utilise your strengths to do this? What does your triumph teach you about your strengths?

2. How can you apply your character strengths to better achieve your purpose and mission in life?

3. Review the goals you have identified for yourself in Chapter 2. Identify how your strengths can help you achieve them.

4. What strength would you like to develop? Choose a strength you would like to enhance or amplify and plan to do so in the next three days.

5. How can you use your top strengths at work and outside of work?

6. What are your loved ones' distinctive strengths and how can you encourage their use?

ENDNOTES

1   Sourced from: http://www.authentichappiness.sas.upenn.edu. Accessed 1 January 2011.

2   Peterson, C. & Seligman, M.E. 2004. *Character strengths and virtues: a handbook and classification.* Washington, DC: APA Press

3   Park, N., Peterson C., & Seligman, M 2004. Strengths of character and well-being. *Journal of social and clinical psychology,* 23 603–619.

4   Buckingham, M. & Clifton, D.O. 2004. *Now, discover your strengths: how to develop your talents and those of the people you manage.* Sydney: Pocket Books.

5   Available on: http://www.strengths2020.com. Accessed 1 July 2011.

6   Linley, A., Willars, J. & Biswas-Diener, R. 2010. *The strengths book: be confident, be successful and enjoy better relationships by realising the best of you.* Coventry: Perfect Paperback.

7   Adapted from: http://www.viastrengths.org/Applications/Exercises/tabid/132/ Default.aspx July 16, 2008 340 Ways to Use VIA Character Strengths. Tayyab Rashid & Afroze Anjum. University of Pennsylvania. Accessed 12 December 2011. Used with permission.

8   Linley, P.A., Nielsen, K.M., Gillett, R. & Biswas-Diener, R. 2010. Using signature strengths in pursuit of goals: Effects on goal progress, need satisfaction, and well-being, and implications for coaching psychologists. *International coaching psychology review,* 5(1):6–15.

9   See the website reference 1.

10 Rath, T. & Harter, J. 2009. *Well-being: The five essential elements.* New York: The Gallup Press.

6

Maintain perspective

Maintain perspective	
Generate positive feelings	Be realistically optimistic
Persevere by being open-minded and flexible	Reach out to others
Connect to your meaning in life	Use your unique strengths

When you go through tough times or when adversity strikes, resilience often wanes. Just when you need to be resilient the most, it's often at its lowest ebb. Your thoughts become negative, and it is very easy to slip into a downward spiral of doom and gloom, which erodes your resilience even further.

At these low points it is particularly important to be aware of your internal world of thoughts. The thoughts you have will either assist in building you back up or break you down further. But being aware of them and their impact is often more difficult than it may seem.

The effect of being negative at work

Leticia had the job of production manager in a pharmaceutical company. She was highly qualified, and had been with the organisation for several years. From the feedback she had received during this time, she was sure that she was on the fast track to the top.

She was, therefore, quite taken aback when she overheard the CEO say that she was negative and unlikely to be promoted further in the organisation.

'How dare he say that? And behind my back!' she raged to herself.

That evening she went for a walk to cool down and reflect on what had happened. Once she had got over her anger, she evaluated her attitude at work as objectively as she could.

> It's in tough times, when you need to be at your most resilient, that your resilience is often at its lowest point.

She recalled incidents when her negative attitude had probably affected her contributions in meetings and the decision-making with the senior team. She slowly realised that she had become increasingly stressed over the past months, and even years, and this had led to her becoming negative and pessimistic.

To her chagrin, she admitted to herself that she had indeed become a negative influence at work.

Where do thoughts come from?

We experience our thoughts, feelings and attitudes all together. At times we have positive thoughts, feel upbeat and have and an optimistic attitude. At other times we may have negative thoughts, feel down and pessimistic.

In order to help us build our resilience, it is useful to understand our thoughts better. In many ways it's artificial to separate thoughts, feelings and attitudes from each other, because they are so integrally linked together. But the value of doing so is that it helps us understand each of their roles in dealing with adversity, as well as in living a life of fulfilment and joy in the face of difficulties. For example, while it is fairly common to experience mood swings, we can't simultaneously have a mixture of both negative and positive thoughts. In other words we can't feel upbeat and happy, while at the same time feel sad and down. This has important implications for how we can deal with and overcome overwhelmingly negative thoughts.

So let's start off asking the question 'Where do thoughts come from?' Some people say they swirl around in one's head and heart and are very difficult to grasp. Others say that their thoughts are heavily influenced by events that happen. A significant happy event causes positive thoughts, while a significant negative event will result in negative thoughts.

Now this does seem to be logical. In other words, a significantly positive or negative event will be experienced as positive or negative in the associated thoughts. This belief can be expressed linearly: as the event leading to a thought, which leads to a feeling, which in turn leads to an attitude.

> Thoughts become emotions.
>
> Emotions become behaviours.
>
> Behaviours become habits.
>
> Habits become character.
>
> Character becomes destiny.
>
> And destiny is who you are and will be.
>
> So mind those thoughts!
>
> *Unknown author*

While this may seem logical, the logic and belief is substantially flawed. Let's look at thoughts differently. Sometimes we have little or no influence over the external events that occur in our lives, despite setting goals and working hard to achieve them. Sometimes we succeed and sometimes unexpected things happen and get in the way. Things happen. Life happens.

> When something bad happens, people sometimes say that they had no choice but to react in a certain way – for example, to lose their temper or to lash out. They may actually say 'When you did that, you made me lose my temper', or 'When you said that, you made me hit you.'

But we do have the capacity for choice. We can choose how we will react to these events and exercising this choice is entirely under our control. This choice is the ultimate freedom we have as human beings: the choice of how to respond to the things that happen to us.

In other words, they feel that they had no choice in the matter. To these people there is a logical and direct link between the event, which caused the thought, which caused the feeling and which resulted in the attitude. Their action was, therefore, beyond their control. From their perspective, there is no personal choice available to them. It's not their fault, because their reaction was caused and forced on them by the actions of others. That logic is used to justify bullying, losing one's temper and even violence.

This argument is, of course, complete nonsense. We do have a choice in how we interpret the events that happen to us. If you momentarily lose concentration in traffic and drive your car into the back of another car, you choose how to interpret the event. Do you choose to see this as an absolute disaster and further proof of how stupid you are? Or do you choose to see this as an unfortunate and really regrettable incident that requires immediate action but doesn't affect the rest of your life?

A much more accurate way of understanding the linking in the sequence of experiencing an event and the related thoughts, feelings and attitude is to see that the event takes place, followed by the *choice* the person makes about how to interpret it. This leads to the thoughts, which leads to feelings and which, in turn, leads to attitude.

In order to deepen our understanding of the choice we have about our thoughts and perspective, let's explore the concept of thoughts further.

Thinking about thoughts

The thoughts we think create us. In this way, we are not a product of what we believe ourselves to be, or what others say we are. We are what we think.

Thoughts are very powerful. A few years ago I was walking in the Drakensberg on the third day of an arduous hike, carrying a heavy backpack. The pack contained camping equipment, a sleeping bag, food and water, all necessary for a multi-day hike.

As I slowly trudged down the well-worn path in the late afternoon, I suddenly saw, out of the corner of my eye, that I was about to step on a poisonous Berg Adder.

I instantly bounced back several steps up the path. My eyes were wide open. My heart was racing, my tiredness gone and I had forgotten the weight on my back.

> We are what we think. All that we are arises with our thoughts. With our thoughts, we make the world.
>
> *Buddha*

Out of immediate danger from the snake, I gathered my courage and cautiously edged forward to see how I could get round it. It was still lying in the path. It hadn't even moved. As I inched slowly closer I realised that it had failed to move for good reason. It wasn't a snake at all. It was an odd-shaped stick masquerading as a snake.

Nevertheless, I took a large step over the stick and only once over it did my heart stop pounding, my breathing slow and the knot in my stomach begin to dissolve.

My mind had interpreted the stick as a dangerous snake and the burst of adrenaline it initiated in my body made me forget my fatigue and aches, as I danced effortlessly back up the path. The fact that the interpretation was erroneous made no difference to how my body reacted. I thought I was in extreme danger, and that thought required me immediately to get out of the way of the threat.

When I interpreted the situation differently, thinking there was no snake, only a stick, a different powerful mind-body response was triggered. The stick held no threat and my heightened physical state of arousal dissipated.

Were the initial interpretation and thoughts about the snake true? No they weren't. But my mind believed they were true, and immediate physical action was required. I didn't think to question my thoughts. To anyone else observing what had happened, my actions may have been odd or even amusing. To me, at that time, they were life-saving.

To experience the power of thoughts yourself, try the exercises on the following page:

Thoughts self-test

First, slowly read the following:

I love apples and eating each one is an adventure. This morning I tried a new variety I had not tasted before. I selected the best looking apple from the fruit bowl. Its size filled my whole palm and fingers. The skin was a smooth golden colour with a slight blush of brownish orange. It had a woody, aromatically flavoured scent.

I bit through the resisting skin, through to the crisp flesh inside. It was very juicy and tasted at one moment mildly tart, and then in another almost sweet. What absolute bliss!

Now, close your eyes, and try to not think of an apple for ten seconds.

Most people who do this exercise say that once they close their eyes, the thought of an apple comes unbidden into their minds. They can see and even taste the apple. This simple exercise illustrates how our thoughts are so powerful and difficult to control.

Our thoughts are often experienced as not only uncontrollable, but also jumbled. The experience can be like a talk-radio show playing in our heads, which we can't switch off. Thoughts pop into our consciousness very rapidly and the negative ones can churn around and easily magnify themselves, until we become stuck, focusing on negative things or a negative incident.

> Don't underestimate the power of your thoughts. Persistent negative thoughts and thinking can create a mental pattern – a groove in which your thoughts run, which becomes your habitual way of thinking and perspective.

When our thoughts go round and round on the same subject and it feels as though we cannot stop them, this is called over-thinking or ruminating. It's a bit like what cows do after they have eaten their fill during the day. They regurgitate some of their feed and chew it over and over again. Chewing the cud serves a useful purpose for cows, ensuring the coarse materials they have eaten are ground down, making it easier for them to be digested. If you have ever seen a cow doing this, you can't help but get the feeling they enjoy it. Our mental ruminating involves regurgitation and chewing the cud of old negative thoughts, which, in contrast, can be quite distressing.

To understand ruminating, imagine your brain as a sandbar in a slow-moving river. The sandbar has recently been exposed by the river, which has receded, and is absolutely smooth. Gentle rain starts to fall onto the sandbar. After some time, there is a build-up of rainwater on the smooth surface of the sandbar.

Water will always find the easiest way to flow, which is, of course, downhill. On the sandbar, the rain water gradually moves down the slight slope in the direction the river is flowing. As it flows, it slowly erodes small paths. As more rain falls on the sandbar, so the rain water flows into and down the paths that have been established. As more water flows down the paths, so the paths are eroded deeper and deeper. Very soon, it's impossible for the rain water to flow in any direction other than in the established paths.

Following this metaphor, negative or unwanted thoughts that are repeated become grooved into or become our habitual way of thinking. Once thoughts get into a pattern or a habit, they become more difficult to break out of, because of the ease in which the thoughts revert to travelling down the paths they have made previously.

The problem with thoughts

Why is it that we have so many negative thoughts? A major reason is that, as human beings, we are more alert to negative rather than positive events.[1] From an evolutionary point of view, this was a survival tool in the face of life-threatening dangers we faced. In our distant past, threats came from animals and hostile neighbours as we roamed the plains of Africa. The individuals and tribes who were the most alert to danger, who reacted quickest and successfully fought, fled or hid, were the ones who survived.

The amygdala area of our brain developed and became highly skilled at recognising and dealing with physical threats. It is the most primitive part of our brain and has a direct role in identifying threat and initiating instant physical reaction. It initiates dramatic physiological changes in our bodies by pumping adrenaline and noradrenaline into our systems. This results in narrowing of our thought process to focus attention on the threat at hand. The resultant tense energy concentrates our attention, so as to deal with a potential life-threatening event.[2]

> Everything we hear is an opinion, not a fact. Everything we see is a perspective, not the truth.
>
> *Marcus Aurelius*

Over time, our predecessors changed their lifestyles from hunter-gatherers to agrarian crop cultivators, living in larger communities and villages. From these beginnings, our 21st-century lifestyle was born. Not only is our present lifestyle radically different from that of our predecessors, but also the thinking our new lifestyle requires is different. In the past, being alert to threats and reacting fast was a survival mechanism that became hardwired in our brains. Fortunately, we now seldom need this ability. In contrast, the thinking that we need today has a long-term time horizon, uses imagination and creates and explores alternatives. Rather than muscular energy, creative energy is needed.[3]

The change in these thinking requirements has occurred extremely rapidly, in the context of evolutionary change. This means that our alertness for danger and physical threat, with the associated narrowing focus of thought to deal with the threat, is still present and part of the hard-wiring of our brains today.

But that's not all. In addition to having to deal with this evolutionary hangover from our past, our thoughts and thinking actually deceive us. We believe that the way we perceive the world and our thoughts is accurate and true. We seldom question our thoughts, as most of the time we experience our thoughts as reflecting reality and being true.

Yet this is not so. We have established that from an evolutionary point of view we are more alert for the negative than for the positive. So the way that we notice and pay attention to the world, and experience it, is through that bias. In addition, our own personal history and experience directs us to see things from our particular personal perspective as well.

In other words, if you are on the lookout for particular events happening, guess what? You will find them along with ample evidence to support what you have found.

So many Volksie Beetles

Richard loves telling the story of buying his first motorcar. It goes back to his father insisting that he always pay cash for big purchases, rather than buy on credit. So he spent months scrimping and saving before he was able to buy a car.

He recalls that, when using public transport or walking, he fantasised having the freedom and prestige of owning his own vehicle. Not only would it save him time and endless hassles, but it would be what he described as a 'babe magnet'. It would spruce up his dismal romantic life.

Finally, when he had saved sufficient to purchase a vehicle, he found an ancient Volkswagen with the old Beetle shape. He was absolutely thrilled when he finally handed over a cash cheque in exchange for the keys. As soon as he drove away down the road, he gave an air punch with a yell of delight. Yes! His dream had come true!

Almost immediately he saw another Volksie Beetle coming towards him from the opposite direction. He flashed his lights and waved. And soon there was another! And then another! He was amazed at how many other Volkswagen Beetles they were on the road that day.

Of course they weren't more Volksie beetles on the road than before. What had happened was that, because Richard was so intensely focused on his distinctively shaped Volkswagen, he became alert and sensitised to them. While in the past they had been just part of a background blur of vehicles, they were now suddenly in acute focus. His frame of reference and his thoughts were dramatically influenced by his purchase. Being more alert to Volksie Beetles, he now 'saw' each one clearly and with greater impact and intensity than ever before.

The more Richard thought about how many Volksie Beetles there were on the road that day, the more he was convinced he was correct. It did not occur to him to question his perspective.

Like Richard, we experience our thoughts as accurate and true. Yet our thoughts, and the way we see the world, are intensely personal. Our view is influenced by our experiences and biases. We construct thoughts to interpret and deal with the world around us. As a result, our thoughts are not grounded in reality. Neither are they the absolute truth.

Ask any policeman dealing with a serious accident. From twenty eye-witnesses, all seeing the accident clearly, he will get twenty slightly different, or even very different, honest accounts of what happened.

A distortion called 'cognitive fusion' occurs when we and the thoughts we have are seen as part of each other and inseparable. This happens when we believe that what we are thinking is actually happening; that our thoughts are true reflections of reality, rather than simply constructs in our mind.

In order to develop resilient ways of thinking, it is useful to understand that our thoughts are just constructs. They are created and biased by who we are, what we interpret and experience. They are not necessarily true at all.

The implication is that you always have a choice. We need to have our thoughts, otherwise our thoughts will have us!

The good news is that with this insight it becomes easier to deal with unwanted thoughts and reduce the impact of them, as well as to increase positive and welcome thoughts.

Your mind-set determines your success

Success is determined by your mind-set, rather than by being lucky or by great intelligence.[4]

People with a success mind-set believe their talents can be enhanced and developed through persistence, education and learning. This is called a 'growth mind-set'. They regard making mistakes as a natural part of learning, and are thus not too fussed when things go wrong. They try to learn from their mistakes and not to repeat them. They mostly understand that change is inevitable and believe they usually have to go along with change in order to keep up and not be left behind. This mind-set enhances their resilience and enables them to persist in the face of setbacks.[5]

This contrasts with people who believe that their abilities and talents are unalterable. This is called a 'fixed mind-set'. These people think and react very differently. They believe that they only have the talents that they are given and there is no way they can be improved. They believe practising, addressing weaknesses, and trying to learn new skills and behaviours will not change much. So they don't do so willingly. Consequently, they become defensive about their abilities or lack of them, try to hide their deficiencies and react defensively to mistakes.[6]

It is not events, but our beliefs about them, that cause us suffering.

Epictetus

This fixed mindset and defensive attitude prevents them from learning from their mistakes, because they are so busy trying to prevent their weaknesses from being revealed. Change is threatening, because they are unlikely to have developed the personality or innate ability to cope with the challenges it brings. Their resilience is diminished, which is shown by their becoming discouraged and giving up easily.

What is really interesting is that the growth mind-set actually produces physical changes in the brain. When new information is learned, the brain forms new connections between neurons and, over time, it physically becomes 'smarter'. This improved efficiency and functioning enables an improvement in the capacity to learn. It helps you in being prepared to receive feedback and to deal with life's challenges. It also assists you to learn new ways of doing things which, in turn, improves the brain's functionality.

Great news if you have a growth mind-set. Unfortunately, it doesn't happen to those with a fixed mind-set.[7]

So what is the real implication of all this for you?

Well, it's further evidence that your thoughts and perspective are very important from the point of view of building your resilience. Thoughts are not just uncontrollable things that enter into your mind, sometimes welcome and sometimes not, and don't really matter. They do matter.

First. It is useful to understand that you are not your thoughts. You are a soul, for the lack of an alternate word, and separate from your thoughts. Your thoughts come and go, are sometimes correct and sometimes aren't, and even though it feels as though they are who you are, they are not *you*.

Second. The perspective you choose influences your feelings, which, in turn, influences your attitude, which has a direct impact on the actions you take.

Third. You can't stop the thoughts that pop into your head. You can, however, change how you interpret events and, thus, your perspective. Although thoughts seem to be true and unalterable, they are open to being influenced, changed and even substituted by others. You can choose the perspective you would like to experience.

People with a fixed mind-set often struggle to accept these assertions. People with a growth mind-set find it easier to accept them and become better able to live the life that they want. Thus, understanding thoughts and perspectives is the starting point of creating a life of happiness and joy; of being resilient in the face of obstacles and recovering from adversity.

Too much positive thinking is dangerous!

The idea of positive thoughts being important has been around for a long time. There is even a movement, founded on the principle of positive thinking, called Positive Mental Attitude – PMA for short. The movement's central philosophy is that one needs to have a positive outlook and positive thoughts to work hard to have *only* positive thoughts. Taken to its conclusion, is the belief is that negative thinking and negative thoughts are bad and only positive thoughts are good.

The idea of thinking only positive thoughts is, at best, problematic and, at worst, dangerously dysfunctional.

Let's take an example. At the time of writing this book, the world is slowly recovering from an economic crisis, precipitated by sub-prime loans granted in America. These home loans or mortgages were issued by large numbers of American banks to people who, the lending officials knew, could not ever pay them back, unless the value of their houses rose with a booming housing market. The bank officials were only thinking positive thoughts. This was naive, as they didn't consider potential risks, the realities of the American economy and the dynamics of global market forces. The result was one of the worst financial crises the world has ever seen.

Like the American banks, people who only want to hear good news and have only positive thoughts run a grave danger of being blindsided by reality. It makes us run the risk of making terrible mistakes. It is much better to be able to accept and understand that we must have negative thoughts, as well as to be able to express our negative opinions to others.

Negative thoughts are, in themselves, not necessarily bad. What is important is how the negative thoughts are expressed in one's own head, as well as how they are expressed verbally to others. Negative thoughts based on fact are important, and should be considered and verbalised. Someone who only expresses positive views and positive thoughts is unlikely to express a balanced view or have their opinions respected and accepted by their audience.

Ironically, the harder one tries to be only positive and to have only positive thoughts, the more likely it is that negative thoughts will occur. We need to embrace both positive and negative thoughts, ensuring that we have a balanced perspective.

When negative thinking is valuable

It is foolish to go through life trying to think only positive thoughts. Negative thoughts obviously have a role to play in life because life is not all positive.

Take, for example, the thoughts associated with regret. When you look back on your life, do you remember things that you regret? People mostly regret things they didn't do, such as abandoning a safe career working for a big organisation and not taking the risky route of pursuing their passion in life. Others may regret things they have done, such as an extramarital affair or buying stock market shares when the market was at its peak.

Regret can be expected in these examples and will, most probably, be associated with negative thoughts. Those negative thoughts are not necessarily wrong or bad.

Let's explore this a little bit further. Regret is a normal part of life, and is useful, because the negative feeling of embarrassment and guilt motivates us to do something about the cause. We need to correct the cause or deal with its impact on our present situation, by changing what we can, or learning from the incident and doing something different in the future. In this way, regret triggers and is part of our personal learning and growth.

> I have come to the frightening conclusion that I am the decisive element. It is my personal approach that creates the climate. It is my daily mood that makes the weather. I possess tremendous power to make life miserable or joyous. I can be a tool of torture or an instrument of inspiration. I can humiliate or humour, hurt or heal. In all situations, it is my response that decides whether a crisis is escalated or de-escalated, and a person is humanized or dehumanized. If we treat people as they are, we make them worse. If we treat people as they ought to be, we help them become what they are capable of becoming.
>
> *Goethe*

Just because you've lost your temper and yelled at the kids, it doesn't make you a bad person. Just because you have strayed in your marriage, even if that has caused great pain, it doesn't mean that you will continue to have pain for the rest of your life.

When asked to reflect on their lives, it is common for women in midlife express regret. For most women, midlife is a time of re-evaluation and even crisis. Some are able to say that they are flourishing while others aren't. Those that flourish are positive in their attitude and thoughts, set goals to change their circumstances and take action to achieve them. They use their negative thoughts as a springboard for change in their lives. This is in contrast to those that want change but wait for change to happen. In their case, the negative thoughts make them feel powerless, so they wait for their situation to improve, unfortunately, often in vain.[8]

We can learn and change based on our past negative experiences. It is what you make of your life today that counts. You cannot change what is in the past, but with effort and determination, you can definitely influence your future.

If we constantly dwell on negative events, and have predominantly negative thoughts, negative thinking can become the hallmark of our lives, with resulting unhappiness and dissatisfaction. Should this happen, we need to change our thoughts and perspective.

Common thinking mistakes

Because we think so fast, and our thinking is not easily apparent, it's easy to make mistakes in thinking which have a big impact on our perspective.

There are five common thinking mistakes. Let's take an example of something that happens and use that to illustrate the five commonest mistakes.

You have just learnt that your partner has crashed into the back of another vehicle. Fortunately, no one is injured, but the car is severely damaged and is in the process of being towed away. The following are examples of faulty thinking and how to avoid them.

1. Over-thinking or rumination

The mistake. Over-thinking occurs when small details are obsessively analysed over and again, until they become blown out of proportion. Small things become big and scary.

Example. 'The entire car is damaged. The wheel alignment will be out. The cooling system will always be suspect. The repair will rust in a short time. Panel-beaters never repair cars the way they should after an accident. They will overcharge me. I hope they don't pinch any of the undamaged parts of the car while it's in the workshop. There is so much that can go wrong. This is a disaster!'

What to do about it: Maintain perspective by writing down each of the concerns and develop an action plan to deal with each of them.

2. Simplification

The mistake. Paying too much attention to one or two areas. This obscures the big picture, which can lead to your thinking becoming inflexible and, ultimately, stuck.

Example. 'This is going to affect our motor insurance premiums. Our no-claim bonus will disappear. We will be a poor credit risk. We will pay more. We will have to cut our spending to survive.'

What to do about it. Maintain perspective by accepting that life is difficult. Everyone makes mistakes and things go wrong. Find the positive in what has happened and look for alternative ways of coping with the outcome.

3. Generalising

The mistake. Believing that, because something is true in one particular case, it is always true throughout life.

Example. 'Driving into the back of another car was my partner's fault. He is obviously a careless driver. If he drives again he will, no doubt, have another accident. He shouldn't be allowed to drive at all.'

What to do about it. Maintain perspective by accepting that what has happened in the past remains in the past and won't necessarily become the future. Examine the thinking that led you to this conclusion to see if it holds true, making sure you keep the big picture in mind.

4. Comparison to other people

The mistake. Comparing yourself to other people who have more than you or who are better than you in some aspect of their lives.

Example. 'Our neighbours have never crashed their car. They don't have the same problems that we do. Why can't we just be like them?'

What to do about it. Maintain perspective by comparing yourself to yourself, rather than to others. Reflect on how you have grown and developed as a human being, improving your weaknesses and developing your strengths. Acknowledge and be at peace with the idea that there will always be people who, in some aspects of their lives, have things that you don't, and others who will be better than you in some areas of life. On the other side of the coin, you have many things that others don't, and are better off than others in many areas of your life.

5. Making things worse (Catastrophising)

The mistake. You make things worse by over-reacting

Example. 'He is completely stupid! He is negligent! He can't be trusted! How did I end up living with this man? He's going to ruin my life!'

What to do about it. Maintain perspective by focusing on the facts. The worst possible consequence did not happen. Devise several different strategies to cope with the situation and, after considering each one carefully, choose the most suitable course of action.

Panic attack at night!

Thokozani had a panic attack last night. She woke in the early hours of the morning with her thoughts out of control: 'The financial markets are in a panic; a world-wide recession is likely; people will lose jobs; crime will rocket; and the impact on individuals, families and livelihoods will be dreadful. My retirement savings will be inadequate; finding work impossible. I will end up selling *The Big Issue* on street corners!'

She couldn't shake these thoughts. Like laundry in a washing machine, her thoughts went round and round, paused, then round and round again. The more she tried to stop them, the more persistent they became. She began to sweat with anxiety.

Eventually she got out of bed and decided to take control of the thoughts before her thoughts took total control of her.

She asked herself how probable were all the catastrophic outcomes. The answer was 'most unlikely'. She then conjured up more realistic and useful thoughts. 'I have been through tough times before and I will be able to get through this' and 'There is very little I can do to influence the stock market, so let me rather think about the how I can change my family's spending patterns.'

She wrote down some ideas about how her family could prioritise their spending. Almost immediately she felt calmer and more in control. She had stopped her downward-spiralling and negative thinking by channelling them into problem-solving.

With relief, she went back to bed and switched off the light, confident that she would be able to go back to sleep and take action the following day.

How to change your thoughts and perspective

In situations where our thoughts have become inappropriately and overwhelmingly negative, is it really possible to stop and change them?

Happily, the answer is that you can change negative thinking and your perspective.

When you become aware that you have more negative thoughts than you would like, simply ask yourself: 'Am I enjoying these thoughts?' If the answer is 'no', then, in essence, there are five options open to you:

- Choose to accept your thoughts.
- Reframe your thoughts.
- Distract yourself.
- Avoid negative-thinking triggers.
- Call out 'Stop!'

1. Choose to accept your thoughts

This rather counter-intuitive approach to maintaining perspective involves accepting the upsetting and unwanted thoughts, rather than fighting against them.[9.]

The rationale is that sometimes the harder you try to control or avoid unpleasant thoughts, the more you focus and dwell on them. This leads to further negative thoughts, such as self-recrimination and guilt. The result is a negative spiral of frustration, anger and despair, which makes the original negative thoughts worse. In other words, the more you try to control your thoughts, the more you will create other negative thoughts, and the less successful you will be.

Let's say you are worried. Very worried. This could be about a significant upcoming romantic date, business meeting, university examination or speech you have to make. The more that you think about it, the tenser to become. You try to stop worrying, but it doesn't work. As the important event comes closer, your worry escalates. Soon it is almost all you think about. At work your output is negatively affected. At home you are distant, short-tempered and you snap at your loved ones. This makes you feel guilty because your work is affecting your personal life. And you feel awful for being distant and impatient with the ones you love. That, in turn, makes you feel helpless and that you can't get your life together. A real negative spiral!

Struggling to control unwanted and unpleasant thoughts is the problem, not the solution.

But how do you stay open and accept negative thoughts and feelings when your natural instinct is to regard them as an unwanted problem and thus fight against them?

This solution is to be mindful and present, to experience what is happening in the moment that it happens. Don't fight the thoughts. Picture a 'struggle switch' in your mind, and switch it into the off-position. Accept and experience the negative thoughts and feelings, without trying to control them, making them worse. This practice is called 'mindfulness'[10] which many people use in a variety of trying situations with great success.

At the heart of mindfulness is experiencing and accepting your thoughts in a non-judgemental way. It involves calming yourself and becoming aware of how your body is reacting and how your body is feeling. This enables you to become completely in touch and aware of what is happening in the moment, and being open to the thoughts and feelings that come to you.

Accept the thoughts and feelings as perfectly normal and a vital part of the experience of being human. Practise noticing your thinking and feelings; view them as your mind's efforts to solve what it sees as a threat to its survival. When you do this, the thoughts and feelings won't go away, but they won't escalate.[11]

Deep breathing is useful to narrow and focus your attention on the physical processes in your body and it helps to calm you. Once you are calm, you can take effective action to deal with the problem.

An easy way of accepting your thoughts through mindfulness is by meditation.[12] Several meditation exercises are outlined in Chapter 9. Here is composite of those meditations which will assist you to be mindful:

BREATHING MEDITATION

1. Sit in a comfortable position in your chair, preferably with your hands on your diaphragm or stomach.

2. Close your eyes and release the tension in your body by tensing groups of muscles for five seconds and then releasing them. Start with the muscle group at your neck; then go on in sequence to your shoulders, arms, stomach, buttocks, thighs, calves and finally ankles and feet.

3. Then, gently focus your attention on your breathing. Be aware of how you breathe slowly in and out, feeling the air flowing into your lungs; pause, and then release it. Feel how it flows into your nostrils and out through your mouth.

4. After you have spent some time becoming aware of your breathing, become aware of your thoughts. Whatever thoughts pop into your mind, accept them, observe and notice them, and allow them to leave. You are not your thoughts, and from a distance you can observe them coming into your mind and leaving. They float away because you haven't hung on to them, or dwelt on them. Like clouds in the sky, they come into your mind; you observe them non-judgementally and with a relaxed attitude, and then allow them to float off into the horizon.

5. Should you become hooked into a thought, and the thought starts to take over the exercise, shift your focus back to your breathing. Allow your breathing to loosen the thought and let yourself observe it.

6. After you have done this for ten minutes or so, gently shift your attention back on to your breathing, and then open your eyes.

There are many variations of these sequences, so change them to find the sequence that works best for you. It's important when practising mindfulness to be non-judgemental about your thoughts and to accept them, as well as to be aware of what is going on in your body. In this way, you differentiate and distance yourself as an entity from the thoughts you have.

A useful mind-set when practising mindfulness is 'I am a soul which is constant and endures. I am not my thoughts. I observe my thoughts as they come into my head, and then leave'.

Sounds complicated? It's actually easier to do than it is to describe, although the discipline of adhering to the process is tough. The following story explains how it works.

Sylvia beats the debt demon

Sylvia was worried about her finances. A large proportion of her salary this month went to pay off the mounting debt on her credit card and her department store accounts. She couldn't make ends meet, and last month missed some payments on these accounts. Just today, she had received two phone calls reminding her that she needed to pay not only this month's instalment, which was due in three days time, but the previous months' outstanding payments as well.

She was becoming increasingly stressed. At first, she ignored the problem, hoping it would go away. Then she tried to take her mind off the problem by spending time with her friends, going to parties and numbing herself with alcohol. These strategies worked for a short time, but in the end added to her financial woes.

The more she tried to work out what to do, the more anxious she became. She tried to control her negative thoughts, but found it very difficult. This, in turn, made her feel guilty and angry at herself: 'I'm so stupid to have got myself into this situation. How could I have been so dumb? I am really pathetic, leading such as sad life.' The harder she tried, the worse she felt.

Sylvia was then introduced to mindfulness. She was encouraged to accept her negative experience of the spiralling debt, to let go of the struggle and put her struggle-switch in the off position. She accepted her frightening negative thoughts and feelings as appropriate to the situation she was in. She did not try to stop them, but stepped back and experienced them from a distance.

She did this by reframing her thoughts, reminding herself that they were just thoughts rather than an accurate experience of reality:

'I am having the thought that my house will be repossessed and I will be thrown onto the street. Thank you mind,' she said to herself. 'I understand you are giving me these thoughts because you are trying to protect me from danger.'

'The thought of being thrown onto the street is only a thought and not reality. My thoughts come and go, and this one will too.'

With practice, Sylvia was able to put some distance between herself and her upsetting thoughts. As she did so, she found that her level of anxiety reduced to the point she was able to take steps to deal with her financial situation. She drew up a budget, cancelled her accounts, cut up her credit card and established reduced minimum monthly repayments. By then, she was well on a path to financial recovery.

2. Reframe your thoughts

Many South Africans watching Barak Obama's inauguration on 20 January 2009 had a sense of *déjà vu* which harked back to the 1994 inauguration of Nelson Mandela. Both were inspiring and produced a palpable feeling of excitement and, most of all, hope. Hope for change. Hope for a brighter future.

It feels wonderful to be positive. Positive thoughts and feelings like these have an opening and a building effect in us. They have a physiological effect by actually changing our body chemistry. We become more open to possibilities, more creative, more expansive in our thinking. We are able to more easily build networks and learn new skills. This, in turn, creates upward-spiralling patterns of positive achievement, followed by good feelings which enable growth and development.[13]

Reframing is a powerful method of disputing negative thinking and correcting it with positive but realistic thoughts. A practical way to do this is to reframe the thinking, for example, by assigning a different meaning to the adversity. 'I believe this is sent to test me and I will be strong to meet it' was the expression a young single mother used when she was struggling with family commitments and increasing financial pressures.

I have found a four-step ATAC reframing model to be the easiest to remember and the simplest to use.[14] The ATAC model is designed to be used to reframe thoughts and perspective after an unhappy event which didn't end the way you would have liked. Step 1 looks backwards over time at what actually happened. Step 2 helps with understanding the thoughts that you had, together with their deeper meaning. Steps 3 and 4 are forward-looking, beginning with trying to find a different way of viewing what happened, with alternative positive beliefs and thoughts. It concludes with moving on to develop an action plan to proactively deal with the situation.

ATAC Reframing Model

Step 1: Adversity – the triggering event

- Describe the events as factually as a camera would record them.

Step 2: Thoughts – thoughts and their deeper meaning to you

- Immediate, uncensored and surface thoughts. They are like talk radio which plays all the time.
- Deeper-meaning thoughts or beliefs that this triggers, which are sometimes experienced as 'hot thoughts' or 'hot buttons'.

Step 3: Alternatives – alternative positive beliefs and thoughts

- What is a better way of viewing this?
- What good can come of this?

Step 4: Commitment – action plan

- What will you do to improve on your past reaction?
- What will you do next time this happens?
- What will you do to prevent a recurrence?

Using ATAC when you are really mad!

Nerine is ambushed

At last month's divisional meeting, Nerine was asked to report back at the next meeting with a written report, collating and summarising the outcomes of all the divisional projects completed in the previous twelve months. This was big task and involved collating the inputs from several project managers. Nerine was proud to have been delegated this important assignment, which would, ultimately, form part of the company's annual report.

It turned out, however, to be a tough assignment. Days before the meeting she was still struggling to get information from the project managers, with some information only received the day before the report back. The upshot was that the report was not completed in time for the meeting.

At the meeting her boss asked why the report was not available. As she started to explain, the boss angrily interrupted: 'That's just not acceptable! That report is absolutely crucial to record our performance in the annual report. You have let us all down. I am really angry!'

Nerine was shocked. Before she could defend itself, the boss had moved on to the next item on the agenda.

Even after the meeting, she felt awful. She couldn't get what had happened out of her mind and vacillated between feeling furious and despondent.

She decided to use the ATAC reframing model to deal with the situation.

A: Adversity – the triggering event.

Describe the events as factually as a camera would record them: *I didn't have the report completed on time. The boss got really angry with me in the meeting. I wasn't able to explain what had happened before he moved on to the next item on the agenda.*

T: Thoughts – and their deeper meaning to you

Describe the thoughts that flashed through your mind on two levels:

The immediate thoughts in your head, heard all the time like a talk-radio station:

That's not fair! The boss always jumps to conclusions without getting the facts. Yelling at me in front of everyone is so humiliating. I will never be able to look those people in the eyes again.

The deeper meaning, thoughts or beliefs that this triggers, which are sometimes experienced as 'hot thoughts' or 'hot buttons':

My attempts at trying to stand up for myself failed. I try so hard to be professional at all times and now everyone thinks I am a failure. I did not even stand up for myself in the meeting. That's typical of me all my life. I am such a coward.

C: Alternatives – alternative positive beliefs and thoughts

What is a better way of viewing this?

I tried to stand up to the boss and give my side of the story. The boss interrupted me and moved to the next item on the agenda, so I missed my opportunity to explain. I was left feeling humiliated and embarrassed. However, it's really good that I did not respond in anger to him and I probably have the sympathy of many of my colleagues who know what really happened.

What good could come of this?

I can use this as a lesson for myself, to be more forceful with other people. From now on, I will not allow other people's non-delivery to negatively impact on my delivery. I will also talk to the boss about what he says in public and how it affects me.

C: Commitments – action to deal with the adversity

Describe the action you will take – this may be to improve on your past reaction, and/or to prevent future occurrence.

I will make an appointment to see the boss and describe the facts about why the report was late. I will acknowledge my role in the report being late. I will explain what I will do in future to ensure the report will be on time. I will also point out some of the problems I experienced where I was not to blame. I will explain the effect his public anger had on me.

Nerine now had an action plan which she felt good about, and was ready to put into action.

We all have times when we are unhappy with our thoughts and thinking patterns. The ATAC reframing process is a simple but very effective way of changing them. It's also a great way of ensuring that your thoughts don't descend into a spiral of negative thinking. The long term payoff of using ATAC is moving forward and creating realistic action plans to deal with the problem. Try it yourself.

3. Distract yourself

Another way of breaking out of negative thinking is through distraction, which puts some distance between the negative thoughts and yourself. It only requires a few seconds' distraction to break the cycle of negative thinking and, amazingly, a distraction of eight minutes can even break depressive thinking.[16]

So how do you distract yourself? Simply remove yourself from the situation or environment which has caused the negative thinking. Other ways of distracting yourself include doing something which you find pleasurable, such as talking to friends, watching a movie, going to a party, having a tasty meal and snacking on treats (with the obvious caution of not overdoing chocolate!)

> Our greatest battles are those with our own minds.
>
> *Jameson Frank*

Nombulelo distracts herself

Nombulelo, a young person struggling with the demands of raising two toddlers in nappies, deliberately chose not to allow her thoughts to dwell on her financial problems. She did this by changing her thinking to some other topic. She found it helpful to do something physical, such as walking to the local library to borrow books. Another technique she used, involved physical actions designed to trigger a different thinking pattern, was to do something which she described as 'happier'. For her this was playing tennis, whistling or simply singing cheerfully.

Another way of distracting yourself is to engage in enjoyable, relaxing and recharging activities. Taking steps to change the scenery, pace and people around you, can provide a counterbalance to the intense demands and naturally narrowing thought focus associated with dealing with adversity. This is variously expressed as 'taking time out for myself"; 'having me-time'; and 'taking time to smell the roses'.

4. Avoid negative thinking triggers

Another useful strategy is to avoid or limit the situations which trigger persistent negative thoughts.

Tembile stops watching the news

Tembile was an HR manager, responsible for talent management in a steel processing company. He found this strategy worked well for him. He identified three types of situations generated persistent negative thoughts in his mind. These were *events* – such as difficult family reunions; *multitasking* – such as dealing with several demanding managers at the same time, and his *physical condition* – such as when he was tired or hungry. Individually, the effect was bad enough, but together they were guaranteed to bring out the worst thinking in him. His simple solution was to avoid these triggers as much as possible.

He also limited the amount of time he spent watching news on television and reading newspapers. He felt that news was overwhelmingly negative and affected his positive mental state. Restricting exposure to the media is particularly useful with deeply upsetting events such as violent riots, terror attacks or natural disasters, when the same graphic footage is repeated, over and over again. An example is the scenes of the planes being flown into the Twin Towers, which remain indelibly etched in people's memories to this day, due to that horrific footage being played and watched repeatedly.

5. Call out 'Stop!'

We have been taught to be analytical in our approach to problems, to identifying symptoms, causes, and then the root causes before developing action plans. While this approach is really useful at work and with complex problems, applying this to our own lives can be problematic, if overdone. Through over-thinking or rumination, we can end up becoming increasingly fixated on the problem. It grows in our minds, until it reaches almost unmanageable proportions[17].

There is a simple but effective method of stopping over-thinking or rumination. Just say 'Stop!' either quietly or out loud to yourself. Although this might seem simplistic, it does work.

I once was out running with some friends before dawn when an unhappy conversation that I'd had the previous day kept on playing, over and over again, in my mind. My thinking was stuck in a negative groove and I felt the same level of frustration and anxiety that I had the previous day. I was being swamped by negative, ruminating thoughts.

Realising that I had become trapped in this negative over-thinking and ruminating cycle, I said 'Stop!' to try break out of it. To my surprise, my running friends immediately stopped in their tracks, and asked me what was wrong.

Rather shamefacedly, I had to explain that I meant to stop my thinking rather than for them to stop running, and my mistake was to have become so wrapped up in my thoughts that I had said it out loud.

Interestingly, the technique did stop my negative rumination at that time and one of my friends now uses it herself, to stop hers when she has a similar experience.

A variation of this method of stopping over-thinking or rumination is to introduce a physical reminder to break the negative thinking pattern. This can be done by wearing an elastic band around your wrist and whenever you need to break out of a negative thinking cycle, pull and sharply release the elastic band. Some people find that the mild sting of the elastic band is sufficient to break the ruminative thinking.

No negative thinking allowed here!

Ralph sat back in his chair with real irritation. Sitting around the large meeting-room table were several of his long-standing colleagues, whom he also counted as his friends. He bit his tongue to prevent himself saying things that he would regret.

After nineteen years service with the company, culminating in his present senior executive position, Ralph had been retrenched two days previously. Ralph was feeling deeply betrayed and humiliated by what had happened to him. He was battling to remain his old positive and upbeat self.

As was their custom, when the factory closed at the end of the week, he and his colleagues had gathered in the meeting room to chat. This had become a regular stopping-off point for many on their way home. An extra attraction was the assortment of beers from the well-stocked fridge in the corner of the room.

The only topic of conversation today was the retrenchments:

'Of all people, how could Ralph be retrenched?'

'If Ralph could be retrenched, who will be next?'

'The process isn't fair. The new CEO is crazy!'

As the conversation became increasingly heated, Ralph struggled against being sucked into the blame and negativity. It felt as if his soul was being increasingly filled with anger and fear. It was seductive to join them in complaining, but he knew that if he did, he would slide into being negative, saying negative things and feeling worse as a result. He really did not want to be as scathing as his colleagues.

He wrote on the meeting whiteboard: STOP! NO NEGATIVE THINKING ALLOWED HERE!

'I need you guys to help me here,' Ralph said. 'I really don't want to get totally negative about what has happened to me. I need to be able to rise above it. To do this, I need you guys to be positive too. I know you want to help me, and the way to do that is to make the best of the situation.'

'But what's good about it?' asked one colleague.

'Ralph gets a chance to move to something better,' suggested another.

After a brief pause, the conversation turned to the good that could come from the renewal process for the organisation, and how valuable it would be if Ralph were part of this transformation as an external consultant.

Ralph smiled for the first time that day. He had succeeded in changing his friends' thoughts and perspective, and felt he could now start making plans for his future.

Exercises

The final exercise in this chapter, about thoughts and maintaining perspective, is designed to bring together the various sections we have dealt with and to tie up any loose ends. Choose one or more questions from the list below to consolidate and apply your learning from this chapter.

Written exercises

---

1. Think back on the adversity you overcame which you described in Chapter 1. How did you maintain perspective? What can you learn from that and apply to the rest of your life?

2. Are you happy with the negative-positive balance in your thoughts and, if not, what should you do about it?

3. In general, what thoughts and beliefs would you most like to change, and how will you do that?

4. Do you make any of the common thinking mistakes and, if so, what can you do about them?

5. How can you apply mindfulness to maintain your perspective?

6. Where would you get the most benefit from applying the ATAC reframing model? Which circumstances and what type of timing make controlling your thoughts and maintaining perspective more difficult, and what can you do about that?

ENDNOTES

1   Fredrickson, B.L. 1998. What good are positive emotions? *Review of general psychology*, 2:300–319.

2   Tugade, M.M. & Fredrickson, B.L. 2004. Resilient individuals use positive emotions to bounce back from negative emotional experiences. *Journal of Personality and Social Psychology*, 86:320–333.

3   Tugade, M.M., Fredrickson, B.L. & Feldman-Barrett, L. 2004. Psychological resilience and positive emotional granularity: Examining the benefits of positive emotions on coping and health. *Journal of personality*, 72:1161–1190.

4   Dweck, C.S. 2002. Beliefs that make smart people dumb. In R.J. Sternberg (ed.). *Why smart people do stupid things*. New Haven, CT: Yale University Press.

5   Good, C. & Dweck, C.S. 2006. A motivational approach to reasoning, resilience, and responsibility. *In* Subotnik, R. & Sternberg, R. (eds.). *The other 3 R's: Reasoning, resilience, and responsibility*. Washington, DC: American Psychological Association.

6   See reference [v]

7   Elliot, A.J. & Dweck, C.S. (eds.). 2005. *Handbook of competence and motivation*. New York: Guilford.

8   Stewart, A. & Vandewater, E. 1999. 'If I had it to do over again …': Midlife review, midcourse corrections, and women's well-being in midlife. *Journal of personality and social psychology*, **76**(2):270–283.

9   For more information on the section which contains details of ACT or Acceptance and Commitment Therapy, the following website has useful resources: http://contextualpsychology.org/. Accessed 12 December 2011.

10 Hayes, S.C., Luoma, J., Bond, F., Masuda, A. & Lillis, J. 2006. Acceptance and Commitment Therapy: Model, processes, and outcomes. *Behaviour research and therapy*, 44(1):1–25.

11 Harris, R. 2006. Embracing your demons: an overview of acceptance and commitment therapy. *Psychotherapy in Australia*, 12(4):2–8.

12 See reference 2.

13 UCLA's Mindful Awareness Research Center at http://www.marc.ucla.edu/ MARC has useful short guided mindfulness meditations. Accessed 23 January 2011.

14 Fredrickson, B.L., Tugade, M.M., Waugh, C.E. & Larkin, G.R. 2003. What good are positive emotions in crises? A prospective study of resilience and emotions following the terrorist attacks on the United States on September 11, 2001. *Journal of personality and social psychology, 84(2)*:365–376.

15 Inspired by the more lengthy ABCDE process described in this article: Schulman, P. 1999. Applying Learned Optimism to Increase Sales Productivity. *Journal of personal selling and sales management.* XIX(1), Winter.

16 See reference 9.

17 Lyubomirsky, S. 2008. *The how of happiness: A scientific approach to getting the life you want.* New York: Penguin Books.

7

Generate positive feelings

Generate positive feelings

Be realistically optimistic	Persevere by being open-minded and flexible
Connect to your meaning in life	Reach out to others
Use your unique strengths	Maintain perspective

Only man clogs his happiness with care, destroying what is, with thoughts of what may be.

John Dryden

The fourth principle of building resilience concerns feelings and the role positive emotions play in getting through tough times. Positive feelings make you feel good. While that's pretty obvious, what isn't so obvious is that they also build the internal buffering resources and capability that underpins resilience. In addition, they actually undo the damaging physical impact that prolonged and intense negative emotions have on our bodies. So there is more benefit from feeling good than just feeling good.

Everyone who goes through tough times, however, experiences strong feelings, which are usually negative. Even resilient people experience negative emotions which reflect the challenge and difficulty of circumstances. The worse the circumstances, the more likely it is you will experience intense emotions such as anger, fear, dread, guilt and grief.

Experiencing intense negative emotions such as these is not pleasant and, if prolonged, leads to feeling overwhelmed. It reduces and even paralyses our mental functioning at the very time when we need to be strong.

So how do you cope with really strong negative feelings? Trying simply to 'be positive' can be dangerous. We are not able to fool ourselves into believing we are what we are not. Instead, we need ways of boosting positive feelings that are genuine and come from our hearts, and use those positive feelings to boost our resilience.

This chapter explores emotions and gives several methods of dealing with intense negative emotion. In addition, several practical strategies to experience genuine positive emotions, even in really tough times, are provided. These tools and techniques will assist you to build your internal coping mechanisms to become more resilient.

The role of negative emotions

It is important to state at the outset that experiencing negative emotions is not 'bad' or a sign of character weakness or failure on your part. You are internalising, and reacting to, the severity of the adversity. Experiencing negative emotions is an absolutely essential part of robust emotional health and wellness. They are so important, that if you don't experience them, you would be well advised to seek immediate counselling.

Negative feelings have evolved as important indicators to us. For example, feelings of frustration are an important indicator that perhaps a goal is unobtainable and needs to be reviewed or altered. In addition, negative feelings such

Negative emotions narrow thoughts and physiologically prepare the body to fight, run or hide.

as sadness and grief are appropriate at times of loss of a loved one. Positive emotions on such an occasion may be so inappropriate as to be perceived by others as a lack of empathy and caring. Negative feelings are thus an important indicator that something in our lives is out of kilter and needs to be addressed. They are part of our internal self-regulating system, which helps us regain our equilibrium.

In a situation of threat, negative emotions result in narrowing your attention and physiologically preparing your body to run, fight or hide. These responses appear to be biologically hard-wired in our brains and bodies and are extremely useful, even life-saving, in times of physical danger.

In fact, this response to danger may have been an evolutionary selection criterion. Groups that responded quicker and more effectively to physical threat were the ones that survived. Through those survivors' breeding, this has become part of the present-day genetic make-up of our species.

The role of positive emotions

Positive emotions have a very different role to negative emotions. They reduce the biological arousal caused by the negative emotions, as well as broaden our attention, thinking and range of behavioural responses, such as playing, exploring and the ability to be flexible.

Positive emotions broaden potential reactions and undo the physiological effects of the changes created by the negative emotions.

Positive emotions actually create changes in the brain chemistry which enable flexible, efficient, creative and open behaviours to occur.[1]

Positive emotions play a critical role in building and maintaining resilience. There is a direct link between enhanced health and positive emotions. These include enhanced functioning of the immune system, better cardiovascular health, recovery from major surgery, increased longevity (the length of one's life), and better psychological health[2].

So when your mother told you that being positive is good for your health, she was right.

The link between broadening of thoughts and thinking ability on one hand, and health on the other, comes about because positive emotions momentarily broaden the scope of our thoughts, together with enhanced and flexible attention, which, in turn, improves our well-being. With repeated cycles of well-being and positive emotions, a broadened mind-set becomes reinforced, until it is part of our behaviour repertoire.[3]

But the power of positive emotions doesn't end there. Positive emotions build buffering resources that can be called on during tough times. This occurs because positive feelings enable openness, curiosity and exploration, which, in turn, actually alter the brain's functioning to enable learning and understanding. These changes become a lasting personal legacy by permanently broadening your mind-set and improving thinking ability. Enhanced genuine positive emotions are so powerful that they are also effective in preventing, as well as treating, mental health problems[4].

In summary, positive emotions create changes in our brains and our repertoire of coping skills that can be called upon in times of adversity. Positive emotions are directly linked to personal well-being, health and flourishing.

Which are stronger: negative or positive feelings?

Negative feelings have an important role to play in our lives. They tell us when things are not right and need attention or change. But they sometimes crowd out positive feelings. Then we are left with an overwhelming feeling of negativity about everything, including the value of our lives. This is really unfortunate, because there is almost always something good and positive in life, even in the depths of despair.

Check the power of negative and positive feelings in your life. Do this by completing the following exercise.

Testing the power of negative and positive feelings in your life

Read the following statements slowly. If you are in a location which will allow it, say them out loud:

· When I think of the person with whom I have a romantic relationship, I feel a little bit of gratitude and love.

· When I think of the person with whom I have a romantic relationship, I feel a little bit of disgust.

Now weigh up each of these statements in your mind and decide which was more powerful.

Most people say that the second statement, which included the word 'disgust', felt more powerful than the first. This is despite the first statement having two of the most positive emotions we can experience: 'gratitude' and 'love'. It is sad but true that negative feelings are more powerful than positive feelings.

The absence of negative feelings does not mean that we have positive feelings and are happy and joyful. The absence of negative feelings simply brings us to a neutral point. We have to create positive feelings that are genuine and come from our hearts. Only then will we experience joy, fulfilment and a feeling of deep satisfaction with our lives.

The profound implication for being resilient and having a joyful life in the face of adversity is that we need to curb the intensity of our negative feelings, such as disappointment, betrayal, distrust, guilt and fear, and generate genuine positive feelings to counter them.

We can't experience both positive and negative feelings at the same time. In simple terms, we can't experience fear and, at the same time, hope. The fact that we can only experience one or the other is good news, when it comes to coping with our strong negative emotions while going through tough times. We can choose to experience positive feelings, such as hope, even in the face of adversity. This will mitigate and drive out negative feelings, such as fear and despair.

Have the rubble roll off you

No dumping on the Common!

Zanele was on her pre-dawn jog around the Rondebosch Common, a large, open piece of ground that has been declared a national monument.

In some deep shadow between streetlights, she was startled by a large dark shape which hadn't been there the day before. On investigation, it turned out to be a huge pile of builder's rubble. Dumped on the Common – what a sacrilege!

On returning home, she alerted the relevant authorities, who told her that she was about the tenth caller to complain since the switchboard had opened thirty minutes previously.

Later that week, she heard from her colleagues at work that a building contractor, working at the University of Cape Town, had dumped the rubble. He claimed he did not know the area was a national monument and had 'inadvertently' dumped the rubble from a building he was demolishing.

However, he was unable to explain his curious working hours – before dawn – and his choice of dumping site.

He shamefacedly removed the rubble and rubbish by the end of the week.

It can feel as if some people carry a huge load of rubble in the back of their metaphorical trucks and are looking for a place to dump it. The load they carry is their accumulated negative feelings of anger, disappointment, betrayal, grief, and unhappiness. It's a heavy load, which makes them even more unhappy. If they can dump it on someone, they feel they have reduced their load.[5]

While that's good for them, it's really not good if they choose to dump it on you. So what should you do if someone dumps on you?

Start by accepting that there will always be people who will try to dump on you. It's about the load they carry. It's not about you. Mostly, you can't stop them from dumping on you.

It is easy to be angry and powerless at being dumped on, particularly when you feel you haven't done anything wrong. But what you do have control over is your choice of how to react. The secret is to not allow them to 'get' to you. If they dump on you, choose to have the rubble roll off you, not stick to you.

So when you meet your loved ones at the end of the day, and one of them has been dumped on, they may, in turn, dump on you. When this happens, ask yourself, 'What do I really, *really* want? Do I want to be right, or do I want a deep and loving relationship? Do I want to ensure that no one, least of all the people I love, take advantage of me, or do I want to be remembered as a loving and tolerant partner?'

Remember, it's completely your choice. You can react with the same intense negative emotion, or choose to let the rubble roll right off you.

The danger in avoiding negative emotions

During really tough times, it can feel as if you are being overwhelmed by negative feelings. If this happens, is it better to control the negative emotions or is it more effective to counteract them by developing positive emotions?

We need to do both. We need to control excessive negative emotions if they threaten to overwhelm us, as well as generate positive ones.

The implication is that while we need to deal with unwelcome negative feelings, creating genuine positive emotions will boost our coping ability. Not only do we feel better, but our internal buffering resources improve.

But a word of caution. An overwhelming emphasis on controlling negative emotions has the potential to aggravate the situation, rather than make it better.[6] This is because a strong effort to control negative feelings, without a balancing action to develop positive feelings and find meaning in life, may only result in more focus on the negative feelings.

Don't create a jack story!

Gareth was driving his car from Cape Town to Johannesburg. He was in the middle of the semi-arid Great Karoo and had just passed through one of the small towns when his steering became quite heavy and the vehicle started to shudder.

'Damn!' he thought. 'A puncture.'

He pulled over and sure enough his rear back tyre was flat. But what made him really mad was that he couldn't find his wheel-jack.

'I told my son to replace it after he used it... and obviously he didn't,' Gareth thought, with clenched teeth.

He locked the vehicle and started walking back to the town he had just passed to find a garage where he hoped to borrow a jack.

He trudged back on the long road, with the sun burning his unprotected head and arms. His attempts to catch a lift, from the infrequent cars that sped past, were unsuccessful.

It really wasn't his day.

Gradually the spires of the town's church appeared on the horizon, but did not lift his mood. 'I hope there's a garage in the town and I don't have to walk further to find a jack,' he thought anxiously. 'And if I do find a garage, I bet they will give me a hard time when I ask to borrow their jack.' 'I hate asking people for favours, knowing they don't want to help,' he thought.

Round and round his thoughts went, as his anger built.

Eventually Gareth located a garage, strode into the owner's office and, in a fit of temper shouted: 'You can keep your jack!'

How do you generate positive feelings ... that are genuine?

Thus far, we've established the importance of using positive feelings to build internal buffering resources which are needed for resilience. We have also established that just simply trying to be positive, ignoring negative feelings, is naive and even dangerous. So the question is 'How do you generate positive feelings that are real and genuine?' And is it really possible to generate positive feelings during tough times?

The answer is a resounding yes. There are four exercises which really work to generate genuine positive feelings. Each of them creates upward spirals of positive emotion, which build buffering resources. Find one or two that work best to enhance your mood and build your resilience:

- Three Good Things exercise
- Gratitude exercise
- Gratitude Letter exercise
- Savouring exercise

1. Three Good Things exercise

This exercise[7] is designed to enhance your self-awareness about the good things that have happened in your life. It helps balance the busyness of our lives which, together with our natural negative bias, can easily lead us to focus mainly on what we have not yet done, the opportunities we have missed, and our problems.

Written exercise: Three Good Things

Find a time in your daily routine when you can be quiet and reflect. For most people it's early in the morning or late at night, and should be carried out daily.

1. *Write down three good things that have happened to you over the last 24 hours.* Review the day and reflect on the positive events that have occurred. Try to be as specific as possible, for example, 'My partner cooked supper for us tonight' is much more valuable than a general statement such as 'The love of my partner'. You only need to write a sentence or two for each of the good things.

2. *It is important now to write a few sentences about why that good thing occurred.* Again, the more specific you are, the more benefit you will get

from this exercise. For example, 'I was feeling really tired and the thought of cooking supper was just too much. When I said this to my partner, he immediately volunteered to take over the cooking and produced a wonderful meal. He is so in tune with my moods and feelings, and goes out of his way to help me when I am tired.'

Rather than just thinking about three good things that have happened to you, writing them down, preferably in a journal and using formal sentence construction, assists you to create order in your thinking. Try to trace the thread back to the origin of the good things that have happened. Some good things happen because of good that you have done to others. Other good things won't seem to have an obvious cause. You just appear to be the lucky recipient of good in the world.

After you have done this exercise for a week or ten days, look back over the reasons you have found to see whether there are any patterns. Ask yourself what you can do in future to ensure more good things happen to you. Your answer may give you ideas on how to enhance your efficacy and self-esteem, as well as live a more resilient, happy and joyful life.

2. Gratitude exercise

It's wonderful to have people around you who are grateful. You will probably have noticed that gratitude has huge paybacks for them and the way they live their lives.[8] Typically, grateful people are less stressed and happier with their lives[9], cope better with difficulties, are better able to reach out to seek support from others[10] and are less likely to fall prey to mental problems such as depression[11].

In addition, because emotions are transmitted like an influenza virus between people, being around grateful people rubs off on you, and you, too, experience the benefits of their gratitude[12].

A grateful attitude is a cornerstone of the teachings of Judaism, Christianity and Islam.

Gratitude is not only the greatest of the virtues but the parent of all others.

Cicero

Having described what gratitude is, what is it not? It is not indebtedness. Indebtedness occurs after a person, who has received help, feels an obligation to repay that assistance. That feeling of obligation may be so uncomfortable that it could lead the person who has received the help to avoid the helper in future. This contrasts with gratitude, which motivates the receiver to seek out the benefactor to deepen their interactions and relationship[13].

Written exercise: Practising gratitude

Find time in your schedule when you are able to spend ten to fifteen minutes by yourself reflecting on the things for which you are grateful.

You probably can think of many things that you are grateful for – the fact the sun is shining today; that you were able to have a hot shower this morning and that you made it to work without mishap, and so on.

This exercise calls for a deeper reflection, however, of those things for which you are truly deeply grateful. It asks you to reflect on the enduring and significant things in your life which you have been given.

As with the previous exercise, it is best if you write your thoughts daily in a journal, as writing has the benefit of slowing and ordering your thoughts into a coherent stream.

Some people who do this exercise end up doing it only twice or three times a week. They say that not forcing themselves to do it every day helps to keep it fresh and interesting. So you too might not want to do it every day.

Johan, who is a regular jogger, says he loves the Gratitude exercise for the benefits it gives him. At the end of his early morning jog, he passes a large tree about five minutes away from home. It is his reminder to think of what he is truly deeply grateful for in his life.

3. Gratitude letter

This exercise [14] is a variation on the previous one. The difference is that with this exercise you actually do something practical with the powerful positive emotions it generates.

Feeling gratitude and not expressing it is like wrapping a present and not giving it.

William Arthur Ward

Written exercise: Gratitude letter

Think of a person who is living and to whom you are very grateful, but to whom you have not recently expressed your gratitude.

Write either in long hand, or using a keyboard, the details of what you are grateful to that person for, and why. Explain how the things that you are grateful for have impacted your life.

Writing a gratitude letter in this way makes you feel great. It generates a huge amount of positive emotion and energy.

But I'd like to suggest that you do one more thing with it. Go to the person and read it to them face-to-face. If it is absolutely impossible to meet, then telephone or Skype them.

Well, you can imagine what happens. Inevitably, there is a lot of emotion and even tears. But these are happy emotions which result in deepening the relationship.

---

4. Savouring exercise

Savouring concerns being aware of the positive aspects of living and involves paying attention to the experience of pleasure. It focuses on the present and being aware of what is happening. It involves mindfulness and appreciation, and it is a simple way of creating positive emotions during tough times and adversity.

It's particularly useful to use when the pace of life threatens to overwhelm you. The effect is to slow things down, as you become aware of your existence in the moment.

Reflection exercise: Savouring exercise

There are four techniques to promote savouring[15]. Try each to find the ones that work best for you:

Sharing with others. Find other people with whom to share experiences. For example, invite your best friend for coffee to talk about how it felt when you got promoted.

Building memories. Reliving positive experiences. For example, keep a picture or a keepsake on your desk which reminds you of happy memories, or set your computer screensaver to show pictures of your most recent vacation. A more formal variation is to create a scrapbook of your vacation, or to arrange your digital pictures into a movie with software like Windows Live Movie Maker.

Self-congratulation. Appreciating yourself for the success that you've achieved. For example, go for a walk and have a conversation with yourself, proudly congratulating yourself on sticking to your diet and losing two kilograms.

Being in the moment. Putting all your attention into your experience of the present; not allowing yourself to be distracted by other things. This is the opposite of multitasking. For example, when your child wants to talk to you about what happened at school, put down what you're doing, look your child in the eyes and listen, giving your full attention to the child.

How much positive feeling should you aim for?

We have established the importance of experiencing genuine positive feelings and their role in health, well-being and resilience. The question that now arises is 'How much positive feeling is needed to have a happy, good life and be resilient?'

The answer is intriguing. There is a 'magic ratio', or tipping point, in the proportion of positive to negative feelings above which flourishing occurs. A tipping point happens when a major change occurs. For example, in physics, it's when water turns into ice or into steam. Due to the strength of negative experiences and emotions, the ratio is weighted towards having more positive than negative. The tipping point ratio is 3:1 positive to negative feelings, and it's then that flourishing occurs[16].

This is not just important for living an engaged and positive life. It also has implications for how long a marriage will last. A crucial factor in marriage appears to be the number of positive interactions versus negative that occur in the relationship. Amazingly, newly married couples who have a ratio of 5:1 positive to negative interactions have a substantially higher chance of remaining married for ten years, than do couples with a 1:1 ratio. Unfortunately for those couples that can only manage a 1:1 ratio, it predicts inevitable divorce.[17]

Experiencing positive feelings has a profound influence on the overall feeling of satisfaction with your life. When positive feelings on one hand and meaning and engagement on the other, are assessed for their impact in creating satisfaction in life, experiencing positive feelings is at least as important, if not more important, than meaning and engagement[18].

Andile loses his mojo

Sunday dawned full of promise for a lovely day – just what Andile wanted, so he could take his convertible for a trip into the countryside. He grabbed his car keys and credit card and was on his way.

What fun. With the vehicle's top down, wearing designer sunglasses and with the wind blowing through his hair, he felt great. A few puffy, white clouds in the sky blew overhead, but were soon chased away by the sun. The road was an easy drive with little traffic. He felt he could literally and figuratively see forever. Life just couldn't get better.

The road turned and went down into a valley. Suddenly he entered a patch of mist. The sun was blotted out. He couldn't see more than fifty metres. His previously safe speed was now dangerous.

Andile braked hard, threw his sunglasses on to the seat next to him and switched on his hazard lights.

After what seemed like many minutes of intense concentration, but, in fact, was probably only thirty seconds or so, the road lifted out of the valley, the mist cleared and he entered sunshine

again. Breathing a sigh of relief, he replaced his sunglasses and tried to recapture his mood.

But no matter how he tried, Andile couldn't recreate the wonderfully positive and upbeat feeling he had had before driving into the mist. He was left feeling drained and slightly negative.

Soon he turned the car around and went home.

A word of caution, however, should be made before we leave this section. You can have too much positivity or too many positive feelings. The point at which too much positive feeling becomes counter-productive is a second tipping point. This occurs at the ratio of 11:1 positive to negative feelings[19]. Above this boundary level, the positivity becomes self-blinding and counter-productive.

Staying positive

It's probably clear by now that bringing positive emotions into your life, even during tough times, has significant benefits for you. But there is a problem with positive emotions that you need to know about. It's the concept of habituation, which means the gradual lessening of the impact of things over time.

The impact of the same positive emotion unfortunately doesn't remain constant and actually reduces over time.

Take, for example, the first time you saw a beautiful view or sunset. Initially you were lost in wonder and awe. After a little time you were aware of its beauty but it didn't make the same impact. All too soon, you took it for granted and you had to remind yourself to look at it.

This process of acceptance, fortunately, does have an upside. It helps us get used to bad things that happen to us, for example, losing the use of your legs or living with permanently impaired health.

The implication of all this is that we need to continually generate genuine positive emotions. One other way of doing this is to consistently remind ourselves of the good things that happen to us and how fortunate we are. Also, the four exercises to generate positive feelings that have been described in this chapter are particularly useful.

Self-affirmations don't always create positive feelings

Self-affirmations are positive statements people repeat to themselves, over a period of time, to develop aspects of their character and so that they become something that they currently are not. An example is 'I am self-confident and have joy and happiness in my life'. This is completely different to positive self-talk which encourages you, for example: 'You did your best, but you didn't win. Only one person can win, and today that wasn't you. Tomorrow will be different, and what's important is that you don't let this get you down.'

The idea behind self-affirmations is that what you say to yourself gets acted out in your life. In other words, the theory is that if you say positive things to yourself, you will live those positive things. And if you say negative things to yourself, you will live those negative things in your life.

The implication is if you have beliefs that cause low self-esteem, you can transform yourself by repeated self-affirmations. Thus, feeling unworthy and unable to cope can be altered by repeating positive statements such as 'I am a strong and powerful and can cope easily with any difficult situation'.

Now there are people who say that self-affirmations help them. The interesting thing is those people almost always have a positive self-image or self-esteem to start with. Their self-affirmations probably help them open themselves up to possibilities and help them to become better able to take action to achieve their goals.[20]

The problem with self-affirmations is that about 30 per cent of the population has low self-esteem, and they won't get these benefits. Their positive self-affirmations feel false to themselves. They look for evidence to support that feeling and when they find it, it reinforces the problems they are trying to solve. When this happens, not only will the self-esteem affirmations not work, but they will probably make the person feel worse.[21]

This happens because we spot falseness easily. For example, even when people are called upon to evaluate and assess others who are negative, but do it in a positive way, their evaluation is felt as false and untrue[22]. The experience of falseness simply reinforces the negative condition felt in the first place.

Everybody wants to be somebody; nobody wants to grow.

Johann Wolfgang Goethe

It's a great pity that simply wanting something enough does not make it happen. It would be wonderful if the formula to create change in one's life were to really want it; to repeat that want frequently and then, magically, it would be achieved. Unfortunately, life just does not work like that.

Other problems with using self-affirmations to create personal change:

- There are some things you just can't change, for example going bald.

- They can lock people into warped thinking, such as believing you are overweight when you are not.

- They can prolong undesirable situations. For example, people in an abusive relationship who use affirmations to try to get their partner to change may find it more difficult to get out of the relationship.

In summary then, if self-affirmations help you get through tough times, that's great. Continue to use them. But be cautious about saying things to yourself which feel false. Saying things over and over again to yourself, that you don't believe, is unlikely to help you change or help you cope in tough times.

How to keep your temper and get out of a bad mood

Picture this: you are late for an important appointment and are caught in traffic. As the traffic creeps along, you eventually can see the building where your meeting will be held. Only one more set of traffic lights.

The traffic light changes and just as you are about to enter the intersection, a taxi overtakes and stops right in front of you. You're now stuck and can't move. You are about to lose it.

At times like this you really need to control your temper. Losing it only makes matters worse. It is interesting that the word 'temper' has its origins in the 14th century, when 'temperament' referred to a person's character. In other words, when you lose your temper, you lose your personality or character. That makes sense because, when you lose your temper, you actually become a different and much worse person.

But not everyone sees it like this. People who often lose their temper say that they only do so when provoked beyond their ability to control their rage. For them, there is a point beyond which losing their temper is justifiable. Which, of course, is nonsense. You have a choice as to how you interpret events and also a choice of how to react. No matter how difficult the circumstances or how trying the situation, you can choose how to react and whether to lose your temper or not.

There are several easy techniques to prevent you from losing your temper, and to deal with strong unwanted negative feelings.

The starting point is to get in touch with what you are feeling. This can be done using the simple grid below:

Green feelings	Feelings are under control. Logic prevails and emotions are expressed constructively, even in difficult situations.
Yellow feelings	Feelings threaten to overwhelm. We struggle to control ourselves, and not do and say things which are later regretted.
Red feelings	Feelings overwhelm us. We do and say things without thinking. 'I lost my temper.' Inevitably we regret what we said and did.

Let's start off identifying what's happening in your body as the level of intensity of feeling rises from green to yellow and finally to red:

Green feelings are associated with even breathing, logic, listening and self-control. This does not mean that you can't have difficult conversations, but it does mean that negative feelings are sufficiently controlled and do not become a problem during difficult conversations.

Yellow feelings occur when the level of emotional tension rises and are associated with more rapid breathing as we struggle for self-control. We start to sweat; hands and knees shake and we may go either red or white in the face. If there are other people involved, the pace of responding to each other increases as the tension rises.

Red feelings are so powerful they swamp logical thought. Voices are raised and your body is ready to fight or run away. You may actually even see red. There may even be a delicious sense of abandon in losing your temper.

How do you deal with powerful feelings to keep them green? Try the exercise on page 57.

Written exercise: How to make sure you don't lose your temper

---

What do you do to make sure that you don't lose your temper?

1. Write down techniques that work for you.

2. Compare your techniques with those other people find useful to see whether any you can benefit from any of them.

Here are some techniques which other people use:

· Be alert for when you feel yourself moving into yellow. Recognise that this is not the time to be brash.

· Decide not to allow your feelings to go yellow or red.

· Take deep breaths.

· Slow down. Don't respond immediately. Counting slowly to ten, before responding, actually works.

· Take a break.

· Get some exercise.

· Get out of the situation.

· Ask yourself:
  – What do I really want?
  – What am I doing?
  – Is what I'm doing working?
  – What can I change? Remember you can only change your own behaviour.

Dealing with bad moods

Having a bad mood affects both you and the people around you. Bad moods can be 'caught' just as you would catch a flu bug. Fortunately, good moods can be caught just as easily.

But let's keep some perspective here. Moods are signposts that point to issues that are going on in your life. A good mood indicates things are going well, and a bad mood shows that perhaps there is an issue that needs attention. Also, good moods are best for promoting confidence, creativity and new ideas, whereas bad moods are best for focusing on the work at hand and ensuring it gets done. Bad moods have this effect because people experiencing them tend to be more realistic, more detail-orientated and self-critical[23].

At work, it can sometimes feel that criticism and being critical is more important than praise and being positive. If you experience this, you're probably right. The higher one goes up the organisational ladder, people who voice negative views are seen as more expert and competent than those who voice positive views[24].

While there is value to being critical and having bad moods, there comes a time when you don't want to be in a bad mood, and you want to get out of it.

How to get out of a bad mood

There are several ways of getting yourself out of a bad mood. Have a look at the following list and try the ones that suit you the best:

- Exercise: playing with a ball, swimming or going for a run is guaranteed to lift your spirits.

- Do something different: distract yourself by changing your activity.

- Talk to a friend. When you do, it's best not to talk about yourself, or whinge, but rather find out how they are doing.

- Talk to someone you trust. If you have a specific problem that's causing the mood, it may be useful to talk to someone who understands you and your situation, who can give you good advice.

- Avoid what seem to be the easy solutions. Shopping, alcohol and drugging may bring momentary relief, but also come with long-term problems.

- Be kind to yourself. Give yourself time to recover from a setback; allow yourself to feel down, and don't get cross with yourself if you don't get over the mood as soon as you would like.

- Speak to your doctor if the mood persists for several days, or interferes with the way that you live your life.

Choosing happiness

This chapter has been concerned with the need to generate genuine, positive feelings, which are useful in helping to cope with tough times and for building buffering resources during good times. So perhaps it is appropriate that the final words are about happiness.

We all want to be happy and have our dreams fulfilled. Yet it's very easy for these ideals to slip away as we struggle to cope with multiple day-to-day hassles, as well as heartbreaking tragedies. If this happens, we end up living a life of quiet desperation.

Happiness does more for you than just make you feel good. At work it's associated with[25]

- better supervisor performance evaluations

- better management performance evaluations

- more income

- increased insurance commission

- boosted creativity

- service providing better customer satisfaction

- enhanced employee health and well-being

- greater satisfaction at work

- reduced staff absenteeism.

In addition, the counter-intuitive finding is that happiness creates these outcomes,

In other words, happiness causes good things to happen in your life.

rather than the other way around. In other words, happiness causes good things to happen in your life. Good things happen to us when we are happy. Success does not make us happy. Happiness makes us successful[26].

What creates real happiness?

One of the foremost researchers into happiness is Martin Seligman. He is one of the most influential psychologists of the present day and, together with his colleagues, has changed the face of psychology by introducing what has come to be called Positive Psychology. They have specialised in researching and understanding what creates happiness.

Seligman believes that there are three pathways to happiness[27]:

- *Feeling good.* This involves thinking and feeling positive about events that have happened in your past, the positive aspects of the present and the future. It also includes trying to minimise the amount of pain experienced, by not mentally revisiting painful memories over and over again. This philosophy stretches back in time to the ancient Greeks and to Epicurus in particular. This is called the *Pleasant Life.*

- *Being engaged.* This comes about by pursuing activities that are so intensely involving that you become immersed in them and derive great satisfaction from what you are doing. This is the mental state of 'flow', which occurs when you lose track of time and feel a deep sense of satisfaction. This is referred to as the *Engaged Life.*

- *Creating meaning.* This is almost always achieved by serving some purpose outside and beyond yourself and has its origins in Aristotle's philosophy of coming to a deep understanding of oneself, and in living life in harmony with one's values. This is referred to as the *Meaningful Life.*

Seligman's scholarly research on the pathways to happiness is relevant to understanding how to build internal coping and buffering resources. It reinforces the idea that purpose and meaning, together with being engaged and feeling good, are the components of real and enduring happiness. This is good news because as we seek out our purpose and meaning in life, it raises our level of deep personal satisfaction and happiness.

What will make me happy?

Hereditary factors have a large influence on our experience of happiness, as does how we were brought up. Interestingly, we probably have a 'set point' which accounts for about fifty per cent of the happiness we experience. Remarkably, only about ten per cent is accounted for by our circumstances. It is such a low percentage because, with habituation, we get used to and accept our circumstances very quickly,

> No matter what the influence of your parents or your upbringing has been, you can increase your experience of happiness through intentional activity.

whether it relates to good fortune or not[23]. It is really encouraging, from the point of view of developing resilience, that the remaining forty per cent is a function of how we live our lives – our perspective, the emotions we choose and our attitude[29].

People are consistently poor at guessing what will make them happy and overestimate how happy a specific event will make them, however much they want it. Examples are when people say they will be happy when they get a promotion at work, or meet their ideal mate, or lose weight, or get out of debt.

Unfortunately, even when these things happen, they do not necessarily create enduring happiness. Happiness may increase for a while, but then it slips back to the level it was before. People who win large sums of money in a lottery have an initial spike in their level of happiness. But soon afterwards, their happiness returns to the same level as before[30].

Reverting to the prior set point also occurs with the experience of tragedy and significant misfortune. As can be expected, at the time of the incident there is an immediate and substantial dip in happiness. But what is surprising is that, with time, happiness levels often rise back to the same level they were before[31].

To compound the problem of understanding what will make us happy, we are very poor at assessing or calculating the odds of something happening. When we do have to make calculations and assess the odds, we are inevitably over-optimistic.

How accurate are you in assessing the chances of something good or bad happening to you? Answer the following questions to find out:

Self-test: How good are you at assessing what will happen to you?

Answer either 'yes' or 'no':
- Do you think you have a reasonable chance of living beyond 100 years?
- Do you think that your marriage will probably last?
- Do you think you have a reasonable chance of raising a gifted child?
- Do you think you are probably above average intelligence?

If you have answered 'yes' to one or more of the above questions, you are probably too optimistic in assessing your chances of the event happening. Statistics have shown that there is a negative chance of all of the above occurring. If you have overestimated any of these events happening however, you're not alone. People commonly overestimate the chances of good things happening, and underestimate the chances of bad things happening.

To counter this natural difficulty in assessing the chances of something happening or not, here is an exercise you can do to quickly identify the things that will make you really happy, as opposed to what you *think* will make you happy[32].

Imagine you only have ten more minutes to live: what would you spend those ten minutes doing? Would you spend the time fighting with your boss, or getting even with that nasty co-worker, or going for a drive in your new motor vehicle, or going for a cycle ride with your children?

Spending quality time with significant people in our lives is always rewarding. The answer to what makes you really happy isn't that difficult after all, is it?

Self-test: Rate your happiness level

If you wish to know how happy you are, in comparison to other people, there is a test you can take to get an answer.

The Subjective Happiness Scale is available for you to assess yourself, free of charge at: http://www.authentichappiness.sas.upenn.edu

Quick ways to alter your happiness

It is important to be aware that there is an activity which is *guaranteed to decrease* your level of happiness. That is to compare yourself unfavourably to others. No matter how successful, attractive, rich, popular or healthy you are, there will always be people who have more than you, or do better than you. Comparing yourself upwardly to such people is guaranteed to reduce your happiness and leave you in a state of funk.

Fortunately, with downward comparison, the reverse applies. No matter how little you have, comparing yourself with people who have less than you will always make you feel better and more grateful for what you actually have.

Try this downward comparison for yourself. Think of specific people you

Happiness is a choice that we make every day for ourselves.

have encountered who have less than you have. Think of what it must be like to live their lives. You will experience overwhelming relief that you are not in their situation, and gratitude for what you have. Downward comparison like this increases one's gratitude and humility. And makes you happier.

A final point about building your level of happiness. Don't rely on doing the same thing over and over again and expect the same result. Repeating the same exercise or activity will result in diminishing levels of happiness through the process of habituation[33].

Exercise

The final exercise in this chapter, about generating positive feelings, is designed to bring together the various aspects we have covered and to tie up any loose ends. Choose one or more questions from the list below to consolidate and apply your learning from this chapter.

Written exercises

1. Think back on the adversity and tough times you made notes of in Chapter 1. How did you generate positive feelings, and how did they help get you through a tough time? What can you generalise from this good experience for handling the tough times?
2. How can you apply the Three Good Things exercise?
3. How can you apply the Gratitude exercise and Gratitude letter?
4. How can you apply the Savouring exercise?
5. How can you apply the Green, Yellow and Red Feelings exercise?
6. What is your most effective way of getting out of a bad mood?
7. What circumstances and timing make generating positive feelings easier for you, and how can you ensure that you do this more often and more effectively?

ENDNOTES

1 Fredrickson, B.L. 2001. The role of positive emotions in positive psychology: The broaden-and-build theory of positive emotions. *American psychologist,* Special Issue, 56:218–226.

2 Tugade, M.M., Fredrickson, B.L. & Barrett, L.F. 2004. Psychological resilience and positive emotional granularity: Examining the benefits of positive emotions on coping and health. *Journal of personality,* 72(6):1161–1190.

3 Fredrickson, B.L., Mancuso, R.A., Branigan, C. & Tugade, M.M. 2000. The undoing effect of positive emotions. *Motivation and emotion.* 24:237–258.

4 Garland, E.L., Fredrickson, B., Kring, A.M., Johnson, D.P., Meyer, P. S. & Penn, D.L. 2010. Upward spirals of positive emotions counter downward spirals of negativity: Insights from the broaden-and-build theory and affective neuroscience on the treatment of emotion dysfunctions and deficits in psychopathology, *Positive clinical psychology*, 30:890–905.

5 Inspired by a post in *Positive Psychology Daily News:* http://positivepsychologynews. com/news/david-j-pollay/20071002426 and related to an event reported in newspapers and on-line at http://allafrica.com/stories/200702010694.html. Accessed 22 March 2011.

6 Kashdan, T.B., Breen, W.E. & Julian, T. 2010. Everyday strivings in combat veterans with posttraumatic stress disorder: Problems arise when avoidance and emotion regulation dominate. *Behavior therapy,* 41:350-363.

7 Seligman M.E., Steen, T.A., Park, N. & Peterson C. 2005. Positive psychology progress: empirical validation of interventions. *American psychologist,* 60(5):410–21, Jul.–Aug.

8 Sheldon, K.M. & Lyubomirsky, S. 2006. How to increase and sustain positive emotion: The effects of expressing gratitude and visualizing best possible selves. *Journal of positive psychology,* 1:73–82.

9 Wood, A.M., Joseph, S. & Maltby, J. 2008. Gratitude uniquely predicts satisfaction with life: Incremental validity above the domains and facets of the Five Factor Model. *Personality and individual differences,* 45:49–54.

10 Wood, A.M., Joseph, S. & Linley, P.A. 2007. Coping style as a psychological resource of grateful people. *Journal of social and clinical psychology,* 26:1108–1125.

11 Wood, A., Joseph, S. & Linley, A. 2007. Gratitude – parent of all virtues. *The psychologist,* 20(1):18–21.

12 Hatfield, E., Cacioppo, J.T. & Rapson, R.L. 1994. *Emotional contagion.* New York: Cambridge University Press.

13 Watkins, P.C., Scheer, J., Ovnicek, M. & Kolts, R. 2006. The debt of gratitude: Dissociating gratitude and indebtedness. *Cognition and emotion,* 20:217–24.

14 See reference 14.

15 Byrant, F.B. & Veroff, J. 2007. *Savoring: a new model of positive experience.* New Jersey: Erlbaum, Lawrence & Associates.

16 Fredrickson, B.L. & Losada, M. 2005. Positive emotions and the complex dynamics of human flourishing. *American psychologist*, 60:678–686.

17 Gottman, J.M., Coan, J., Carrère, S. & Swanson, C. 1998. Predicting marital happiness and stability from newlywed interactions. *Journal of marriage and the family*, 60:5–22.

18 Peterson, C., Park, N. & Seligman, M.E.P. 2005. Orientations to happiness and life satisfaction: The full life versus the empty life. *Journal of happiness studies*, 6(1):25–41.

19 *Fredrickson, B.L. 2009. Positivity: Top-notch research reveals the 3 to 1 ratio that will change your life.* New York: Three Rivers Press.

20 Diener, E. & Diener, M. 1995. Cross-cultural correlates of life satisfaction and self-esteem. *Journal of Personality and Social Psychology*, 68:653–663.

21 Wood, J.V., Perunovic, E. & Lee, J.W. 2009. Positive Self-Statements: Power for Some, Peril for Others. *Psychological science*, 20:860–866.

22 Swann, W.B. Jr., Hixon, J.G., Stein-Seroussi, A. & Gilbert, D.T. 1990. The fleeting gleam of praise: Behavioral reactions to self-relevant feedback. *Journal of personality and social psychology*, 59:17–26.

23 George, J.M. & Zhou, J. 2007. Dual tuning in a supportive context: Joint contributions of positive mood, negative mood, and supervisory behaviors to employee creativity. *Academy of Management journal*, 50:605–622.

24 Amabile, T.M. 1983. Brilliant but cruel: Perceptions of negative evaluators. *Journal of experimental social psychology*, 19:146–156.

25 Lyubomirsky, S., King, L. & Diener, E. 2005. The benefits of frequent positive affect: Does happiness lead to success? *Psychological bulletin*, 131(6):803–855.

26 See reference 13.

27 Seligman, M.E.P. 2004. 'Can happiness be taught?' *Daedalus,* Spring.

28 Brickman, P., Coates, D. & Janoff-Bulman, R. 1978. Lottery winners and accident victims: Is happiness relative? *Journal of personality and social psychology*, 36:917–927.

29 Lyubomirsky, S. 2008. *The how of happiness: A scientific approach to getting the life you want.* New York: Penguin Press.

30 See reference 26.

31 See reference 9.

32 See reference 9.

33 See reference 12.

8

Be realistically optimistic

Be realistically optimistic	
Persevere by being open-minded and flexible	Reach out to others
Use your unique strengths	Connect to your meaning in life
Maintain perspective	Generate positive feelings

This chapter concerns attitude in the face of adversity. Even though life is difficult, and despite disappointments, heartache and pain, we can experience joy and fulfilment. It is important, however, that our optimistic beliefs are realistic. Unrealistic optimism is very disappointing, risky and even dangerous.

At the heart of this principle is the strong belief that you can influence the direction of your life and that the inevitable problems encountered along life's journey can be solved. Viktor Frankl[1], who survived Nazi death camps during the Second World War, describes this eloquently:

> *We who lived in concentration camps can remember the men who walked through the huts comforting others, giving away their last piece of bread. They may have been few in number, but they offer sufficient proof that everything can be taken from a man but one thing: the last of the human freedoms – to choose one's attitude in any given set of circumstances, to choose one's own way.*
>
> Viktor Frankl

Some fortunate souls are born more optimistic than others, and show this with their sunny disposition, focusing on the good rather than the bad in life. But what is particularly interesting is how they interpret the happy as well as well as the unfortunate things that happen to them. They see the good things as permanent and affecting everything, whereas they experience bad things as only temporary and having a limited effect on their lives.

Pessimistic people on the other hand, have a completely different interpretation of what happens to them. Good things have only a temporary and limited effect on their lives, whereas the bad things have a permanent, negative impact and affect everything in their lives[2].

> The optimist proclaims that we live in the best of all possible worlds; and the pessimist fears this is true.
>
> *James Branch Cabell*

In other words, the difference between optimism and pessimism lies not just in the view that 'the glass is either half full or half empty'. It is much more profound. Optimists and pessimists actually have a different interpretation of the world and what happens in their lives. For those pessimistic individuals, with a more curmudgeonly approach to life, and who would like to become more optimistic, the good news is that optimism can be cultivated and developed. Several strategies are outlined in this chapter.

Our attitude to life is reflected in our stories that we tell ourselves and others, as we make sense of our experience of life. Our stories are made up of particular events we select from our past, disregarding many others, linking them together to create a narrative about our lives. It's as though we are the authors of a book that we write, or the film that we direct, of our lives. This is explored in this chapter, together with strategies, to develop realistically optimistic stories.

Carrying hurt from the past can be a significant drain on our resilience. Some people struggle with forgiving others, some struggle with forgiving themselves. Practical advice is provided in this regard.

Disabled in body but not in mind

The attitude of being realistically optimistic is epitomised by Mildred. She was severely disabled by polio early in her married life. After five operations involving transplants, she managed to gain the use of some of the fingers of one hand, and to walk, though with a marked limp. She was cared for by her husband, who modified the steering of a motor vehicle for her. This enabled her to drive and to carry out all the usual chores of a mother raising two children and involved in charity work.

Forty years later, and in her eighties, she had a bad fall, closely followed by her husband's sudden death in a motor accident. At the time I interviewed her, as part of the research on resilience, Mildred was confined to a wheelchair with 24-hour care to assist with daily living. She still remained as active as ever, undertaking various charity works, reconditioning Christmas cards to raise funds, teaching and exhibiting her creative knitting.

Recently, she had even started writing her own blog and had developed a small but thriving business with her caregivers, breeding and selling earthworms for gardeners.

She describes herself as tough ('I am not a lovey-dovey person'), determined ('I don't give up easily, like learning to use the computer…I try, try, try!') and positive ('I don't like pictures to be taken of me. I don't want to see myself as disabled and for people to treat me that way. It's intimidating!').

Optimism in a time of pessimism

We live in a time when there is much to worry about. And rather than getting better, so much seems to be getting worse.

Take, for example, work and employment. Youngsters worry about finding a job; people employed in jobs worry about their skills becoming redundant, and people at the end of their working careers worry about whether they'll have enough money for retirement.

When people get together in business meetings and on social occasions, it's often an opportunity to sound off about all the things they see wrong around them: corruption; the state of the roads; the lack of service delivery; the worsening economic and political situation. This sort of group-complaining often leads to a downward spiral of negativity.

Problems are magnified. Solutions aren't easy. People feel trapped. The result is increasing feelings of helplessness and despair, until eventually they give up looking for solutions. This is called 'learned helplessness'[3].

Before we go any further, it is important to note that pessimism does have a useful role in our lives. From an evolutionary point of view, pessimism was necessary when we lived in makeshift shelters and caves. Survival required being on the lookout for negative events such as the arrival of dangerous animals or hostile tribes. But, in our modern world, being pessimistic and having pessimistic people around you is, at the very least, simply not pleasant. At the very worst, ongoing pessimism is detrimental to your emotional stability and equilibrium.

Your attitude of optimism or pessimism directly influences the perceptions you have of your experience of life, and how you live it day to day. But, in addition, your attitude of optimism or pessimism influences your future. Whatever you expect to happen, be it good or bad, focuses your attention on those outcomes. As you look for those outcomes, you will find evidence that supports your beliefs, which then reinforces those beliefs.

In other words, through self-fulfilling prophecies, we anticipate, look for and select experiences to back up our beliefs. In this way, when you believe good or bad things will happen to you, they do.

Putting it simply, you create your future.

> The optimist sees the rose and not its thorns; the pessimist stares at the thorns, oblivious to the rose.
>
> *Kahil Gibran*

How pessimism can spread in organisations

If you have worked in a company, I am sure you will have come across pockets, and even entire departments, where the staff are more pessimistic than the rest of the organisation. Why is that?

Well, there are several organisational forces which have the potential to create and sustain negativity. Take, for example, the influence the manager has on his staff. It's much easier and less risky to turn down suggestions and requests from staff than it is to agree to them. This is because managers seldom get into trouble by saying 'No', even if that does lead to a drop in the morale of their staff.

Criticism sounds smarter than praise, and highly critical people are perceived as more intelligent than those who praise.

Being negative and critical is a tactic people use when they are intellectually insecure[4]. For newcomers to a group, for example, when joining a new team or department at work, critical and negative comments make the person seem wiser than if they were positive and upbeat.

The role of a manager can inadvertently enhance this negative bias. Managers constantly need to be on the lookout for potential risk and problems. With a wide span of control, they are forced to manage staff by exception, paying most attention to people whose results don't match what was planned. In this way, problems and risks get more attention than successes.

Tea and smoking areas become hotbeds of negativity, pessimism and cynicism in times of organisational and personal adversity.

This also applies at regular team and department meetings held to review performance against annual targets. Those areas that are not meeting targets become the focus of attention. Areas of underperformance are identified and exposed, and the causes rigorously dissected. Miscreants and culprits are identified and given appropriate censure.

Too much optimism is simply dangerous and can result in taking dangerous risks – for example, believing there won't be negative consequences from drinking and driving or having unprotected sex with multiple partners.

A little bit of pessimism is not a bad thing, particularly when it translates into saving for retirement, or limiting unhealthy food intake or adhering to an examination study timetable.

It is for this reason that this principle of building personal resilience concerns being *realistically* optimistic, rather than just optimistic. It is the kind of realism where you expect the best, but prepare for the worst.

Living with optimism and pessimism

Our neighbours were a friendly, elderly couple whom we got to know very well. The wife was pessimistic, while the husband much more optimistic. Towards the end of the husband's life he developed Alzheimer's disease. I used to visit them regularly on Saturday mornings for tea, but the progression of the disease made it difficult for him to participate fully in our conversations.

He would often say to me: 'Tell me a happy story.' He loved hearing about what had happened earlier that week, and would laugh heartily at anything even vaguely amusing.

However, I found it quite difficult to find a happy story to tell him every week. Sometimes I repeated stories or merged some previously told stories to create a new one. He never noticed or, if he did, he didn't complain. I loved seeing his face become animated as I related some escapade. The stories made him happy and I felt happy too.

The wife, on the other hand, was much more pessimistic. She sometimes cautioned me at the end of a happy story that I shouldn't expect the good thing that I had related to last for long, or that, perhaps, the motives of some person who had been kind to me were actually suspect.

The wife saw her environment and living situation becoming worse, and she did not believe it would improve. She interpreted events in her life in a negative light.

I'm sure that, in her mind, the negative expectations she had of how things would turn out were fulfilled.

Learning to be optimistic

If realistic optimism is so much more desirable than pessimism, can one develop optimism? Is it learnable or do we have an unalterable set point of optimism and pessimism?

We all start life with a personal quota of optimism or pessimism, which differs from person to person. You can see this in babies, some of whom have a sunnier disposition than others[5]. Their genetic inheritance of optimism or pessimism is modified as soon as they begin to understand language. They listen to and absorb the stories people tell as they make sense of their experiences in the world, particularly from their mothers and people who spend significant time with them. These stories, called 'explanatory style'[6], reflect the storyteller's optimism or pessimism. Young children are impressionable and adopt the underlying beliefs of the stories as their own.

To illustrate the power of explanatory style, let's take the different responses of two mothers driving their cars in traffic, with a young toddler strapped into a car seat in the back. Each crashes into the car in front. The first mother curses out loud and says:

- *'I can't believe it! How could this have happened to me? I looked away for a second. It's my fault that I hit his car!'*

- *Thank goodness my baby and I are unharmed.*

- *'I've been driving for five years since my last accident. I must have travelled over 250 000 km accident-free. What rotten luck to have looked away, just for a second, just when he stopped!'*

- *'I need to get hold of our insurance company and find out what I should do next to get the car repaired. What a relief to have paid insurance premiums all these years without a claim.'*

Contrast this with the second mother, who also curses out loud, and says:

- *'I can't believe it! How could this have happened to me? I looked away for a second. It's my fault that I hit his car!'*

- *'My baby and I could have been killed through my stupidity! When my partner hears about this he's really going to go off the deep end.'*

- *'I always do such stupid things. This is just one more in the long list of dumb things I have done.'*

- *'And now I have to get the car repaired through the insurance company. I will lose the no claims bonus I have had all these years, and my insurance premiums will increase.'*

- *'I can't believe I'm so stupid. I really am living a sad life.'*

Same event; different reactions. This is because the first mother has an optimistic explanatory style while the second has a pessimistic explanatory style. The toddlers in the backseat learn their mothers' explanatory style and use it to explain other events in their lives.

Optimistic people experience good things as permanent and pervasive. In other words, they experience good things happening frequently and these events positively influence and affect many other aspects of their lives. And when bad things happen to them, optimistic people experience them as mostly temporary and as not having a broad, negative influence on other aspects of their lives.

Optimistic and pessimistic people have very different ways of describing the good and the bad things that happen to them.

Pessimists experience the direct opposite: the good things that happen don't last long, and don't have such a pervasive impact on other areas of their lives. In contrast, the bad things that happen, which occur frequently, have a much more permanent impact and affect many other areas of their lives.

These different reactions are shown in the table below[7]:

	Experience good things as:	**Experience bad things as:**
Star-gazers (Optimists)	Permanent and have broad impact	Short-lived and have limited impact
Mud-gazers (Pessimists)	Short-lived and have limited impact	Permanent and have broad impact

We have seen that optimistic thinkers tend to expect good things will happen to them. They are alert and expect good things to happen, and actually seek out information to support these beliefs. They are, therefore, not surprised when they find them.

This creates positive feelings which lead to positive expansive actions:

- joy in the urge to play
- interest in the urge to explore
- contentment from the urge to savour and integrate
- love of a recurring cycle of each of these urges[8].

These positive thoughts, feelings and attitudes build our resources and buffering ability to cope with any present, as well as future, negative emotional experiences. In other words, they help you cope today as well as help build the resources to cope with tough times tomorrow.

Did you miss the bus … or did the bus miss you?

Let's start by exploring the attitude required to be realistically optimistic. People who believe that they are able to influence their world through their actions are described as having 'an internal locus of control'. Others see events in their world being caused by chance and luck, rather than being able to be influenced or caused by them. They have what is called 'an external locus of control'.

To explain this, let's take the example of missing a bus. How do these different people explain what has happened to them? Or, putting it another way, what is the story they tell themselves about what has happened?

One interprets missing the bus as not having reached the bus-stop in time, and the bus left without them. 'I missed the bus,' they say. Their explanation may include insufficient planning, not realising the walk to the bus stop would take so long and other factors within their control.

The implication is that when they consequently arrive late for work, they will want to make up for their lack of punctuality by working during lunch hour or staying late to catch up on lost time.

The other has a different interpretation, with a dramatically different outcome in the workplace. Typically, they interpret not having reached the bus-stop in time as due to bad luck, or the bad weather having caused the walk to the bus stop to take longer, or to not having a wristwatch. 'The bus missed me,' they will explain, because it's not really their fault as they had little or no influence over what happened.

When they arrive late for work, they don't have a similar desire to make up for lost time. In fact, they may need a cup of tea or cigarette before starting work, because it's been such a stressful start to the day. That is learned helplessness in action, which will make it difficult to have a realistically optimistic attitude.

Exercises to create a positive attitude

Here are three simple exercises you can use that will help create a positive attitude no matter what your locus of control. They will also help you to be more realistically optimistic in the longer term.

Exercise: Creating a positive attitude

Method 1. An easy, effective way of creating a positive attitude is by using self-fulfilling prophecies. To do this, prime yourself before an event by imagining in detail the positive outcome you would like to achieve. For example, before an important presentation, think through how the audience will be seated, their state of mind, receptiveness to your topic and the atmosphere in the room. Then imagine yourself giving your best possible talk. You have prepared well; you are relaxed; you establish eye contact with individuals in the audience. Your examples are relevant and understood, and your answers to difficult questions are precise and to the point. You see yourself doing a thoroughly professional job, connecting to the delegates and meeting their needs.

Priming yourself for a positive outcome like this sets you up to anticipate and be alert for good things happening. As you notice them occuring, it reinforces your belief that other good things will also happen, which, in turn, helps you anticipate them. In this way, you set up your own positive self-fulfilling cycle of events.

Of course, you can't skip doing the required preparation simply by just having a positive attitude. It's still important to do the necessary work required for the talk.

Method 2: Associate with and surround yourself with positive people. Positive people radiate and enhance energy that you feel and 'catch' through the process of social contagion. The flip side is to try to avoid negative people and naysayers who drain your energy and positivity.

Method 3: Some people react well to physical stimulus, such as the colour of walls, music, pictures of loved ones, real or toy animals and motivating quotes. If you're such a person, then use this attribute of yours to create an environment around you that is upbeat and positive.

Forgiving and asking for forgiveness

Harbouring intense negative feelings from the past such as hurt, resentment, anger and even hate is debilitating. If we choose not to forgive, we end up carrying a huge burden of negative feelings. We then suffer the double whammy of having experienced the great hurt in the first place, which is then compounded by reliving the pain over and over again. It is only when the person who has been wronged forgives that they are able to get on with their life and move forward.

> How can you be realistically positive if you are suffering great anguish from injustices and deprivations from the past? And anyway, is it appropriate to forgive and forget?

Forgiving others is enshrined in the beliefs of Judaism, Christianity, Islam, Buddhism and Hinduism. Yet we all know that to forgive a major transgression is extremely difficult. It is for this reason that forgiveness is not something that weak people do; it is only achieved by strong people.

> Forgiveness is the willingness to let go of one's legitimate right to anger and hurt in order to move on.

If you are interested, you might like to take a free website questionnaire to see how you compare to average adult Americans when it comes to forgiveness. The questionnaire is free and called Transgression Motivations Questionnaire, which can be found at the following web address: http://www.authentichappiness.sas.upenn.edu

The REACH Model

What should you to if you would like to forgive someone who has wronged you, but are finding it difficult?

A practical yet simple model[9], with the mnemonic REACH[10], has five steps in the form of pyramid that one climbs in the process of forgiveness.

R: Recall

Recall the anger and pain that you have suffered. Forgiveness can only take place when you fully acknowledge the impact of your feelings. Feel once again the intensity of your emotions and values that were brought into play by the intensity of the event. It may help to fulfil this step by completing the following sentences for yourself:

- 'When I think about ...' (identifying what actually happened).

- 'I feel...' (the actual emotions that you feel).

- 'Because ...' (the reason why this is an issue for you; the moral values that you hold dear).

E: Empathise

Empathise with the person who has hurt you. Just as you have identified and lived through your feelings and pain, this step requires you to try to understand what was going through their mind and heart at the time. What motivated the person to do this to you and what thoughts and beliefs do you think they had? It may help to fulfil this step by completing the following sentences for yourself:

- 'When I think about ...' (identifying what actually happened from the other's perspective).

- 'They may have felt ...' (the actual emotions that they may have felt)

- 'They may have done it because ...' (the reasons, values, needs and expectations that they may have and hold dear to them).

A: Altruistic

The gift of forgiveness that you give the other person is not because they deserve it but because you have been forgiven in the past and you would like to reciprocate. You want to move on with your life. You are forgiving voluntarily and because it's part of the moral code or beliefs that you hold to do so. It may help to fulfil this step by completing the following sentences for yourself:

- 'I want to forgive what happened ...'

- 'My reason for forgiving them is ...'.

C: Commit

Commit to forgiving now and not reliving it later. You don't have to actually tell the person they are forgiven, because telling could be unwise, unsafe and even lead to further hurt. It may help to fulfil this step by completing the following sentences for yourself:

- 'I commit to forgiving them now and not reliving this in the future. I will particularly remember this commitment when ...'.

H: Hold

Hold on to the fact you have forgiven the person. This is particularly important when the negative feelings come back again and again. This is why the model is in the form of the pyramid which has to be climbed several times. Don't allow yourself to backslide into the dark well of negative feelings that you have let go of.

Some general points should be made about forgiveness:

- The REACH model of forgiveness, in common with many other models, aims to change intensely negative feelings that are experienced to neutral feelings. Any positive feelings that result from the forgiveness are a bonus.

- Just because you decide to forgive someone doesn't mean to say that the intense negative feelings won't come back sometime in the future.

- Forgiveness is something you do for yourself, not for the person who has wronged you.

- Forgiveness takes work, lots of work, but it gets easier with the passage of time.

- Forgiving someone doesn't mean that you have to trust them again.

- Forgiving someone very often involves forgiving yourself too – as we forgive others, we ourselves are healed.

- Forgiveness is not excusing or condoning what the other person has done, nor does it require you to re-establish the relationship you had with the person.

A parent's worst nightmare

Amy Biehl[xi] was born in America and grew up with a passion for human rights, particularly in South Africa. She came to South Africa as a Fulbright student, studying at the University of the Western Cape and working with various ANC heavyweights on women's issues and the Bill of Rights. She started to study Xhosa and spent time with local black South Africans in Cape Town, in their townships homes and reggae clubs.

On 25 August 1993, it was two days before she was to fly home to be re-united with her family and her long-time boyfriend in California. What she didn't know was that her boyfriend intended to propose to her on her return. This was not to be, as she was murdered by a mob in Gugulethu township, outside Cape Town.

Four young men were arrested, convicted and sentenced for her murder. They applied for amnesty from the Truth and Reconciliation Commission and, with the support of both of Amy's parents, they were successful. They were released from jail and were granted amnesty for their crimes. Amy's parents were able to do the almost unthinkable – let go of their anger and hatred and forgive the individuals who had murdered their daughter.

Amy's parents went on to establish the Amy Biehl Foundation, with its mission 'to weave a barrier against violence'. The foundation offers programmes to children to supplement what they learn at school with workshops that let them express themselves and think independently. The foundation serves 1500 underprivileged youths (aged six to eighteen) a week in many of the townships around Cape Town. The foundation was funded by USAID until December 2005, when it came to the end of a seven-year contract.

Two of the four youths who were sentenced for murdering Amy work in the foundation. Amy Biehl's mother, Linda Biehl and one of the youths, Ntobeko Peni, address audiences and groups about forgiveness and reconciliation. Amy's mother says that she regards Ntobeko as part of her family.

Asking for forgiveness when you have been in the wrong

What about when you have done something wrong and you want forgiveness? Perhaps you have done something that you regret, and you would like to ask the other party for forgiveness. It could be that you are substantially in the wrong, or it could be that there was wrong on both sides, but in either case you would like to ask for forgiveness in order to initiate the healing process.

Here are the four steps to ask for forgiveness:

1. *Take responsibility.*
   Acknowledge, without being defensive, where you have erred and the implications of that for the other person.

2. *Identify their feelings and the impact on the other person.*
   Describe what you understand is the impact and implications of the incident on their needs, values and expectations.

3. *Express your feelings about what has happened.*
   Explain your feelings and regret.

4. *Ask for forgiveness and make restitution.*
   If appropriate, this may include actually asking for forgiveness and exploring with the other person how you can make restitution.

It is really helpful to maintain your dignity and respect as well as that of the other person at all times during this conversation. Doing so will help keep the conversation from being derailed into accusations, blame and side issues.

Forgiving in tough circumstances

There are times, however, when a face-to-face conversation either to ask for forgiveness or to forgive someone is either impossible, for example when the person has died, or is potentially dangerous – as is the case with an evil person with whom reconnection could put you at risk.

In these cases, have the forgiving conversation in your mind in as much detail and as realistically as possible. Imagine going through all the steps and notice the relief you feel as you obtain forgiveness. Going through this process in your head is not easy, however, and may require several attempts in order to derive the feeling of forgiveness and release that you seek.

Alternatively, you can write a letter to the other person, following the steps, but do *not* send it. Rereading it again each day for a week will reinforce your forgiveness, help bury the past and enable you to move on.

Recharging your batteries

It is now generally accepted that it's important to maintain a life-work balance and you need to take time out for yourself. Yet the irony is that, while everybody knows this to be true, many people find it difficult to achieve. How often haven't we cancelled family outings to finish a report for work, come back early from annual leave to attend a meeting, or cancelled some planned family or sporting activity to meet with members of our community or religious committee? This happens because we often put the needs of work and others ahead of our own needs.

The pernicious effect of living a life of high stress and continual multitasking is that the adrenaline rush it creates becomes addictive, and we end up feeling it is normal. There is a risk, however. Living at too fast a pace can eventually lead to a breakdown in your health, in your loving relationships and mental well-being.

To maintain a realistically optimistic outlook and prevent overload, we need to regularly recharge our batteries by engaging in enjoyable, relaxing and re-energising activities. Taking steps to change the scenery, pace and people around us was cited by some people, in my study of resilience, as a useful counterbalance to the intense demands of dealing with adversity. They called this 'taking time out for myself', having 'me-time' or 'taking time to smell the roses'.

Specific activities that people found useful were

- spending time with loved ones and good friends
- going for a walk or some other physical activity
- playing games with friends
- going to the gym
- shopping with friends
- watching a movie or play
- reading a novel
- partying
- listening to live or recorded music.

Try to find the activities that work for you, to dissociate from adversity and recharge your batteries. You will then be able to deal with the stress and difficulties you face in life with renewed vigour.

The value of exercise

Exercise is probably the simplest and easiest way of dealing with stress and recharging one's energy. Walking, cycling, aerobics, gym, swimming, jogging, running, basketball, netball, baseball, cricket – the list is endless. It's less important what exercise you do than doing the exercise.

Exercise can benefit you from many perspectives:

- *It protects against the ravages of stress.* It helps burn off excess adrenaline, which is associated with anxiety and tension. Cortisol is released at times of stress to enable the body to instantly prepare itself to fight, run or hide, which was potentially life-saving in our past. However, in the present we seldom use up this powerful hormone. When it is not used up, it can lead to high blood pressure, ulcers, depletion of energy, hypertension and reduction in the metabolic processes of digestion, growth, reproduction and even maintenance of the immune system. Exercise wards off these dangerous side-effects by making use of excess adrenaline and cortisol.

- *It produces a natural chemical high.* Serotonin, which is released by exercise, is thought to enhance mood, sleep, appetite and even libido.

- *Increases energy.* Energy levels are enhanced through an increase in overall cardiovascular capability and fitness.

- *Makes you feel good.* It builds confidence and self-esteem and produces a sense of accomplishment as personal goals are achieved.

So go on, try it. Find the exercise that you enjoy the most and which fits in with your time constraints. You won't regret it.

Exercises to enhance realistic optimism

Earlier this chapter I asked whether optimism could be developed. This section outlines exercises to develop realistic optimism that are easy and have fantastic results.

Exercise: Imagining your dreams have come true

Start by selecting a category that most interests you. Then imagine that all that you wish for in that area of your life has come true: your dreams have been fulfilled; you have achieved all your goals and you have fulfilled your potential[11].

Categories:

- Loving relationships
- Spiritual
- Friends and social
- Career
- Health
- Wealth
- Sport and recreation
- Community

Picture in your mind all the details of what is happening. What are you doing day to day? What are you feeling and thinking? What is happening around you? What are other people doing?

Some people say they find it helpful to write down their thoughts as they live out and experience this attractive future. Write in the present tense, as though things are happening right now.

Once you have completed writing how it feels, discuss your answers with significant people who will be part of and affected by these achievements. This will most likely be your loving partner and perhaps close friends. Encourage them also to write their own story about this category and share it with you.

You will find that it's very exciting to feel what it's like to live in the future where all you wish yourself has come about. The picture or vision of your desirable future will draw you and your significant people to it. The energy and enthusiasm it creates will naturally lead you to start planning and then implementing the steps needed to bring it about.

The above exercise can easily be applied to make important changes in your life, as the following story illustrates.

Barry helps Louise to live her best future

By the time Louise and Barry's children had finished their university studies and left home, Louise was very ill with myalgic encephalomyelitis or post-viral fatigue syndrome (PVFS). Barry was rattling around their large double-storey home, while Louise, with her impaired health, was battling to cope with the stairs, let alone run the house. Downsizing seemed an obvious solution, which they did as soon as Louise was finally well enough to cope with selling the house and all the packing up which went on around her.

Several months after moving into their smaller house, they were sitting in the kitchen after supper one evening talking about Louise living with PVFS. She was passionate about embroidery and particularly pulled-thread and drawn-thread techniques. Barry really wanted to ensure that she had all her embroidery materials and equipment easily accessible in the room they had chosen for this purpose.

However, the discussion was proving more difficult than Barry had expected. Louise was overwhelmed by all the minor decisions that were needed, about the layout of the room, cupboards and placement of machines. The PVFS was preventing them from optimising their new home and environment. The conversation got bogged down. They weren't getting anywhere. It seemed as though the whole rationale for the move, which was to make life easier for both of them, was just not working out.

A few days later Barry tried a different tack. He wrote down how he saw himself spending his time five years hence, with all his dreams having come true. He described trail-running in the beautiful Cape mountains; paddling on his wave-ski off the beaches of False Bay; working in his specially designed home-office and running workshops for clients. The more he wrote, the more energised and enthusiastic he became about the future.

He read out loud what he had written to Louise. She became enthused by his excitement and energy. Picking up the challenge of doing the same for herself, she wrote about experiencing huge fulfilment and satisfaction working in her ideal home office; creating embroidery pieces; teaching others at the local Embroidery Guild; regularly writing a blog, and having a book published.

As she read to Barry what she had written, her eyes sparkled with her passion for the embroidery. Then she suddenly stopped and said: 'But the room that I want to use is small and dark.'

The solution was obvious. Within a few months the room was transformed with large windows, loads of artificial light, and cupboards incorporating areas designed for her specialised equipment.

Barry and Louise had both lived in their best possible worlds, feeling and experiencing their dreams having been fulfilled. This produced the energy and motivation for Louise to make the changes needed. The best possible world that they envisaged was so powerful and motivating that it temporarily overcame the PVFS, and it was almost as if it created itself.

What is the story of your life?

We all have a story to tell about ourselves that helps us make sense of what we have experienced in life. These stories can be happy or sad, humorous or tragic, focused on recent events or far back. We tell these stories to our friends, partners, business associates and children. And most frequently of all, we tell the stories to ourselves.

Steve Jobs, the extremely talented founder of Apple Computers, had this to say about his life in a commencement address at Stanford University[12]:

> *I dropped out of Reed College after the first six months, but then stayed around as a drop-in for another eighteen months or so, before I really quit. So why did I drop out?*
>
> *It started before I was born. My biological mother was a young, unwed college graduate student, and she decided to put me up for adoption. She felt very strongly that I should be adopted by college graduates, so everything was all set for me to be adopted at birth by a lawyer and his wife. Except that when I popped out they decided at the last minute that they really wanted a girl. So my parents, who were on a waiting list, got a call in the middle of the night asking: "We have an unexpected baby boy. Do you want him?" They said: "Of course". My biological mother later found out that my mother had never graduated from college and that my father had never graduated from high school. She refused to sign the final adoption papers. She only relented a few months later when my parents promised that I would someday go to college.*
>
> *And 17 years later I did go to college. But I naively chose a college that was almost as expensive as Stanford, and all of my working-class parents' savings were being spent on my college tuition. After six months, I couldn't see the value in it. I had no idea what I wanted to do with my life and no idea how college was going to help me figure it out. And here I was spending all of the money my parents had saved, their entire lives. So I decided to drop out and trust that it would all work out OK. It was pretty scary at the time, but looking back it was one of the best decisions I ever made. The minute I dropped out I could stop taking the required classes that didn't interest me, and begin dropping in on the ones that looked interesting.*

It wasn't all romantic. I didn't have a dorm room, so I slept on the floor in friends' rooms, I returned coke bottles for the five cent deposits to buy food with, and I would walk the seven miles across town, every Sunday night to get one good meal a week at the Hare Krishna temple. I loved it. And much of what I stumbled into, by following my curiosity and intuition, turned out to be priceless later on. Let me give you one example:

Reed College at that time offered perhaps the best calligraphy instruction in the country. Throughout the campus every poster, every label on every drawer, was beautifully hand written. Because I had dropped out and didn't have to take the normal classes, I decided to take a calligraphy class to learn how to do this. I learned about serif and sans-serif typefaces, about varying the amount of space between different letter combinations, about what makes great typography great. It was beautiful, historical, artistically subtle in a way that science can't capture, and I found it fascinating.

None of this had even a hope of any practical application in my life. But ten years later, when we were designing the first Macintosh computer, it all came back to me. And we designed it all into the Mac. It was the first computer with beautiful typography. If I had never dropped in on that single course in college, the Mac would have never had multiple typefaces or proportionally spaced fonts. And since Windows just copied the Mac, it's likely that no personal computer would have them. If I had never dropped out, I would have never dropped in on this calligraphy class, and personal computers might not have the wonderful typography that they do. Of course it was impossible to connect the dots looking forward when I was in college. But it was very, very clear looking backwards ten years later.

Again, you can't connect the dots looking forward; you can only connect them looking backwards. So you have to trust that the dots will somehow connect in your future. You have to trust in something — your gut, destiny, life, karma, whatever. This approach has never let me down, and it has made all the difference in my life.

How we frame stories from our past

Each time we tell a story about our past, we select particular events, stringing them together to make sense of what has happened. By focusing on particular events from our past, and ignoring a vast number of others, we actually create a simplified and selected picture of our past.

Two really intriguing points arise. First, we believe that the story we create about our lives is completely and one hundred per cent true. In reality, however, we select specific events while ignoring many others to suit the story we wish to tell at that particular time.

Second, we make interpretations and draw conclusions from the story and then act as though they are completely representative of our entire lives. To compound this, we actually become alert for events and information that occur in the present to support our conclusions.

Thus the stories about our past that we tell others and ourselves are actually select recreations of our past and not necessarily representative of all the events of our past. Our stories are just that part we wish to highlight at a particular point in time. But with each telling of the story, we feel the emotions more strongly, which, in turn, builds our belief of the truth of the story.

An example of how this works is the story of the fish that was caught but got away, and which grows in size with each telling. The fisherman may, at some level, be aware that the story is not a hundred per cent accurate. But each time the story is retold, the more it is experienced as true, reinforced by repeatedly experiencing the powerful emotions associated with almost catching the fish.

Put simply, the story we tell ourselves creates ourselves.

In summary, through telling our stories, we actually re-experience prior events, with all the original emotion, as though they were happening in the present. In this way, we perpetuate the story from our past into the present and also project it into our future.

Thus, if you are on the lookout for good things to happen, interpreting events in a realistically optimistic way, then the story you create for yourself is one of happiness. Such stories have the potential to create upward spirals of happiness and resilience.

On the other hand, if you are on the lookout for negative things to happen, and interpret events in a pessimistic way, the result will be a story that you tell yourself of doom and gloom. These stories will reinforce past hurts and insults, creating downward spirals of negativity and despondence.

Exercises

Exercise: Telling your story

This exercise assists you to tell the story of your life and to join the dots, looking backwards as Steve Jobs did, in a way that is realistically optimistic. In order for it to become part of you, it must be created by you and, most important, believable to you. To do this, follow the instructions below:

1. Write down a minimum of three and a maximum of five major obstacles you've had in your life.

2. Tell the story of your life out loud (how these events occurred) but tell the story with the obstacles reframed as stepping stones to a new phase in

your life. Explain how, when you look back to join the dots, each of these events enabled you to obtain new insights, and how new opportunities were opened up to you.

3. Listen to how you explain your past to yourself. Listen to how you are interpreting and recreating your past and, by so doing, opening up a different future for yourself.

4. Practise telling this new story about your past. Do this by telling the story to yourself a couple of times, and by relating it to trusted friends and loved ones. The more you tell it, the more real it will become.

Exercise: Listening to your and others' stories

This is a simple exercise and you will be amazed at how easy it is to recognise the types of stories people use, to create and reinforce the picture they have of their lives:

· Every time you meet with friends, ask how they are. Listen carefully to the story they tell you, which explains and make sense of their life experiences and in this way creates them.

· Ask yourself: are they creating a positive story, in which they strong and proud, or is it a negative story full of anger, pain and regrets? Which story would you choose?

· Then tell them how you are. Select events in your life which tells your story in which you are strong and realistically optimistic. Listen to yourself creating the life you would like to live.

The final exercise in this chapter is designed to bring together the various aspects we have covered and to tie up any loose ends. Choose one or more questions from the list below to consolidate and apply your learning from this chapter.

Written exercises

1. Are there people you need to forgive, and f so, how will you do so?

2. What physical relaxing and recharging activities should you do more of?

3. Identify the stories you tell yourself about yourself. Are you happy with the stories and, if not, how would you like the stories to be different?

4. What can you do to tell yourself accurate and resilient stories about yourself?

5. What can you do to be more realistically optimistic?

ENDNOTES

1 Frankl, Viktor E. 1963. *Man's search for meaning*. New York: Washington Square Press, Simon and Schuster. (p. 63.)

2 Seligman, M.E.P. 1998. *Learned optimism: How to change your mind and your life*. New York: Free Press.

3 See reference [ii]

4 Jared Sandberg. *The Wall Street Journal*. 'Negativity is a tactic people use when they're insecure'. *Deseret News*. Salt Lake City. FindArticles.com. 24 Jun. 2011. http://findarticles.com/p/articles/mi_qn4188/is_20061029/ai_n16811511/. Accessed 29 August 2011.

5 Seligman, M.E.P. 1996. *The optimistic child: Proven program to safeguard children from depression and build lifelong resilience*. New York: Houghton Mifflin.

6 See reference 2.

7 See reference 2.

8 Fredrickson, B.L. 2001. The role of positive emotions in positive psychology. *American psychologist*, 56(3):218–226.

9 Worthington, E.L. Jr. & DiBlasio, F.A. 1990. Promoting mutual forgiveness within the fractured relationship. *Psychotherapy*, 27:219-223.

10 Worthington, E.L. Jr. & Drinkard, D.T. 2000. Promoting reconciliation through psychoeducational and therapeutic interventions. *Journal of marital and family therapy*, 26:93–101.

11 Sheldon, K.M. & Lyubomirsky, S. 2006. How to increase and sustain positive emotion: The effects of expressing gratitude and visualizing best possible selves. *Journal of positive psychology*, 1:73–82.

12 Source: *http://news.stanford.edu/news/2005/june15/jobs-061505.html*. Accessed 6 June 2010.

9

Persevere by being open-minded and flexible

Persevere by being open-minded and flexible	
Reach out to others	Connect to your meaning in life
Maintain perspective	Use your unique strengths
Generate positive feelings	Be realistically optimistic

Obstacles are great incentives.

Jules Michelet

Deciding what to do in the face of adversity is often difficult. We know we need to make decisions and 'do something' or 'change something', but we feel paralysed. Emotions like anger, fear and grief can rob us of our usual rational thinking and decision-making abilities.

During my research on resilience, people related stories about when they had faced adversity and triumphed. They dealt with tough times by taking action, by doing things to address or change the situation. They did not just sit back, hoping that things would get better. They described how they had continually tried to find better ways of dealing with their situation, of coping and of making things better. They were action-focused, looking for solutions with an open and flexible mind-set.

These stories reflected a high degree of tenacity on the part of people to seek solutions and deal with issues, rather than accept things as they were and giving up or ignoring the problem. Their actions reflected open-mindedness and flexible approaches to problem-solving, which enabled them to change tactics and even strategy as they thought necessary. They took action to address both the causes and effects of the adversity. Thoughtful risk-taking also came to light as a part of their successful coping with adversity.

This was in marked contrast to the stories about when they weren't resilient. Those reflected a fixed mind-set – not listening, tunnel vision, and using brute force to deal with the adversity. Many stories described a great deal of drive and energy, but there was an almost despairing acknowledgement that it was often 'action for the sake of action' rather than pursuing a creative solution. Other stories were about being almost paralysed by fear or anger and not taking action.

Perseverance is the key to taking action in the face of adversity. We need mental toughness to grit our teeth and not succumb or become disabled by adversity. If we don't, we lapse into inactivity and even depression.

On the other hand, too much perseverance results in a blinkered and bull-headed drive to 'do something' for the sake of action. In such cases, there is often poor listening and a fixed mind-set. The result is decisions and actions that are unlikely to be creative and may even make the situation worse. This happens because the anxiety caused by adversity narrows thinking and reduces creativity. In simple terms, it's almost impossible to be creative when you're afraid.

The antidote to this is for perseverance to be balanced with an open-minded and flexible approach. This will enable you to still push for action, but to do this in a creative way, listening to views different from your own, and being open to changing tactics and even strategy.

Now, at first glance, it may appear that this is a contradiction in terms. How is it possible to persevere, which requires dogged determination, and at the same time be open-minded and flexible?

The remarkable thing is resilience requires both. You need to have both the determination and persistence to stay the course, and also the ability to be creative, open-minded and flexible. Like much in life, it is an enigma. This chapter provides some help on how you can do just that.

> Success in the affairs of life often serve to hide one's abilities, whereas adversity frequently gives one an opportunity to discover them.
>
> *Horace*

Adam perseveres by being a lateral thinker

Perseverance, together with open-mindedness and flexibility in building resilience, is illustrated by the different courses of action taken by two pharmacists, Adam and Daniel[1]. They owned and managed their own independent pharmacies, approximately two kilometres apart. They both faced the promulgation of new legislation, controlling the prices charged for prescription medicines. The implication for them was, at the very least, that they faced substantially reduced profit, and at the worst, bankruptcy.

Adam dealt with this adversity by advocating for changes in the legalisation through the local chapter of the Pharmaceutical Association and then, later, at national level. He was instrumental in getting court interdicts to stop and ultimately alter the legislation.

During the many months while this dragged on, he changed his pharmacy's focus to become more customer-orientated, to take advantage of the increasing tourist trade. Today, Adam has the highest turnover in sun-screen protection sales in his geographical region. He makes more profit from the retail side of the business than from the sales of prescription medication of the past.

The other pharmacist, Daniel, faced the identical adversity but reacted with less open-mindedness and flexibility. His strategy was to boost pharmacy sales by encouraging repeat business from his existing client base, by means of mailed flyers, lowering the prices of some of his non-prescription lines and introducing a motorcycle delivery to customers.

Deep down, he felt that these actions were not very creative and would not have the desired effect. As his worst fears were borne out, he stopped introducing new ideas and became increasingly despondent. Daniel eventually sold his pharmacy at a low price to a national retail chain and, with great relief, took early retirement.

Even though the adversity Adam and Daniel faced was the same for both, and their circumstances were remarkably similar, their reactions were very different. Adam persevered with creativity and lateral thinking and, over several years, was ultimately successful. Daniel, on the other hand, allowed the adversity to overwhelm his thinking and natural optimism, and eventually it almost crushed him.

Roles people play during adversity

Tough times can be made even worse by negative interactions with others. Have you ever been involved in negative conversations that seem to go round and round? And no matter what you do, it seems as though you can't break out of the negative cycle?

While these negative conversations can occur at any time, there are specific times when you are at your most vulnerable, for example, when tired, hungry, making a transition and multitasking. Many working mothers experience all of these at the end of the day, returning from work to home, preparing the evening meal and dealing with demanding and excited children who have been at crèche or school all day.

Familiar? If so, this section will help you when you are at your most vulnerable, to recognise and break out of toxic conversations.

A very useful and simple model, for understanding the dynamics of negative conversations, is that of the Drama Triangle proposed by Stephen B. Karpman, MD[2] He showed that people can get stuck playing roles when interacting with others. You know you are in a negative role when you feel yourself falling back into old, undesirable ways of interacting and behaving, that you don't particularly want to, but somehow do anyway. Karpman explains that these toxic roles arise from negative experiences during our childhood and upbringing, and we continue to play them in our adult lives.

There are three typical roles that people can play – Victim, Persecutor and Rescuer. As individuals avoid taking responsibility for their own needs and behaviours[3], these roles come into existence and are fuelled by blame and guilt[4].

The roles are easy to slip into and, because they feel so familiar and comfortable, it's difficult to break out of them. Once you start playing one of these roles, you start a 'drama' which, inevitably, then hooks someone else into playing one of the roles too. We get hooked into playing these roles because we've been practising them since childhood, and it's very easy to revert back to them. In addition, playing the role has a short-term payoff, even though in the long term they don't serve you well and have a negative impact.

Most people have a 'default role' which they are most comfortable playing, and a secondary role which they commonly switch to. The remaining role is usually the one that they are most afraid of and most manipulated by.

The three roles of the Drama Triangle

PERSECUTOR: 'IT'S ALL YOUR FAULT!'

The Persecutor blames, criticises and threatens because they're so convinced they are right. The role is characterised by blaming others and frequently giving vent to their anger. They often go through life angry at the world, blaming everyone else for their problems. They try to change others by guilt, shame or force. They are rigid and inflexible.

The Persecutor role hooks a Rescuer response from the other person, when the Rescuer wants to prevent conflict and smooth the interaction. The Persecutor can also hook a Victim response, if the Victim responds by feeling hopeless, shamed and belittled by the persecutor.

RESCUER: 'I'LL MAKE IT BETTER.'

The Rescuer comes to the rescue because it feels good and correct. The Rescuer tries to smooth things over, keep harmonious relationships and avoid conflict. They feel guilty if they don't rescue, but often feel unappreciated and even manipulated when they do. Underlying their rescue attempts is low self-esteem with a deep feeling that their own needs are not important and that their value is created by helping others. Rescuers often have career roles such as teacher, social worker, nurse and HR practitioner.

The Rescuer hooks a Victim response from the other person, which is resented by the Victim who experiences it as 'saving them', by belittling them and keeping them helpless. Rescuers can also hook a Persecutor response from the other person, if the Persecutor recognises and is infuriated by the martyr feelings of the Rescuer.

VICTIM: 'POOR ME!'

Victims feel oppressed, helpless and often ashamed. They feel they don't have the ability to change their lives. Consequently, they don't have to take responsibility for their own problems. They feel powerless, picked upon and wallow in their suffering. As Victims, they deny any responsibility for their failure – it's all someone else's fault or due to factors beyond their control.

The Victim hooks a Rescuer response from the other person, which is given with feelings of guilt and sometimes even anger, expecting that the rescue attempt will fail. They can also hook a Persecutor response from the other person, if the other reacts angrily to the helplessness and hopelessness implied by the Victim.

How roles come into existence

Roles are usually learned in childhood and particularly in our families as we grow up. Each toxic role hooks and reinforces another toxic role, played by the other person. Playing each of the roles has a pay-off for the role player. The Rescuer gets appreciation and gratitude from the Victim. The Victim gets support and sympathy from the Rescuer. And the Persecutor ends up blaming each of them.

These payoffs help keep the toxic conversation going, even though the role players may wish to break out of them.

These roles have a really debilitating impact. The Victim grovels for help and feels incapable. The Rescuer resents giving up meeting their own needs in order to meet those of the Victim. The Persecutor feels better when blaming everyone else, rather than taking responsibility for their own feelings and behaviours. At the heart of these interactions is a lack of honesty and taking responsibility for oneself.

Get out of your habituated roles

It is difficult to get out of these roles. But it can be done. The following tables show how you can get out of the roles, and also how to use an alternative Harmony role.

Drama Triangle roles	Getting out of the toxic roles
Persecutor	Either give clear structure as to what you think should happen, or move away entirely and allow the other people to sort things out for themselves. Avoid lecturing, giving advice and intervening when not asked.
Rescuer	Be careful about taking action before being asked in order to prevent rescuing when other people don't want it. Resist the temptation to smooth things over or jump in and sort things out. Just let other people know that your help is available if they want it.
Victim	Acknowledge your vulnerability and own up to your fears. Don't blame others for your circumstances. Take responsibility for what you can do and acknowledge what is beyond your control.

Turning toxic Drama Triangle roles into Harmony roles

Getting out of the Drama Roles is a start, but not sufficient. You need to convert your understanding of that role into a Harmony Role. Use the following table to identify what you could do to change from a toxic role to a Harmony:

Alternate Harmony roles	The value of the Harmony role	How to stay in the Harmony role
Persecutor becomes Driver	Gets things done, sets the pace and accomplishes objectives. This role is particularly useful in times of adversity when taking a leadership role and persevering to get action and change.	Listen, check your understanding and summarise. Get consensus for your actions. Make sure that people don't feel their opinions have been ignored. Keep your strong feelings in check.
Rescuer becomes Nurturer	Assists and helps people where and when they need it, without taking over and assuming responsibility for others.	Show your concern for others by asking questions and letting them know you're available to them when they ask for your assistance. Step back and allow others to solve their problems themselves, even if you could do it better and quicker for them.
Victim becomes Owner of the Problem	Lets other people know where you are at. Fears and concerns are voiced in a strong manner. Takes action to deal with problems and issues.	Identify and own your feelings. Voice your concerns and feelings clearly, without feeling embarrassed or guilty. Use problem-solving skills to deal with issues you encounter. Develop solutions and test them with others to ensure you're on the right track. Understand that you learn and develop from your mistakes.

Governing principles for Harmony roles

There are four governing principles or simple rules for engaging in effective conversations to break out of the Drama Triangle and use the Harmony roles. These governing principles have their basis in being honest and authentic in the conversation, and taking responsibility for your own behaviour and your own life:

1. TAKE RESPONSIBILITY

At the heart of a productive conversation is the willingness and ability to take responsibility for one's own actions and one's life. This means owning up to mistakes that you have made. It also means taking appropriate ownership of what is happening in your life, and changing those things that are within your control that you don't like. It's a kind of steely-eyed, realistic view of life.

2. STAY COOL

The more intense a conversation, the greater the temptation for one's negative emotions to interfere and even hijack the conversation. You need to ensure that you don't say or do things that you later regret.

This does not mean that you should not express your feelings. On the contrary, labelling and explaining how you feel will not only help the other person understand your perspective, but will help you feel better too.

3. MAINTAIN DIGNITY

Maintaining the dignity and self-respect of both parties is the foundation of a productive conversation. This will help you craft your responses so that you don't get hooked into toxic roles.

4. SEPARATE FACTS FROM FEELINGS

In order to effectively solve problems and make decisions, you need to separate facts from feelings. The facts need to be identified and separated from opinions, assumptions, impressions and general wishes. Feelings are important to be identified and raised. With a holistic picture of relevant facts and feelings, you are now best positioned to deal with tough issues.

Breaking out of the Drama Triangle

Let's now look at an example of the toxic roles in action. A mother, father and their daughter Julie are at home at the end of the day. Julie has just fled to her bedroom in tears, slamming the door behind her, after an argument with her mother about whether she could watch TV before doing her homework.

Read the script below and notice how each toxic role hooks another toxic role response.

Drama Triangle: Roles in action

Dad	Look what you've done! Why do you always pick on Julie? Can't you see that she just wants to watch TV?	*Persecutor*
Mom	I am just trying to do the right thing for all of us. She needs to do her homework before she's too tired. Please don't shout.	*Rescuer*
Dad	You are always having a go at her. Why don't you just let her relax at the end of the day?	*Persecutor*
Mom	I really don't want to upset either you or her. Let's just leave her for a while and I'm sure she'll be fine in a few minutes.	*Rescuer*
Dad	That's your problem. You're always trying to control everyone's lives!	*Persecutor*
Mom	Let's not argue about this now. Let's have supper together and be a happy family together.	*Rescuer*
Dad	How can I be happy when my baby girl is crying? I have had a terrible day at work and then come home to her crying!	*Victim*
Mom	Well, that's what I'm saying. Let's just have supper and be a family together.	*Rescuer*
Dad	This is really too much for me to cope with. Complaints at work. Fighting at home. You just want too much from me.	*Victim*
Mom	Sometimes you make me sick! All you do is whinge and complain. If you don't like how I deal with Julie, do something about it!	*Persecutor*
Dad	I've got a job I hate. When I get home all I want to do is read the newspaper, watch TV and relax.	*Victim*
Mom	You think that you are the only one that has a difficult job? I also have a difficult job and have to pick up things after you around the house.	*Persecutor*
Dad	Look, I know I haven't fixed all the things that you want me to, but I will get to them.	*Rescuer*
Mom	You never take out the rubbish. You never offer to help with the cooking. And all you do is criticise the way I handle Julie.	*Persecutor*
Dad	Let's just forget all about it and pretend that hasn't happened. Julie will have finished her homework soon.	*Rescuer*
Mom	I really don't know how I survive in this family! I can't seem to do anything right. I have to do all the chores myself – no-one else helps out.	*Victim*

This argument can go on forever. The mom and dad seem, in a perverse way, almost to enjoy the argument. This is because the short-term payoff for each role helps perpetuate the argument. As the conversation moves to new topics, each with its own hurt and anger, the conversation gets new energy to continue. And if one adds alcohol to this noxious stew, there is the potential for the conversation to last for hours and even days.

So how would you break out of this Drama Triangle? Practise by completing the exercise below:

Written exercise: Breaking out of the Drama Triangle

Read the script of the Drama Triangle roles in action again. Notice how the toxic roles hook each other, and how they change in response to each other. Now answer the questions below:

1. Imagine that you are at the end of the script. What would you do to break out of the Drama Triangle? Answer this question first in the role of the mom, and second in the role of the dad. Write down the actual words you would use to break out of these toxic Drama Triangle roles.

2. Having written down your responses, using the actual words that you would say, review your responses against the section 'Getting out of the roles', and the section on 'Turning the Drama Triangle roles into Harmony roles' to ensure that they meet those criteria.

3. Reflect on a conversation you have had recently which involved the Drama Triangle. Identify the roles you and the other person were playing. Review the section 'Getting out of the roles' and the section 'Turning the Drama Triangle roles into Harmony roles' and write down the actual words you could use to break out of the roles you were playing.

Creating inner calm during adversity

Persevering, in an open-minded and flexible manner, even in the face of adversity, is easier if you have inner calm. To achieve this, you need to be able to quieten your anxieties and frustrations, and centre yourself to find inner calm. You can do this despite what is going on around you and even inside you.

Here are four exercises which will help you achieve inner calm:

1. *Physical relaxation exercise*

    This is a useful exercise to use in conjunction with the other exercises which follow, but also works on its own and can be done at any time and place.

    This exercise will also help you fall asleep quicker and remain in a deep sleep. In addition, should you wake up in the middle of the night and find it difficult to get back to sleep, it will help you to disassociate yourself from your worries, relax your body and make it easier to fall asleep.

    – Tense the muscles in your feet and toes, and then release them. Do this three times.

    – Tense the muscles in your calves, and then release them. Do this three times.

    – Tense the muscles in your thighs, and then release them. Do this three times.

    – Tense the muscles in your buttocks and groin, and then release them. Do this three times.

    – Tense the muscles in your stomach, and then release them. Do this three times.

    – Tense muscles in your shoulders, arms and hands, and then release them. Do this three times.

    – Tense the muscles in your neck, and then release them. Do this three times.

    – Tense the muscles in your face, and then release them. Do this three times.

    – Tense all the muscles together in your legs, abdomen, shoulders and arms, neck and face. Do this three times.

    – Breathe slowly in and out three times and feel relaxed and calm

2. *Breathing exercise*

This simple exercise can be carried out at work and at home. I have even done it with good results in my parked car before an important presentation to a client.

- Sit upright in a chair, as far away from noise and distractions as possible. Place your hands on your stomach.

- Close your eyes, and begin to breathe deeply in and out through your nose. When you breathe in, feel your hands moving closer into your body, as your lungs expand and your body lifts to accommodate the air. Then breathe out through your mouth, deflating your lungs and feel your hands moving on your stomach, as you exhale deeply to the bottom of your lungs.

- Notice the air as it enters your body through your nose. Feel it in your nostrils as it gently caresses them as you breathe in, and again feel the air as you breathe out through your mouth.

- Slow your breathing by pausing for two heartbeats when you have finished inhaling, and again for two heartbeats when you have finished exhaling.

- Take ten deep breaths in this way, noticing the air entering your lungs through your nostrils, pausing when your lungs are full, and slowly exhaling through your mouth – until your lungs are empty – pausing once again before you inhale fully.

- When complete, slowly open your eyes, feeling refreshed and calm.

3. *Breathing exercise with instruction*

This exercise is a variation on the previous one, with an additional component to help you relax.

- Find a place to sit upright in a chair, as far away from noise and distractions as possible. Place your hands on your stomach.

– Close your eyes, and begin to breathe deeply in and out through your nose. When you breathe in, feel your hands moving closer into your body, as your diaphragm empties and your body lifts to accommodate the air that is expanding your lungs. Then breathe out through your mouth, deflating your lungs and feel your hands moving on your stomach outwards, as you exhale deeply to the bottom of your lungs.

– Notice the air as it enters your body through your nose. Feel it in your nostrils as it gently caresses them as you breathe in, and again feel the air as you breathe out through your mouth.

– Slow your breathing by pausing for two heartbeats when you have finished inhaling, and again for two heartbeats when you have finished exhaling.

– As you breathe in, say silently to yourself 'Let …' and as you breathe out, say silently to yourself '… go'.

– Take ten deep breaths in this way, each time saying 'Let …' as you breathe in, and '… go' as you breathe out. Each time you breathe in, feel any negative feelings you may have being brought to the top of your lungs. Each time you breathe out, feel them expelled from your mind and body. Feel all your cares and worries leaving your body.

– When complete, slowly open your eyes, feeling refreshed and calm.

4. *Guided meditation exercise*

This calming exercise uses a more creative relaxation technique. Think of a place that you know which is beautiful and peaceful. It's your special place. For most people, this is somewhere in nature, such as a secluded beach, a river, a lakeside or a waterfall. It must be a place that you know well and are able to visualise clearly your mind.

Once you have chosen your special place, follow each of the following bullet points in sequence, taking about thirty seconds on each:

- Imagine yourself on the path approaching your peaceful place. Feel the earth beneath your bare feet as you walk slowly towards it. Become aware of how the grains of sand, or the blades of grass, feel warm and smooth on the soles of your feet.

- Feel the warm sun on your face and arms. It feels good. Feel the cooling breeze through your hair and on your skin. It feels so good. Hear the faint calls from the birds high up in the sky, as they wheel and soar in the beautiful, clear air.

- Imagine now walking closer to your special place. And there, in front of you, it appears in all its beauty. You are in awe of how wonderful nature is to have created such a peaceful and restful place. Everything is in harmony. Everything is at peace.

- You feel so privileged to be part of this beautiful and special place. You soak up the beauty, opening yourself to incorporating the beauty into yourself. You feel yourself an integral part of this beautiful spot of nature.

- In the blue, clear sky above you, there is a small, white, puffy cloud near the horizon. As you watch, it gets smaller and smaller until eventually it disappears. You are at peace, calm and relaxed.

- When you are ready, slowly open your eyes, and feel rested and at peace.

Making risky decisions

Coping with adversity and bouncing back, almost always requires making decisions to do something or to change something. Making decisions, however, involves risk: the risk of being wrong and the risk of making the situation even worse if the decisions don't work out.

In times of adversity making decisions is even more difficult than usual. That's because we're often not emotionally and mentally strong when we have to make the decision.

But let's put this into context. Living involves taking decisions. And taking decisions always involves some element of risk. We take a risk when we cross a busy road, take medication prescribed by a doctor, marry and have a child. We take risks all the time and often we don't even think about the risks involved.

Virgil is reputed to have said (Fortune sides with him who dares).

So how can we make sensible and intelligent decisions in times of adversity when, typically, we are stressed and anxious? In other words, how can we be open-minded and flexible, at the very time when we may be at our weakest?

A simple and yet effective process to assist you make effective decisions is to analyse the risk for potential upside and potential downside. Then embrace the decisions where the risk for the upside is substantially greater than the potential downside. In other words, look for the decisions to deal with adversity which involve little in the way of investment and potential downside, but with lots of potential upside. They are the ones that are the most attractive and should be considered first.

Make decisions where the potential upside is substantially greater than the potential downside.

Let's say that you are struggling to make ends meet – your previous month's salary comes to an end before the end of the following month. Your costs are rising and your pay just isn't going far enough to cover all your expenses. You feel despondent and helpless. How can you tackle this adversity in a way that maximises the potential upside and limits the potential downside?

Here are four alternative decisions open to you. Each is analysed in terms of the potential best-case upside and potential worst-case downside:

- *Ask for a salary increase, job transfer or promotion.* The worst-case downside is that you're told that it is not possible. Best-case upside is that you get more salary.

- *Generate income from your hobby in your spare time.* Worst-case downside is that you find that there is no market or that the financial returns are too small. Best-case upside is that you create a meaningful second income.

- *Carefully analyse your expenditure with your family to find how to cut back.* Worst-case downside is that there is little you can do to cut your spending. Best-case upside is that the family together reduces unnecessary and luxury expenditure.

- *Seek debt counselling.* Worst-case downside is that you're embarrassed. Best-case upside is that your budget is brought under control and eventually your expenses match your income.

However, even when you identify the worst-case downside and the best-case upside, and make your decision based on those criteria, you are not guaranteed that every decision will be successful.

But that's okay. It's often better to make a decision and be wrong than to be paralysed by indecision and not take a decision at all. Not taking a decision is a decision in itself. So it's acceptable to make mistakes, as long as you learn from them, recover and persevere. And preferably not make the same mistake twice.

Also, don't be discouraged if your failures outnumber your successes. Keep a long-term perspective. Sometimes you have to endure a lot of failures in order to reach a breakthrough. That's just how it works. Success and breakthrough are often just around the corner.

Connecting to your meaning, which was discussed in Chapter 4, will give you the strength to persevere and not give up too soon. Make decisions in alignment with your meaning. Analyse the risk and choose a course of action where the best-case upside is greater than the worst-case downside.

That's open-minded and flexible thinking in action.

Exercises

The final exercise in this chapter is designed to bring together the various aspects we have covered and to tie up any loose ends. Choose one or more of the questions from the list below to consolidate and apply your learning from this chapter.

Written exercises

1. Which of the three Drama Triangle roles are your primary and secondary roles? What can you do to ensure that you don't fall into these roles? And if you do, how can you get out of them and play one of the Harmony roles?

2. Which of the calming exercises suits you best and when should you use it?

3. What is your greatest unhelpful tendency when facing adversity? Do you tend to freeze and not make decisions, or do you tend to quickly come to a decision, and then persevere to the point of bullheadedness, not wanting to review your decision? What can you do to address your tendency?

4. How can you make careful and effective decisions in the face of adversity?

5. When would it be useful to analyse the risk of your decisions in terms of the best-case upside and the worst-case downside?

ENDNOTES

1   Warner, R.B. 2009. Seven principles of building personal resilience: practical ways of growing through adversity. *People dynamics*, September.

2   Karpman, S. 1968. Fairy tales and script drama analysis. *Transactional analysis bulletin*, 7(26):39–43.

3   Stephen B. Karpman, MD has a wonderful website with loads of free material on the Drama Triangle that you can download: http://www.karpmandramatriangle.com/.

4   Choy A. 1990. The winners' triangle. *Transactional analysis journal*, 20(1):40–46.

10

Reach out to others

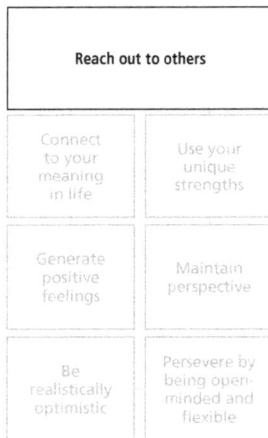

Reach out to others	
Connect to your meaning in life	Use your unique strengths
Generate positive feelings	Maintain perspective
Be realistically optimistic	Persevere by being open-minded and flexible

'Other people matter' is the pithy comment of highly respected psychologist, Christopher Peterson[1]. During tough times, the advice, assistance and support of others can be invaluable. A burden shared is a burden halved, as the saying goes. This chapter covers giving and getting support, which is the seventh and final principle of Building Resilience.

As human beings we have a natural inclination to help and assist others in difficulty. This inclination is formalised in many of the roles we play, such as parent, manager, coach and loving partner. Assisting others enhances the self-confidence of the person giving help and makes them feel good about themselves. If they are also going through the same tough times, helping others enables the helper to disassociate from their own experience of the adversity, and also helps put the experience into perspective.

Assisting others in need boosts your own resilience, even when experiencing adversity yourself.

To effectively give support, you need to be sensitive to the feelings, needs and motivations of others. Responding by acknowledging and showing understanding is useful. Also, sharing your own experiences and emotions demonstrates your identification and support of the other person.

Asking for help, however, is different. It is usually experienced as more difficult than offering help. This awkwardness can result in delaying asking for help, which often causes the problem to worsen.

> There is as much benefit to those who give help and assistance to others, as there is to the people who receive it.

Reasons for this reluctance and what we can do to overcome it are explored in this chapter. In addition, the chapter covers how emotions are 'caught' by others, and how we can reach out to give and get support in the most effective way. The chapter concludes with a section on coping with significant loss and grieving.

The importance of significant relationships

If you were asked what have been the highlights of your life, what would you say? Would you talk about achievements such as promotion at work, academic success, victory in sport and acclaim from hobbies? Or would you talk about memorable times with other people, such as when you fell in love or the beginning of a significant relationship?

And what would you say if you were asked about the worst possible moments of your life? Would you cite failure at work, school or academic circles; losing at sports or defeat in other areas of your life? Or would you respond by saying they occurred within a social context, such as when you fell out of love or when a significant relationship ended?

With our Western society's focus on material acquisitions, consumerism and individualism, it's easy to conclude that individual achievements mark both the highest and the lowest points in one's life.

However, this is belief is faulty. It's the interaction with significant other people in your life that will bring you the most happiness, as well as carry the potential for the most pain. Social connections to others, particularly with intense emotion, such as falling in and out of love, or when a loved one suffers and dies, are the most memorable and significant in our lives[2].

> It's a bit embarrassing to have been concerned with the human problem all one's life and find at the end that one has no more to offer by way of advice than 'Try to be a little kinder'.
>
> *Aldous Huxley*

Relationships are important from an early age. The number of significant friendships at school is a predictor of increased remuneration in adult employment. In fact, for every person you have considered to be a close same-gender friend at high school, your earnings in adulthood are increased by two per cent compared with the norm[3].

The importance of significant relationships also extends into the workplace. If you are able to say that you have a best friend at work, you are four times more likely to describe yourself as being engaged, productive and successful compared to people who don't[4].

Even when it comes to retrenchments, managers will do their utmost, within legal constraints, to protect their friends from being fired. They prefer to have those on their teams that they know and trust, rather than unknown people.

In simple terms, other people matter. People, and particularly significant people, matter in both the good and the bad times in one's life, much more than achievements and accolades.

Calamity strikes Thandeka

It was end of a long week, and Thandeka couldn't wait to leave work and get home. She lived in a small house, in a vibrant but noisy suburb, in one of the poorer areas of Cape Town. She usually found the daily commute by rail between her home and the city centre difficult, but today the trip had been particularly traumatic.

Standing packed together with other commuters on the train, she had been pick-pocketed. Her purse with cash, identification document, bank savings card and monthly train ticket had been stolen.

She usually struggled to make ends meet on her meagre salary and this loss was really disheartening. In addition, the thought of the hassle and time it would take to replace her identity document and bank card was almost too much.

As she slowly walked from the station to her home, she saw the side window had been smashed and the burger bars ripped from the wall. On top of everything, her house had been burgled!

Rushing in, she was horrified to see that many of her treasured possessions, of which she was so proud, had been damaged and others were missing.

Two robberies in one day – she burst into tears.

At that point, her two teenage daughters got home from school and ran to their mother.

They held each other tightly and cried together.

After a little while, Thandeka raised her eyes to her children and said, 'At least we are safe. We weren't in the house when the robbery occurred and were not hurt by the robbers. We still have each other.'

Through her tears she smiled at her children. 'We've still got each other. We are more important than our possessions. Come, let's clean up the mess.'

Together they started to clean and repair the damage. Dealing with this calamity together brought them closer as a family and reinforced their love for each other.

Giving advice and assistance

Managers and team leaders are required by their roles to give assistance and support to their staff. They normally do this through coaching and mentoring. In fact, progressive organisations provide training in how to coach and mentor, how to engage the other person, give feedback and generally develop staff. Once these skills have been learnt, most managers and team leaders will say that giving advice and assistance is relatively easy.

What keeps us from easily asking for help?

With all the advice and assistance that is being given by skilled managers and team leaders through coaching and mentoring, you could be forgiven for concluding that it must be easy to ask for help.

However, this is not the case. Most people say they find it difficult to ask for help, both in their personal lives and about work issues. The more personal and complex the problem, the more difficult it is to ask for help.

Reasons commonly given are:

- I will feel embarrassed.
- It will make me look stupid.
- The person won't respect me afterwards.
- The person won't want to help me.
- I am reluctant to ask for help, and so the problem gets worse, which in turn makes me feel helpless.
- I will be surrendering control to another person.
- The other person may ask for something in return.

Each one of these fears has its origin in some small grain of truth. However, each these fears have grown out of proportion and are now mental barriers to asking for help.

How gender and seniority affects asking for and offering help

When researching resilience, I was told by the people I interviewed that issues of gender and seniority in organisations complicated even further their general reluctance to ask for help.

As a broad generalisation, males have more difficulty than females in asking for help. And when they do ask for help, it is often only after some considerable delay, which often ends up making the issue even worse.

A senior manager referred to this as the 'cowboys don't cry attitude' that was common in the upper echelons of his organisation. He felt that people in senior positions were concerned that, if they admitted to problems and asked for help, it would be seen as a sign of weakness.

As another broad generalisation, I found that women are increasingly reluctant to ask for help the more senior they become in the organisation. A senior manager explained that after having worked so hard to reach the top levels in the organisational hierarchy, she feared being branded a 'weak female' or a 'girlie-girl' who couldn't take pressure.

Women leaders face additional difficulties. The Barrett Values Centre examined the values, strengths and areas of personal development of 100 leaders in 19 countries. They found that 'female leaders … appear to have a tendency to overextend, to be too hard on themselves and others, with long hours, demanding organisation/ time management and stress management'[5].

In addition, 32 per cent of the women they studied had controlling and demanding values, as opposed to only 20 per cent of men. This counterintuitive finding about female leaders can perhaps be explained by social role theory. This has identified that, at a young age, males are socialised and encouraged to be outgoing and achievement-orientated in marked contrast to female children, who are expected to be more emotionally-orientated and reserved in their relationships. Thus, when females reach senior organisation positions, they may have a propensity to overcompensate, resulting in these findings[6].

Asking for help in a powerful way

So, given that it's difficult to ask for help, which is compounded by gender and seniority in organisations, what can one do to overcome these fears? How can you ask for help in a way that the other person is impressed with you, feels good about the conversation, and their opinion of you is enhanced?

There are two preparatory steps you must take before meeting with the person you are going to ask for help.

THE FIRST PREPARATORY STEP

Make the decision to ask for help. Deal with the little voice in your head that says you are not worthy; you are stupid; no one will want to help you. Remember the times you have helped others, and how you have enjoyed assisting them. Accept that now it is your turn to ask for help, and people will gladly reach out to help you too.

Approached correctly, almost everyone will respond graciously, freely giving time and advice, just as you have done to others. So get your mind right. People will want to help you, and will even experience it as a privilege to do so, provided you go about it the right way.

So ensure you ask for help early. Don't delay asking for help, resulting in worsening the problem.

THE SECOND PREPARATORY STEP

Decide who would be the best person to consult. In making this choice, bear in mind factors like the insight that the person needs to have to be able to help appropriately; their availability; the background knowledge and experience they need; whether you prefer to consult a person who is a complete outsider or someone with in-depth knowledge of the problem.

Once you have identified the most suitable person, you should set a time to see them. Use the following four-step process to ask for help in a powerful way:

STEP 1: START WITH A SPECIFIC REQUEST.

Be specific. For example, is your request to come up with a solution to a problem; or to find the best solution from solutions you have developed; or to get a second opinion on your thinking; or to work through a mess of issues, to try and identify the underlying causes?

STEP 2: SET UP A MEETING TIME.

Agree on a specific starting and finishing time, as well as a venue where you can discuss your issue without interruptions and time pressure.

STEP 3: CONDUCT THE MEETING.

- Open by thanking the person and check that they are still available until the closing time on which you have previously agreed. Then repeat your specific request for the meeting. This orientates both of you to the objectives to be achieved.

- Explain your issues, problem or challenge. Outline the pertinent facts, and the feelings you have about the situation. Give the details and information needed to meet the request you have made. But be careful not to flood them with unnecessary background information.

- Explain the alternatives you have considered. Explain succinctly how you see the issue, the facts you have considered, and the conclusions you have drawn. In other words, make your mental reasoning visible. This is when you come across in a powerful manner. Showing the mental work you have done demonstrates that you aren't a helpless and despairing victim of circumstances.

- Describe the solution you have in mind and make your request. Explain your reasoning and then make your request for the advice that you seek.

- Listen and be open to solutions you haven't considered. You may get solutions that are ideal or you may not like them at all. Whatever the other person comes up with, listen respectfully and carefully consider what is being suggested.

STEP 4: THANK THE PERSON, WHATEVER THE OUTCOME.

In the best case, you've got the information and encouragement you need to deal with the issue. In the worse case, you haven't received insights or alternatives. In that case, you're no worse than when you started.

Whatever the outcome, thank the person for their generosity of spirit, and assure them that you will think very deeply about what they've said.

After the meeting, the person who gave you the advice will really appreciate being told the outcome of your conversation. In most cases, it will be a pleasure to explain how their insights and recommendations helped.

But even though you have asked for their recommendations and advice, you don't have to take it. After all, you probably have a good understanding of the situation, as well as what will and won't work. So if their recommendations don't feel right to you, don't take them.

But then, what should you tell the person who gave you the advice?

Try this. Initiate a conversation with the person. Say that the consultation you had with them gave you a great deal of food for thought. It helped you clarify your thinking and eventually you came to a conclusion. Although the conclusion was different from what was suggested, the conversation was nonetheless helpful.

Using this approach will ensure that the other person feels good about having given you advice and your relationship with them will be maintained or even enhanced.

Written exercise: Asking for help in a strong and positive way

Think of some advice or guidance that you would like to receive about the problem you're facing. Apply what you've learnt about approaching people for advice and assistance, by writing out your answers to the steps below:

1. Describe the advice or guidance you would like concerning the issue or problem you are facing.

2. Decide who is the best person you can approach, for advice and input. Decide in terms of their insights, availability, background knowledge and experience and your relationship with them.

3. Prepare to make a request for a meeting with the person by summarising in one or two sentences the outcome you'd like to achieve. Also, estimate how much time you could reasonably request from the other person for the meeting.

   Having done your preparatory work, now go and have the interaction:

   • Make the request for the meeting, agreeing on a suitable time and venue.

   • Hold the meeting following the steps outlined above.

   • Don't forget to give them feedback on what you have done subsequent to the meeting.

How behaviours and emotions spread

How often have you seen pictures on television of large numbers of people looting, burning and rioting? When a person is in an unruly crowd or a member of a gang, they can do nasty and even terrible things which they wouldn't do as individuals. Just as with catching a virus, such as a cold or flu, which is spread by people, so we 'catch' behaviours and attitudes from people around us. This even applies to catching lifestyles from others such as obesity and loneliness[7].

Fortunately, this also applies to positive behaviours too. Deeds such as kindness, generosity and altruism are spread from person to person to person. It seems that once someone has been kind and generous, it affects the next person to do the same, even if they don't know each other. Happiness and even stopping smoking are also spread and 'caught' by others in this way[8].

Positive connections like this are so powerful that they are probably responsible for us flourishing as human beings. In ancient times, generosity, altruism and love were spread through our social contacts and community groupings. These powerful emotions are believed to have formed the foundation for the ideas and innovations which led to our conquering of the world and developing civilisations[9].

Catching emotions from others

Not only are behaviours caught from other people, but so are emotions. Consciously and unconsciously we tend to mimic the actions, gestures, facial expressions and postures of others. This is called emotional contagion[10]. It probably occurs because the brain interprets and feels what other people are feeling. In some special way, via mirror neurons, our brains are linked to each other, and we experience what the other is feeling. This means that we actually feel the positive and negative emotions of other people[11]. Through this process happiness and joy or, alternatively, doom and gloom, quickly spread through groups of people and even organisations[12].

In the best of times our days are numbered. And so it would be a crime against nature for any generation to take the world crisis so solemnly that it put off enjoying those things for which we were assigned in the first place . . . the opportunity to do good work, to fall in love, to enjoy friends, to hit a ball and bounce a baby.

Alistair Cooke

So what can you do to influence the people around you to be positive in bleak and distressing times?

The answer starts with the quality of the contacts you have with people. It's perhaps obvious that the more significant the relationship, the more impact you can potentially make. But what is less obvious is that even casual and fleeting interactions have an impact. For example, the tone of your e-mail, the way you greet a colleague in the passage, and how you listen to a colleague or friend – all have the potential to create positive feelings which are picked up and spread to other people through emotional contagion.

You can influence the moods of others relatively easily through your behaviour and interactions. In addition, if you are a leader at work, or have a loving relationship, or are a parent, that role will enhance your ability to influence the mood of others[13].

> Greet other people, smile, make eye contact and listen. Your positive emotions will be sensed and reciprocated by the other person, and by so doing, you will influence others for the better.

Associating with other positive people will help you be positive. You will be influenced by their positive energy and they, in turn, will be influenced by your positive energy. The outcome is upwardly spiralling cycles of positivity. Through this process, individuals, groups and teams generate energy and commitment useful to rise above adversity, and to experience joy and fulfilment in their lives.

But what about those people who are perennially negative and who spread doom and gloom? How should one handle them so as not to lose your positive energy and outlook?

The answer is to avoid or ignore them where you can. However, this is not so easy to do if the person is your team leader or you must work closely with them. In such cases, avoiding and ignoring them should be more in terms of attitude than physically doing so. In addition, take particular care not to get involved in group complaining – a pity party.

Four ways of responding to good news

Your relationship with others is particularly important when you want to reach out to give or get support and encouragement. Researchers Shelly Gable and Harry Reis have found that the way you respond to another person can either build or erode your relationship with them, and they have some practical advice on how to connect to and encourage others[14].

They found that there are broadly four ways that people respond to good news, but only one makes a real difference in the relationship. The four ways of responding are:

DISMISSIVE (PASSIVE AND DESTRUCTIVE)

The listener seems uninterested and doesn't seem to pay attention. Typically, they turn away and even change the subject.

DISAPPOINTING (PASSIVE AND CONSTRUCTIVE)

The listener seems happy for the person, but doesn't ask questions, and doesn't show that they are listening and involved in what is being said. Typically, they show little or no emotions while the other person is talking.

DISCOURAGING (ACTIVE AND DESTRUCTIVE)

The listener seems to be negative and highlights potential problems. Typically, they frown, grimace or purse their lips while the other person is talking.

ENCOURAGING (ACTIVE AND CONSTRUCTIVE)

The listener seems excited and engages by asking questions and listening to the responses. Typically, there is eye contact, smiling, and laughing.

It is probably no surprise to you that only the Encouraging response enhances the relationship between two people. Through emotional contagion, both parties experience elevated spirals of positivity, their relationship is deepened and, ultimately, they experience more happiness and joy in their lives[15].

How working moms can be Encouraging prior to supper

Working mothers often find that the period from when they get home after work, until the family sits down for supper, is very stressful. During this time a mother typically multitasks, reunites with excited children, undertakes minor chores around the house, interacts with her partner and on top of all this, prepares the evening meal. From a personal perspective, the mother making the transition from work to home responsibilities is tired and hungry. All of which adds to her vulnerability. No wonder this is a stressful time for her.

Working mothers often say that, during this period, they put their children's needs ahead of their own. They feel guilty about working and compensate by trying to make themselves completely available to their children. A mother expressed this by saying: 'To me, love is spelt T.I.M.E.' and went on to say that she felt she had to make up to her children for not being available during the day.

However, due to the demands on their time during this busy period, many working mothers also said that they felt they did not give their children their full attention. They felt that, despite their best intentions, their interactions were often fairly superficial. This sets up a cycle of guilt and frustration, leading to putting the needs of the children first and, when not meeting them, increasingly putting the children's needs ahead of her own.

There are two unintended consequences of this. The first is that the children do not learn to be considerate and respectful of the needs of their siblings, parents and other adults. If this happens, the best intentions of the mother will come back to haunt her.

> Any mother could perform the jobs of several air traffic controllers with ease.
>
> *Lisa Alther*

As her children grow older, they will act out in problematic and disrespectful ways to others. Also, the working mother's own needs are sacrificed for others.

So what should working moms, who love their children, do at this tough time of day?

Try establishing a time to engage with your children when you are able to give them your full attention. During this special time with each child, they become your sole focus of attention. You will be able to engage with your child by asking questions and showing that you are listening. The special time can be as you get home, or after the family meal has been prepared. But remember that whenever it is held, it must be with your full attention on the child.

Once you have scheduled each child's special time, it's then okay to explain to a child who is clamouring for immediate attention: 'I really want to see your painting that you did at school, but right now my hands are full of the food. If I look now, I may spoil the painting and also ruin the supper. As soon as we've had supper, I would like to see your painting and would like to hear all about what you did today. Is that okay with you?'

Remember that it's critically important that, having promised to spend time with the child after supper, you keep that commitment. Engaging with the child and asking questions about the painting in an Encouraging manner will ensure that any disappointment the child initially experienced is more than made up by the quality of the attention and interaction they experience from you.

> Women do not have to sacrifice personhood if they are mothers. They do not have to sacrifice motherhood in order to be persons. Liberation was meant to expand women's opportunities, not to limit them. The self-esteem that has been found in new pursuits can also be found in mothering.
>
> *Elaine Heffne*

Regular special times when you are Encouraging can also be scheduled for each child on weekends or on holidays, when the child is the total focus of attention. Then you and they can do things together which deepen your bond and connection. In this way, the child experiences family time, when everyone in the family talks, and private times when just one parent and child talk together with the child as the focus.

The long-term effect is that the child learns that other people also have needs. These people include their siblings, parents and other adults. The child learns that just because they have needs, it doesn't mean they can expect them to be immediately gratified. Other people's needs may have higher priority, in which case theirs should be met first. To balance this, they also learn that when their parents engage with them, particularly during their special time, they experience the deep love their parents have for them.

Listening is more difficult than hearing words

It's really frustrating when you not listened to. This often happens in an argument, where the more you tell the other person, the less they listen. Rather than listen, they seem just to be waiting to say what they want to say.

It's easier to be aware of others not listening to us than to our own lack of listening. It's actually more difficult to listen than it seems, particularly when it is to a view that you don't agree with. Thus, it's easier to remember when other people didn't listen to you, rather than when you didn't listen to other people.

Hearing words is not the same as understanding the message. Added to this, the person talking may not be fluent; may not have their ideas well structured; may be emotional or you may be emotional. All of this makes listening difficult.

To add to the problem, we think far faster than we can talk. Thus we can have many rapidly formed responses echoing around in our heads, while the other person is talking. These internal voices can drown out the other person's voice. If this happens, we end up either pretending to listen, or listening selectively.

In contrast, effective listening requires special effort on your part in order for you to really understand, beyond the words, what the person is actually trying to communicate.

> I tell you everything that is really nothing, and nothing of what is everything, do not be fooled by what I am saying. Please listen carefully and try to share what I'm not saying.
>
> *Charles C. Finn*

So what can you do to listen better when you are reaching out to give or to get help, advice and assistance in tough times?

The best way to be an effective listener is to interact with and respond to the speaker as they are talking. This forces you to listen attentively. Do this by asking questions and checking to see if you have understood what they are saying. Engaging in this way helps keep your attention on the message. They will gratefully rectify where you have misunderstood, or where they have been vague.

Four levels of listening

There are various levels of listening, each with an associated type of interaction. They are presented here in the form of a hierarchy, with the higher levels representing more effective, although more complex, ways of listening and responding:

LEVEL 1: ACKNOWLEDGING

'Yes'; 'I see; 'A-ha!'

LEVEL 2: REACTING

'I don't believe it!'; 'That's not right'; 'What you should do is ...'

LEVEL 3: PARAPHRASING

'So what you're saying is ...'; 'Let me see if I understand this ...'; 'So you believe ...'

LEVEL 4: REFLECTING THE FEELINGS

'So you were angry that ...'; 'It really annoyed you when ...'; 'You are hurt that ...'

> No one really listens to anyone else, and if you try it for a while you'll see why.
>
> *Mignon McLaughlin*

To listen effectively, you should use all four levels of listening. The best way to do this is to suspend your own assumptions, criticisms, recommendations and solutions. Focus intently on what the other person is saying, rather than on what you would like to say in response. Try to hear beyond the words, to pick up what the other person is actually trying to communicate. Checking your understanding by paraphrasing and reflecting the other's feelings is a very useful way of doing this.

Feedback in times of adversity

Think of a time when you were going through difficulties in your life. Did you have trusted people alongside you? If you did, the path was no doubt easier.

On the other hand, small frictions and irritations during difficult times can easily fester if they are not addressed. Yet people shy away from doing so, particularly if it feels that trying to address a sensitive issue will only make it worse. Then people just bite their tongues and hope the problem will go away.

It's when times are tough, and perhaps you're feeling down, that it is difficult to give feedback that is heard – also, to receive feedback without becoming defensive. This is because both giving and receiving feedback is toughest when you are sad, angry or scared.

So how do you do this? In other words, how do you give and receive feedback at the most difficult of all times – in the face of life's difficulties and adversity?

What and Why feedback model	
WHAT	• Data • Information
and	
WHY	• Implications • Impact • Consequences • Feelings

There is a very simple model that helps give structure to both giving and receiving feedback, both of which can be either positive or negative. It is called the 'What and Why' feedback model and can be applied equally to both giving and receiving feedback. If used successfully, the model assists in creating harmonious relationships, increased productivity, learning and development.

Giving positive feedback

Let's start off considering praise. Effective praising is not easy and, if you are on the receiving end of praise that doesn't feel sincere, you feel awkward and uneasy. Rather use the What and Why model to give positive feedback. It is much less likely to be experienced as awkward.

Start with the What. State the data and information you have about the issue. Be specific and to stick to the facts.

Then move on to the Why aspect. Explain the implications and significance of what was done, outlining the impact and consequences. Describing your feelings about what has happened also helps the listener better understand the impact on you of what has happened.

An example of positive feedback is: 'You handled that angry customer very effectively. You listened to her angry story without interrupting. (*What*). You kept eye contact with her and didn't argue with her version of what had happened. (*What*). You were patient and kept your cool throughout the conversation. (*What*). The way you listened enabled her to explain her entire complaint and express all of her frustration. (*Why*). She was then able to rationally consider how we could fix the situation. (*Why*). I think you have turned her into a customer for life'. (*Why*).

Using both What and Why in this way, for positive feedback and praise, is most likely to be well received. That's because it's rich with detail and does not contain any puffery.

Giving negative feedback

Now let's turn our attention to negative feedback. The purpose is to share ideas in a way that minimises any associated negative emotion that both parties may feel. In addition, the purpose is to create understanding about the issue and achieve acceptance of its impact.

So it's important to understand that the purpose of negative feedback is not to enable you to give vent to feelings such as irritation, frustration, anger and guilt. Negative emotions such as these complicate and get in the way of giving feedback. If you do have strong negative feelings, and you fear that they may intrude and make giving feedback more difficult, it is best to wait until you've had time to compose yourself before speaking.

To give effective negative feedback, use the same sequence as with positive feedback. Start with the What aspect, with a description of the behaviour you have observed, without interpreting it or criticising: just giving the data and information you have. Then move on to the Why aspect of the model, explaining the implications, impact and consequences of what has happened. Labelling your feelings and explaining why you felt like that adds to the significance of the issue.

An example of negative feedback is 'Last night you came home after midnight. (*What*). You told me you would be back by about ten. (*What*). I lay awake in bed waiting for you, worrying about whether you were safe. (*Why*). Even when you had come back, I still lay awake for a long time. (*Why*). If you don't stick to the agreements that we have, it makes it difficult for me to trust you. (*Why*). I am upset and disappointed that you didn't stick to your word (*Why*)'.

In conclusion, giving positive and negative feedback using What and Why does not guarantee that it will be heard and received the way would like, but it does gives you the best chance that it will be.

'Thank you for explaining so nicely!'

Gillian-Ann is the vice principal and teacher of Grade 1 children in a small private school. Last year she had an extremely disruptive child in her class. The child wouldn't listen; interrupted her as she tried to give instructions to the class; wouldn't sit down when there was a group activity and even ran out of the classroom when he was unhappy. She privately thought that he was the most disruptive child she had ever taught, and that the child clearly needed professional help.

Gillian-Ann had had several meetings with the parents about the child's behaviour. She recommended the child be taken for psychological evaluation to see whether there was an underlying problem. The parents were reluctant and, if anything, his behaviour in the classroom worsened.

Finally, she called a special meeting with the parents. Once again she told them how disruptive their child was in her class. She gave several detailed and recent examples of his disruptive behaviour.

At the end, the father responded with a disarming smile. 'Yes, I know. We've talked about that before.'

Gillian-Ann was flabbergasted by the parents' lack of concern and understanding. She realised she wasn't getting through to them.

She then explained the impact of his behaviour in detail: he was falling behind the rest of the class; other children were having their learning hindered; some children were even imitating him and he was becoming class clown.

The impact on her, as the teacher, was that she often ended the day with a severe headache and sometimes even a migraine. If his behaviour continued to affect not only his own learning but also the learning of the children around him, then he could not remain in her classroom. The school would ask for him to be removed.

The father listened quietly. After a pause he responded, 'Thank you for explaining so nicely.'

The parents agreed to have their child and his learning difficulties evaluated. This started the process of assisting the child curtail his disruptive behaviour which, fortunately, enabled him to remain in Gillian-Ann's class.

The change started when the parents finally heard how serious the situation had become.

Receiving feedback

What about when you are given feedback? What is the best way to listen and respond to someone who wants to give you feedback about your behaviour?

The 'What and Why' model of feedback can also be useful for you, as the receiver of the feedback, to best understand what is being said and why it is of concern to the other person. It applies equally well to both positive and negative feedback.

Start with the 'What' part of the model. Listen for data and information, asking for examples to fully understand the issue. Then move on to the 'Why' aspect. Try to understand the impact, consequences, implications and feelings from the other person's point of view. Ask questions to show you are listening and that you respect what is being said. Reflect what you have heard to check your understanding.

If the feedback is negative, you might need some time to digest the information. Just because you are given feedback, doesn't mean to say that it is true, nor that you have to change in the manner the other person would like you to. You must decide how much of the feedback is true; how much of your behaviour you are prepared to change, and how you wish to respond. What you do with the feedback and any change that you make is entirely up to you.

> Among my most prized possessions are words I have never spoken.
>
> *Orsen Rega Card*

That brings us to the question of what you should do if you receive negative feedback which, from your perspective, is incorrect or misplaced.

You don't necessarily have to defend yourself, or justify your actions. It is more important to show the other person that you have understood their point of view, by asking questions and paraphrasing.

If the negative feedback is so blatantly incorrect that you need to reject it, you can do it in a manner similar to the way insurance companies tell you to react in the event of a car accident: stay calm, listen intently and ensure you understand the other person's point of view. Don't argue about who was right or wrong. Don't admit liability. In extreme cases, walk away.

Coping with significant loss and grieving

Everyone loses something really precious to them at some stage of their lives. It may be when a marriage ends in divorce or a loved one dies. Or it could be some other significant loss, such as decline in health, a miscarriage, loss of a job or even the death of a loved pet. Grief turns your whole world upside down and fills you with pain. If this happens, it is useful to understand the following:

- Grief is your natural response to significant loss. It's the emotional suffering that is caused by something you hold very dear being taken away from you.

- Sometimes people try to avoid grieving rather than work through it. This seldom works, because grieving is the human process of acceptance and, ultimately, healing that everyone who suffers a significant loss needs to go through.

- You can't hurry the grieving process, and you need to allow yourself to take the time you need to heal.

- Although everyone grieves, they do it differently. Some people grieve publicly and others privately.

- You may find that your productivity and concentration levels fluctuate wildly while grieving, and there are interruptions in your normal physical routines, such as when you feel hungry and when you're able to sleep.

- Grieving doesn't go through predictable stages, such as denial, bargaining and depression[16]. The grieving process is more like a rollercoaster ride, with ups and downs, highs and lows. It is not a linear and incremental process, where one gets a little better each day. With time, however, the difficult periods do become shorter and less intense.

Making sense of what has happened

Significant loss is often bewildering. If you follow a religious faith, this is the time to use those connections and follow the rituals. Speak to members of your faith who are trained to assist in these times. They'll be able to help you with the practical issues, as well as deal with spiritual questions that you may have, particularly if you are questioning your faith.

Young children often blame themselves for significant loss. They may feel if only they were not so naughty, mommy and daddy wouldn't have divorced, or granny wouldn't have died. Talk openly and frankly with your child about their loss and how it impacts on them. Find out what they are worried about, and answer their concerns as frankly and openly as you are able.

Healing after loss

Sometimes it is tempting to avoid thinking about and dealing with the loss. Throwing yourself into work and other activities, postpones feeling the pain and coping with the reality of what has happened. But avoiding your feelings only postpones the grieving process and can potentially lead to other difficulties, such as depression. In order to heal, you have to accept that the loss is real, to feel the pain and adjust to the life changes which it has brought about.

During this time, you need to look after your physical health, by getting enough sleep, eating properly and exercising. Be kind to your body which will be reflecting physically the emotional pain in your heart. As tempting as it is to use alcohol, drugs and food to cope, these are short-term solutions and are destructive in the long run.

In essence, be kind to yourself.

It's okay to grieve and even cry in front of your children. That legitimises their feeling and expressing their grief. Be kind to them and encourage them to be kind to themselves too.

Asking for support when you have suffered a loss

It's very important to reach out to other people for support at a time of loss and grief. It is not a good idea to try to grieve alone. Sharing your feelings helps make the burden lighter, and helps find perspective when you are in emotional turmoil.

> When you are sorrowful look again in your heart, and you shall see that in truth you are weeping for that which has been your delight.
>
> *Kahil Gibran*

Your family and friends will want to comfort you. They will expect you to lean on them and will be looking for opportunities to assist and console you. Take their help even if your sense of pride makes you hesitant to do so.

Also, be sensitive to the needs and reactions of your loved ones who are affected by the loss. People cannot read your mind and, likewise, you can't read theirs, so good communication is really important. Find out how they are experiencing grief and grieving. Talk about what you are going through, and discuss what is helpful and not helpful to them.

Consider joining a support group and talking to other people who are going through the same things you are. The people in these groups will be able to provide emotional support, as well as practical suggestions about what helps at this time.

When to seek professional help

An experienced psychologist or a leader in your faith can help you gain perspective; assist with the grieving process; help you let go and move on. That's what they are trained to do. Consulting a professional is a sign of strength on your part, not weakness.

If you persistently experience any of the following, however, you should consult your medical doctor without delay:

- Feeling life isn't worth living
- Feeling numb and disconnected from life
- Being unable to perform your normal daily routine and activities
- Being unable to properly function at work and/or at home
- Having intense feelings of guilt and/or hopelessness
- Having thoughts of suicide.

Supporting someone who has suffered a loss

It can feel quite awkward when someone close to you suffers a significant loss. You may feel that your words are inadequate and you fear that you may just make things worse.

Be assured that your presence and support is exactly what they need, and they understand that finding the right words is very difficult. In fact, listening and doing small things to help are more important than trying to find the most appropriate words for the situation.

Listening, helping with the practical arrangements and being there for the person will be really appreciated:

SUPPORTING BY LISTENING

- The grieving person may or may not want to talk about what has happened. If they do want to talk, you should simply listen and be with them. It's important for them to feel that they are able to express their feelings without judgement or criticism.

Alternatively, if they don't want to talk, be willing to sit in silence with them.

HELPING WITH PRACTICAL ARRANGEMENTS

As we have been discussing, people generally find it difficult to ask for help. So it's best to offer your help. Make specific suggestions, such as doing the shopping, helping the children with their schoolwork, watering the plants or taking borrowed books back to the library.

BEING THERE

Providing emotional support is hard work. Grieving and getting over a loss always seems to take longer than everyone expects. After the initial flurry of activity over the loss has subsided, you need to commit yourself to providing help and support over the long term. If the loss is a death, stay in touch, dropping in from time to time, and offering support on vulnerable occasions, such as birthdays and anniversaries which bring back the pain of loss. In the case of divorce, offer to look after the children, do the shopping and clean the house.

Phrases to avoid when someone is grieving

In trying to empathise with the grieving person, there are several phrases that can be particularly insensitive and should be avoided:

- *'I know how you feel.'* It's highly unlikely you know how the other person is feeling. Rather ask them how they are feeling and if they would like to talk about it.

- *'Call me if you need anything.'* The grieving person is unlikely to call you. Rather make specific suggestions as to what you can do to help them, such as picking the children up from school or taking out rubbish to the dump.

- *'Put this behind you and get on with your life.'* If the person is grieving, no amount of criticism or cajoling will hurry the process. With a divorce, they may still be struggling with feelings of guilt or being scared to trust again. In the case of the death of a loved one, they may never get over it, but with time will learn to accept the loss. Rather let them know that you are their friend and will continue to support them through their healing process.

- *'You should ...'* or *'You will ...'* statements. It's not helpful to tell the grieving person what they should do or what will happen if they don't do something. Rather reframe these statements as questions such as 'Have you thought about ...' or 'Could it be that ...'.

- *'You are looking strong.'* The grieving person may experience this as pressure to hurry the grieving process and not express their feelings. Rather allow them to grieve and heal at their own pace.

- *'He's in a better place now – it's part of God's plan.'* This is likely to evoke a strong negative reaction if the grieving person doesn't share your belief. Rather keep your beliefs to yourself.

Helping children to deal with grief

Children may require extra patience and understanding as they struggle to come to terms with their loss. Even very young children experience loss and grief. Take their feelings seriously and don't let them be sidelined with all the attention on adults. Talk to them openly about what has happened and how they are feeling. Answer their questions as directly and honestly as possible. Don't use euphemisms about death such as 'Daddy's gone to be with the angels'. Rather say 'Daddy has died'.

Talk to them about what the loss means to them in practical terms, such as 'Daddy won't be able to read your story at night any more, but I will do that in his place'. Or 'Mommy and Daddy aren't living together anymore, so you will only see your Daddy on the weekends. But that won't stop him still loving you and still being your Daddy'.

Exercises

The final exercise in this chapter is designed bring together the various aspects covered in this chapter and to tie up any loose ends. Choose one or more of the questions from the list below to consolidate and apply your learning.

Written exercises

1. From whom can you request support and assistance?
2. What can you do to expand your circle of support to both give and get help and assistance?
3. With whom do you have toxic interactions that you need to repair? How can you repair the relationship and, if that's not possible, avoid the person?
4. To whom can you offer support and assistance?
5. What do you do well when you listen and support? What do you need to work on?

ENDNOTES

1 Peterson, C. 2006. *A primer in positive psychology*. Oxford: Oxford University Press.

2 Jaremka, L., Gabriel, S. & Carvallo, M. 2011. What makes us feel the best also makes us feel the worst: The emotional impact of independent and interdependent experiences. *Self and identity*, 10:44–63.

3 Conti, G., Galeotti, A., Mueller, G. & Pudney, S. Popularity. *ISER Working Paper Series 2009–03*.

4 Buckingham, M. & Coffman, C. 1999. *First, break all the rules*, New York: Simon & Schuster.

5 Lee, H. 2011. Understanding the battle of the sexes: The effects of gender on leadership style. Barrett Values Centre www.valuescentre.com. Accessed 30 August 2011.

6 Budworth, M. & Mann, S. 2011. Becoming a leader: The challenge of modesty for women, *Journal of management development*, p. 181; as referenced in Lee, Hannah, 'Understanding the battle of the sexes: The effects of gender on leadership style', Barrett Values Centre www.valuescentre.com. Accessed 30 August 2011.

7 Christakis, N.A. & Fowler, J.H. 2007. The spread of obesity in a large social network over 32 years. *New England journal of medicine*, 357(4):370–379.

8   Christakis, N.A. & Fowler, J.H. 2010. Social network sensors for early detection of contagious outbreaks. *PLoS One*, 5(9): e12948. doi:10.1371/journal.pone.0012948, September.

9   Fowler, J.H., Settle J.E., & Christakis, N.A. 2011. Correlated genotypes in friendship networks, PNAS: *Proceedings of the National Academy of Sciences*.

10 Hatfield, E., Cacioppo, J.T. & Rapson, R.L. 1993. Emotional contagion. *Current directions in psychological science*, 2:96–99.

11 Van der Gaad, C., Minderaa, R.B. & Keysers, C. 2007. Facial expressions: What the mirror neuron system can and cannot tell us. *Social neuroscience*, 2(3-4):179–222.

12 Goleman, D. 2007. *Social intelligence: The revolutionary new science of human relationships*. New York: Bantam Books.

13 Dutton, J. 2003. *Energize your workplace: How to create and sustain high-quality connections at work*. San Francisco: Jossey-Bass.

14 Gable, E.L., Reis, H.T., Impett, E.A. & Asher, E.R. 2004. Capitalizing on daily positive events, *Journal of personality and social psychology,* 87.

15 See reference 10.

16 Friedman, R. & James, J.W. 2008. The myth of the stages of dying, death and grief. *Skeptic magazine,*14(2).

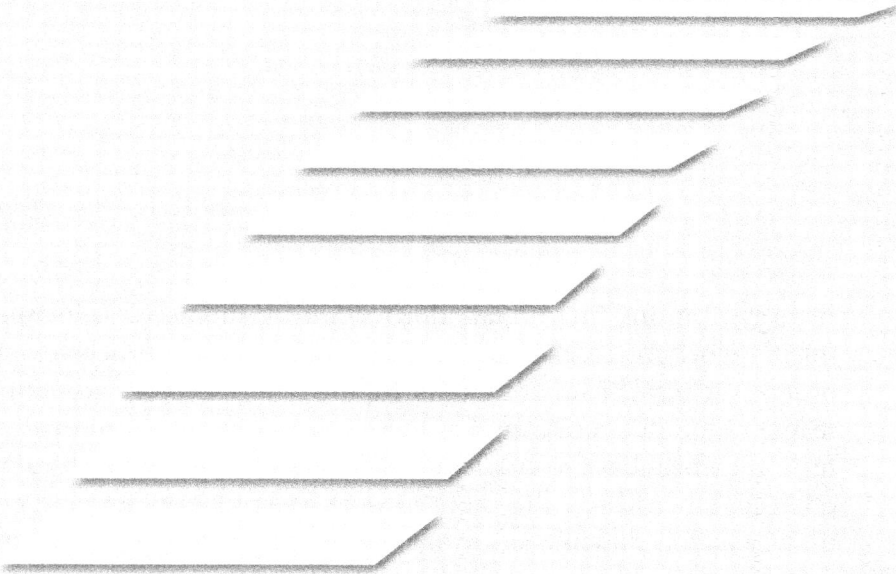

PART THREE

11

Building resilient work teams

In organisations individuals don't work by themselves. People mostly work in teams structured around workflow processes in order to achieve business outputs, for example, a debtors' accounts team or a production team. For these teams to function optimally, team members have to cooperate and work in harmony with each other. In other words, they need to work as a properly functioning body, which is difficult, as anyone will tell you who has worked in organisations.

To compound their problems, teams face organisational difficulties, such as changed processes, downsizing, outsourcing, the introduction of new technology and even rivalry from other teams. To cope, not only is it important for the individual team members to be personally resilient, but for the team to be resilient too.

If individuals are personally resilient, but work in a team that is not resilient, they will find their personal resilience wanes. They become disengaged at work. Disengaged staff are not just unhappy and lack passion for their jobs, but their work outputs are substantially reduced and they can even undermine their colleagues' engagement[1]. By contrast, staff who are engaged at work, and enjoy their work, are committed to it and do it well. Organisations benefit with lower turnover, higher sales growth, better productivity, better customer loyalty and other indices of superior performance[2].

A high percentage of staff in organisations is thought not just to be unengaged, but actively disengaged: 71 per cent in the United States of America[3], 80 per cent in the United Kingdom[4] and 88 per cent in Thailand[5]. The worryingly implication of these statistics is that only 20 to 30 per cent of staff is performing optimally.

This leads to the question – what can be done to enhance engagement and build resilience in teams, so that they perform at their peak, recover from setbacks and thrive in the face of difficulties?

This chapter gives practical suggestions on how to enhance engagement and build powerful, resilient teams at work. It draws from Positive Organisational Scholarship[6] and Positive Psychology[7] which aim to understand the mechanisms that lead to flourishing[8].

How to create purpose and meaning for teams at work

A very important, but largely unrecognised, task of a team leader is to guide the team to find meaning in the work they do. If team members identify a higher meaning in their work, and have a personal connection to it, then alignment is created between their personal mission and values and those of the organisation. The outcome is deep personal satisfaction from doing meaningful work and from working with co-workers who are also committed to the team's higher purpose[9]. These 'hot teams' are committed to the work they do and are best able to take obstacles, disruption and change in their stride[10].

So, if you are a team leader, what can you do to identify and sustain purpose and meaning in your team? Here are four levers you can use:

1. **IDENTIFY THE HIGHER PURPOSE AND MEANING FOR THE TEAM'S WORK**

As the team leader, create an uplifting and engaging purpose for the team. Admittedly, this is not easy if the team's work is tedious, routine and pressurised. But even in situations like this, a higher purpose can be created as was done in the following examples:

Finding meaning for a benefits payments team

A life insurance company had three large benefit payments teams. Their functional mission was to make benefit payments to qualifying beneficiaries. The team's performance was rigorously assessed against criteria such as complete documentation from the client; accuracy of payouts and adherence to time standards.

These performance criteria were very important to the organisation, but they were not particularly motivational to the team. Consequently, compliance did not enhance the team members' engagement.

To discover the team's higher meaning in the work they did, the team leader got them to review their outputs from the perspective of their clients who, in this case, were policyholders. This elicited a very different view of the importance of their work. They told stories of how they went out of their way to help clients. Some told stories of how they helped semi-literate, grieving families complete the detailed claims forms. Others told stories of how they assisted and gave advice on the easiest way to obtain missing identity documents and death certificates. Some stories were just about being kind and sympathetic to grieving people.

With the perspective of their clients in mind, they crafted a new purpose and meaning for themselves: *to help people at the worst times in their lives – when they urgently need money – by paying the benefits they deserve speedily and accurately.*

Finding meaning for an IT department

A fast-moving consumer goods organisation had an information technology (IT) department made up of 37 individuals. The IT department's role was to improve existing IT software and to develop new software to support the introduction of new product lines. The department had problems with high absenteeism, low morale, higher than usual staff turnover and work outputs seldom meeting deadlines. Several initiatives were instituted to try to deal with these problems, but none was particularly successful.

Then a team leader decided to try a different approach by creating meaning at work.

She sought out staff members in the company whose day-to-day jobs were impacted on by the IT systems her department developed. She asked the individuals to talk about their experience with people in her department and how the IT system impacted on their day-to-day work.

The stories were videotaped and shown to the IT team. Some of the stories were positive, although many were negative. A common theme was that the IT department had a profound impact on the way staff worked and on their enjoyment of their jobs.

The discussions about the impact of their work continued over several months. The team leader continued to highlight the link between what they did and the impact on the day-to-day lives of others. Slowly but surely, the attitude of individuals and then that of the entire group changed, until there was a noticeable difference in dedication and commitment to their jobs. This had the welcome effect of better adherence to work deadlines and reduction staff turnover.

2. CREATE PRIDE IN THE TEAM'S WORK

Deep down everyone wants to be proud of their work, to exceed expectations, be recognised and valued for what they do. Most people enjoy working cooperatively in teams, particularly in a winning team.

As a team leader, you can capitalise on these motivations by showing your pride in your team. Keep records to track your team's performance, and use the results to praise their accomplishments and build their confidence and self-esteem.

Explain how the work of your team is linked to the organisation's mission. Outline how, even though they may only be a small cog in the bigger organisational machinery, they assist the organisation deliver on its promise to its customers.

You may, unfortunately, have to fight turf battles and defend your team's interests. If this happens, bear in mind that it's important for your team to see you identifying with them, and that you have their best interests at heart.

3. INSTIL A SENSE OF BELONGING IN THE TEAM.

As team leader, you should create and sustain emotional bonding as well as a sense of community in your team. For example, once a month encourage everyone to have tea or lunch together. If you have the budget, 'away days', where the whole team meets off-site for planning sessions or teambuilding, can enhance the sense of belonging.

Find ways of giving recognition to people who go out of their way to assist and help each other, for example, by choosing or electing an employee of the month. Celebrate. Find opportunities to recognise team achievements such as targets being met, long-service awards, and team members' birthdays, marriages and births of their children.

4. IDENTIFY OPPORTUNITIES FOR PERSONAL GROWTH AND DEVELOPMENT.

People need to feel that their skills and talents are recognised, and that their skills and abilities are being stretched and developed. This helps build the team members' commitment and motivation.

You can develop your team members by allocating tasks to those who are less experienced. To ensure their success, either you or another experienced team member should work alongside to mentor and coach them. Be sure to recognise and praise the contributions of both the person who is learning and the more experienced mentor.

Organisational change also presents opportunities for enhancing personal growth and development. As a team leader, you should frame organisational change initiatives as opportunities for personal growth and the development of new skills, rather than as obstacles to be overcome.

The outcome will be enhanced and sustained resilience in the face of organisational difficulties[11].

Introduction of an Internet-based procurement system

A large sugar refining company decided to replace their outdated, paper-based, procurement process with an Internet-based system. Senior management were enthusiastic because it promised to speed up the process, increase controls and reduce costs. Their enthusiasm, however, was not matched by everyone in the organisation.

The procurement team particularly resisted the change, because they felt the new system was much more complicated than the existing one. As a result, the procurement team leader was called in by senior management and told that the attitude of his staff was retarding the rollout of the new system, and he was instructed to 'sort your team out'.

He spoke to each of the team members individually, describing how their job would be affected and how the new process would give them the opportunity to learn new skills and develop themselves. He reframed the threat as an opportunity for personal growth and development for each team member.

He personally volunteered enthusiastically for training, and became a vocal proponent of the new process. With his encouragement, most of his team members also attended training and he coached those who struggled to get to grips with some of the more complicated aspects.

Within a few months, all the staff members had developed sufficient competency for the old system to be switched off and be entirely replaced by the new system.

A year later, the procurement team spoke with pride about their migration to the new system, which is regarded as an example of best practice.

How to use strengths to build team resilience

Everyone has their own unique combination of strengths. Using personal strengths at work is uplifting, invigorating and deeply satisfying.

Fortunately, the particular personal strengths a person possesses do not force one into a particular career. This is because strengths can be exercised in almost any situation at work.

Take, for instance, the strength of love. At first glance it may seem that it is a 'soft' strength, compared to bravery or perseverance. But consider how useful it would be to an industrial relations consultant, who has to make tough calls about hearing and weighing evidence before reaching conclusions in disciplinary cases.

Or an accountant team leader, with the same strength, who deeply understands the difficulty his non-specialist accounting staff experience with sales and expenses forecasting, and takes this into consideration to initiate a new annual budgeting process.

As the team leader, you should also be careful not to abuse or overuse individuals' strengths. This can happen if teams regularly allocate the same task to a particular member who has strengths in that area. If this happens, the person may feel they are being exploited. Take, for example, a team member who has the strength of high attention to detail and always goes the extra mile to ensure everything is just right. If they are frequently asked to use that strength to sort things out, when the team gets into difficulties, it may feel that the team does not value the role and automatically dumps it on the team member.

How to recognise and encourage the strengths of a team

Just as with individuals, teams also have unique strength combinations. If they are recognised and used in team functioning, the team members collectively experience this as uplifting and deeply gratifying. Strengths in teams are important: 55 per cent of high-performing teams believe that using their strengths is the secret of their success, as compared to 37 per cent of a national USA sample; 42 per cent of high-performing teams report that they discuss their strengths with their managers, as opposed to 24 per cent of the national USA sample[12].

Using the team itself to identify its own strengths reinforces the value of the strengths-based approach, as well as creating buy-in and understanding. This is because the team is more likely to support the outcomes they have been involved in creating than those they haven't.

Here's how to identify your team's strength combinations:

STEP 1

Begin by identifying and ensuring that your team members understand their own personal strengths. This process is described in Chapter 5.

STEP 2

Assemble the team and ask each person in turn to reveal and explain their strengths to the group. After each person has discussed their strengths, ask the team to give examples of when they saw that team member's strength in action. Give appropriate recognition and praise.

STEP 3

Explore the strengths of the entire team together. You can do this by brainstorming a list of the positive attributes of the team by asking one or more of the following questions:

- What special insight, skills or knowledge would the organisation miss most about this team if we disappeared off the face of the earth?

- Give an example of this team at its best.

- Give an example of when you feel most energised and powerful in this team.

- What creates high-spiritedness in this team?

- How can we build on our high-spiritedness?

When answering these questions, have the team members record each of their ideas on a separate piece of paper. Large Post-It notepads are ideal for this purpose. Stick all the individual pieces of paper onto a wall or large glass window of the meeting room in a random fashion, so that the team members can see all the responses.

STEP 4

Encourage everyone in the team to move the pieces of paper so as to group together those that are similar or related. Aim for about seven clusters of strengths, although the process can work with as many as nine or as few as five. As you can imagine, it's a rather messy process, but at this stage everyone's participation is more important than accuracy.

STEP 5

There are two ways of exerting one's strength; one is pushing down, the other is pulling up.

Booker T. Washington

Once the team is satisfied that all the responses are appropriately grouped together, ask the team to come up with a name and description for each group or cluster of strengths.

The outcome is a list and definition of the team strengths, as experienced by the team members and described using their words. There will be high buy-in and excitement at the end of this exercise

A VARIATION OF THIS EXERCISE

If time allows, obtain comments from clients and other teams about their experiences of your team, and incorporate that information into the exercise. This external view brings realism and richness to the process.

This is best done by eliciting positively phrased comments in order to prevent finger-pointing, justification and denial by the team members. Three useful questions to ask clients and other teams are:

- What do you really appreciate about this team?

- When the team is at its best, what do you experience?

- What would you really appreciate from this team in the future?

FOLLOW UP ON THIS EXERCISE

In order to keep the team's engagement and motivation high, you should review and extend the outcomes of the exercise. Here are two powerful ways of achieving this.

1. Hold a follow-up meeting at which you ask: 'What can we do to apply our team strengths to re-craft our jobs, so that we are more effective, engaged and resilient?'

2. Other useful follow-up questions are: 'How can we apply our team strengths to contribute to the greater good of the organisation?'; 'How can we apply our team strengths to contribute to the greater good of society at large?'

The conversations which follow will reinforce the team strengths and help your team enhance their meaning and purpose in the work they do.

Leveraging the strengths of teams at work

Having helped your team identify their own unique strengths, the next step is to help the team enhance their strengths, in order to use them for even greater effect.

Here are three ways of achieving this:

1. Start your usual weekly or monthly team meeting by asking team members to give examples of when the team strengths have been used since the last meeting. Complement the individuals involved and reinforce the power of using their natural strengths.

2. At the beginning of the team meeting, hand out cards with the name and description of the team strengths on them. Request each team member use that strength when contributing during this team meeting. At the end of the meeting, ask team members how it felt to deliberately use those strengths. Compliment team members on effective use of the strengths.

3. During team reviews of progress on projects or tasks, ask the members which team strengths were used and what impact it had on the outcomes. Compliment team members on using strengths to achieve work outputs.

All of these activities will reinforce your team's understanding and use of their strengths.

How to generate positive feelings and energy in your team

Building Resilience Principle 3 is *Generate positive feelings*, which is covered in Chapter 7. The principle applies as much to individuals as it does to teams, particularly those who face organisational change, uncertainty and adversity. Feelings quickly spread through the team by social contagion[13], whereby team members actually 'catch' positivity or negativity from each other like a flu virus.

Resilient individuals deliberately generate genuine positive emotions during adversity to cope with and counterbalance their negative emotions. Positive feelings also assist in creating open and flexible ways of thinking and mind-sets[14], even in the face of tough times[15]. In a nutshell, creating genuine positive emotions moderates the negative experience and fosters resilience[16].

The power of negative over positive is so great, however, that for individuals interacting interpersonally, it takes three positive expressions to balance one negative expression[17]. In order for teams to flourish, the effect of a single negative expression needs to be counterbalanced with between seven and thirteen positive expressions. In addition, the team needs to maintain an equal balance between enquiry-to-advocacy and self-to-other talk[18].

In addition you, as team leader, should be positive yourself and show this in your interactions with the team. The team will pick up on your positive attitude and it will rub off on them too.

But let us be clear that negative feelings and experiences are not all bad and often are useful and necessary. For example, negative feedback about performance is absolutely crucial for developing insight and facilitating change in behaviour to enhance performance. Also, negative experiences, mistakes and even failure can be valuable lessons if they lead to wisdom and, ultimately, better decision-making and resilience. Indeed, without some degree of failure, teams may never learn to become more resilient[19].

Increasing energy in teams

As with positive feelings, team leaders have a substantial impact on the energy in their teams. If the team leader deals with staff members in a way that is encouraging and respectful, the team members experience such high-quality interactions as uplifting. We quickly sense when people are sincere and interested in us. It's almost as if we are hardwired to pick up people's reaction to us. High-quality interactions result in people feeling more engaged, open and competent. This enhances the team's positivity and energy.

On the other hand, we intuitively know when the other person is not really listening, is unengaged or disrespectful. Low-quality interactions like this erode people's ability to learn, to show initiative and to take risks[20]. If this is sensed from a team leader, it quickly depletes and erodes the team's energy[21].

There are many things you can do to enhance your team's energy with high-quality interactions with your team members.

Try the following:

GREET PEOPLE AT WORK BY ENGAGING WITH THEM

A brief comment or question about their clothes, the weather, their children or the impact of local news item will help make a connection between you and the other person.

SHOW YOUR RESPECT FOR PEOPLE

Show your respect for people with whom you interact by looking in them in the eyes and listening intently. Really listening, as opposed to listening while thinking of other things, is probably the greatest respect you can show another person.

EMAIL WORDING

Be careful not to send quick e-mails with curt responses, as the tone of e-mails is notoriously easy to misunderstand.

DISCLOSE PERSONAL INFORMATION ABOUT YOURSELF

Disclose personal information about yourself that is non-sensitive and appropriate to the situation, which allows team members to see the real person behind your role. This shows your authenticity and, in return, you will encourage disclosure and authenticity from them.

TELL STORIES WITH POSITIVE MESSAGES

Tell stories with positive messages that you would like reinforced, for example, an occasion when the team faced great obstacles and what they did to emerge triumphant. Skilled team leaders tell the same story over again until it becomes part of the folklore and history of the team. This is a fun way of embedding the team's feelings of competence and self-efficacy.

DO SMALL THINGS FOR OTHERS

Small things from a team leader mean a lot, particularly when people are under pressure. For example, take a colleague a cup of tea or coffee when they are very busy; help carry files; assist setting up the data projector before an important presentation.

SPREAD SMALL POSITIVE MESSAGES

Make a point of thanking people for their contribution, recognising work well done, and congratulating achievements. A few sincere words are more impactful then effusive generalities.

Your team members know and understand you probably better than you appreciate. Even if you don't get all of these suggestions right all of the time, they will anyway appreciate your motives. It's therefore better to err on the side of trying several of these suggestions rather than on only cautiously trying a few.

Meeting openers to enhance positive emotions in teams

Meetings that start on a positive note make it easier for the people attending to relax and to participate more freely. This, in turn, enhances the quality of the conversation and commitment to the decisions taken in the meeting. Even meetings where tough issues are to be discussed will benefit from starting a positive note.

Here are some suggestions on how to start a meeting in a positive and energising way:

WHAT HAS OCCURRED SINCE LAST MEETING FOR WHICH YOU ARE GRATEFUL?

'Before we start with the agenda for the meeting, I would like us to spend a few minutes reflecting on what has happened since the last meeting. I know that each of you have been very busy working in your areas of responsibility. And I am sure there has been noteworthy progress in many areas. So let's start off with each person taking a minute to describe what has happened in their area for which they are grateful.'

WHAT IS GOING RIGHT IN YOUR AREA?

'In our meetings we often focus on uncovering areas where we are not meeting targets, and sometimes take difficult decisions about them. In other words, our focus is on all the things that are going wrong. Before we start this meeting, I would like us to set a more balanced picture for our conversations. Please will each person in turn describe those things in their area that are going right. For example, talk about where your area is meeting its targets; where your projects are on track, or where your initiatives are working.'

NAME THREE THINGS WHICH HAVE INSTILLED YOU WITH PRIDE.

'Let's start this meeting by talking about some of the things that we don't normally have time to cover. Would each person describe three things that they are really proud about that have happened in their area since our last meeting.'

WHAT PROBLEM HAS BEEN RESOLVED IN YOUR AREA SINCE THE LAST MEETING?

'Before we start the meeting, I would like to say that I'm aware that there has been a great deal of work in resolving many of the issues raised in the last meeting. Let's start off by requesting each person in turn to take a few minutes to describe a problem that they have overcome or solved. Who would like to start?'

Don't be put off if, the first time you try these meeting openers, you are met with blank looks and surprise. If people usually go to the meeting expecting haranguing and criticism, it can be very disconcerting to suddenly have to think about positive things. Therefore persist and don't give up as the outcomes are worth it in the end.

Dealing with negativity in and outside your team

What can you do if the loudest voices in your team are predominantly negative, pessimistic and cynical? As the team leader you should nip the negativity in the bud before it spreads. On encountering inappropriate negativity, try the following:

STEP 1

Listen intently to understand the team members' perceptions and fears. Separate in your mind the facts from the assumptions they are making. Do this by checking your understanding and ensuring that you are also not making assumptions. Ask questions such as 'Am I correct that you are concerned that ...?' and 'So, from your point of view, this change will result in ...?'

STEP 2

Reflect to the team what you have heard their understanding to be. Ensure the team members agree that you have correctly and comprehensively understood their perspective, beliefs and fears before moving to the next step.

STEP 3

Correct any faulty information they have or incorrect conclusions they have made.

STEP 4

Reframe their perspective. Present the facts from a different point of view which is either less threatening, or has a silver lining, or will enable them to learn and develop themselves. Explain that you can't change what has happened or the situation the team faces, but you all have control over your reaction to it.

To illustrate the process of how to reframe, let's take the example of a team who has just learned it has been outsourced and the reaction by the team members is overwhelmingly negative. The team leader could attempt to reframe their perceptions by asking:

- What could be a different way of looking at the situation?
- Is there any possible good that could come of this?
- Is there a hidden benefit in this for us?
- In what way could this be to our advantage?
- If we look back in five years time, and the best possible outcome has been achieved, what would we say that we had done?

If the team is paralysed by fear or self-pity, the initial responses to these questions may be overwhelmingly negative. If that happens, you will need to continue to ask these questions every time you meet with your team.

Recognise and praise the individuals who are coping. Take the people who are really struggling aside and spend time listening to understand their fears and concerns and the deeper meaning to them of what is happening. Gently point out to them the effect their negativity has on the rest of the team, so that they can become aware of the impact they have on other team members. Hopefully, this will lead them to moderate what they are saying.

Don't allow yourself to take part in pity parties which spread gloom and despondency. Walk away from people who are complaining and are overwhelmingly negative. By doing this, you will be modelling the reframing you have encouraged to your team members to do.

By listening patiently and working with the team's mindset and perspective, you may be able to get the team to see the calamity as an opportunity.

How to deal with a negative relationship outside of your team

If, as the team leader, you have a really bad relationship with a senior colleague or superior, it can spell trouble for your team, if they feel the tension and animosity between the two of you. It makes the team feel they are victims of circumstance and events over which they have no control.

Despite the risks, in most cases it's better to take action to deal with a toxic relationship like this, rather than do nothing. If left to fester, a toxic relationship at work can become increasingly debilitating and also negatively impact on other areas of your life. No matter how difficult the relationship, or senior the person, or entrenched the problem, there is always something you can do to improve the situation.

Try using people you trust as a sounding board to strategise how to deal with the situation. One of the solutions is to remove yourself totally from the influence of the other person. If this is not possible, you should reduce your contact with and your reliance on the person. For example, find ways of dealing with them that are less personal, or perhaps appoint someone to deal with them on your behalf. Also, find ways of reducing the interactions the team has with the negative person.

From a different perspective, it is advisable to ensure that your positive networks are working and strong, in order to build your own internal buffering resources to cope with this situation. High-quality interactions will counterbalance the toxic interactions.

How to energise your strategic business planning process

The annual strategic business planning process is a pain for most people. The process is frequently experienced as complicated and tedious. Typically, groups of people plod laboriously through an analysis of strengths, weaknesses, opportunities and threats. The gaps between where we are now and where we plan to be are analysed and actions plans drawn up on how to close them. The outcome is endless flipcharts and an alarmingly high number of actions on to-do lists.

Once completed by the senior managers, the arduous process starts of getting the rest of the organisation aligned to achieve more difficult targets than the previous year – with fewer resources. For many people the strategic planning process itself is an adversity which requires a great deal of resilience.

Fortunately, there are alternative ways of conducting the strategic planning process. The two methods which follow will achieve engagement, commitment and even better strategic planning outcomes.

Using Appreciative Inquiry in the strategic planning process

Appreciative Inquiry focuses on what is already working in the organisation, rather than what is not. It helps people develop a shared vision of a positive and desirable future by focusing on what is possible, rather than what needs to be fixed[22].

STEP 1

Ask the delegates to work in pairs and, for a few minutes, to tell each other stories about a time in their lives when they felt most energised and engaged at work. Debrief the exercise for the delegates' feelings and learning.

STEP 2

Ask the delegates to select a different partner. Working in pairs, each person should take about fifteen minutes to tell the other about an experience they had when their team was working at its best, when members felt most confident and productive. They should also explain what made it such a good experience; what the team was doing and thinking; what enabled them to reach this pinnacle of success, and how this impacted on the team members themselves. Debrief the exercise for delegates' feelings and learning.

STEP 3

Request the delegates again to select another partner and for each in the pair to tell the other about the best experience they had working in a team which outperformed all expectations. They should outline their role in the team; what caused the great performance; how it was sustained; the feelings of the team members, and the reactions of customers. Debrief the exercise for delegate's feelings and learning.

STEP 4

Ask the delegates to a choose, yet again, a different partner and for each in the pair to tell the other three wishes they have for this team, department or business unit – in order for it to be the best possible place to work, and for it to achieve exceptional results. Debrief the exercise for delegate's feelings and learning.

STEP 5

Request the delegates to assemble in groups of five or six and to identify the key themes that have arisen from the conversations. An example could be customer service or energised staff. Once complete, share their findings with the entire group in plenary, and draw up a consolidated list of key themes.

STEP 6

In plenary, create provocative propositions[23] for each of the key themes. These are positive, challenging and stretching statements in the present tense, which key clients will be saying about the team. A provocative proposition for customer service could be: 'We delight customers by meeting their expectations every time'. A provocative proposition for energised staff could be: 'Our high energy and passionate commitment enables us to exceed our production targets'.

STEP 7

You will now have team members who are enthusiastic about the provocative propositions they have created. Use this positive energy to engage in the strategic planning process by asking questions such as:

- How can our provocative propositions influence the way we see our strategic goals?
- How can we use our provocative propositions to create new strategic goals?
- How can we use our provocative propositions to reduce costs?
- What new areas of business can we expand into by using our provocative propositions?
- What more can we do to delight our customers, using our provocative propositions?
- With our provocative propositions, how can we meet and exceed our strategic plans?

- How can we leverage our provocative propositions to create an engaging and resilient work environment?

The conversation that ensues will sustain the enthusiasm and energy of the team to meaningfully participate in the strategic planning process. The outcome will be stretching strategic goals and objectives to which the team is committed.

Using the team's strengths in the strategic planning process

This process is similar to the Appreciative Inquiry process in that it gets participants enthusiastic and motivated, but differs in that it directly feeds into the strategic planning process of setting goals and targets.

STEP 1

Identify the unique strength combinations of your team, department or business unit, using the process outlined earlier in this chapter.

STEP 2

Ask the team members to identify examples of how each team strength has been used recently. Celebrate and praise each of the examples cited, building the team's enthusiasm and belief in their competence.

STEP 3

Request the team to divide into groups of about five people. Ask each group to use a metaphor to describe their understanding of the team's unique strengths combination.

Strengths like an onion

An advertising and marketing team came up with the metaphor of an onion. Their team's core strengths were creativity and perseverance, which enabled them to produce award-winning designs, despite intense time pressure.

The team's other strengths were teamwork, humour and open-mindedness. Like the outer layers of an onion around its core, these strengths prevented the core strengths from becoming too dominant. Teamwork, humour and open-mindedness also helped ensure that their working relationships were productive and fun.

A humorist commented that when their strengths weren't used effectively, the results were also like an onion, but which caused tears.

STEP 4

When there is a good understanding of the workings of a team's unique strengths, transition to the strategic planning process and brainstorm how each of the strategic areas in the business plan can be positively affected by the team strengths. Questions which help in this process are:

- What new areas of business can we expand into with our particular team strengths?

- How can we use our amazing team strengths to meet and exceed the new targets?

- With our unique team strengths, how can we reduce costs?

- What more can we do to delight our customers, making use of our team strengths?

- Given what we are so good at doing with our team strengths, how can we meet and exceed our strategic plans?

- How can we leverage our team strengths to create an engaging and resilient work environment?

The outcome will be strategic plans with objectives and goals, which are possibly as challenging if not more challenging, than would have been created using the more traditional approach. The crucial difference, however, will be that delegates are engaged and committed to using their strengths to achieve excellence at work.

Helping your team cope with change

Our organisations are constantly changing. We have all experienced having to improve processes; introduce new products; implement new ways of doing business and, the most common change of all, cut costs. Some of us have even lived through company mergers and takeovers. All of these changes are felt keenly by the people and teams who either have to implement the change or are recipients of the change.

If your team experiences what they feel is too much change that also comes at them too fast, then they become what is politely called 'change weary'. Put simply, this means they become shell-shocked, fearful and resist the change any way they can.

When this happens, organisations often battle to successfully implement organisational change, particularly large-scale change.

To prevent this, your team needs to be resilient and change-ready. To give you insights into the present state of your team's resilience and change readiness, you can use the Team Change-Acceptance questionnaire which follows.

Team Change-Acceptance Questionnaire

Directions: For each statement use the scale to select the number that best describes your team, function or the entire organisation in terms of their acceptance of change. Choose a generalised score for each statement that, overall, best describes your team. Record that number in the column at the end of each of the twenty statements which follow.

1	2	3	4	5
Not True	Sometimes True	Moderately True	Often True	Very True

Questionnaire

No	Statements	Rating
1	Overwhelmed	
2	Eager beginnings but implementation problems	
3	Overly critical	
4	Growing and developing	
5	Feels let down by management	
6	Disillusioned when the going gets tough	
7	Narrow thinking	
8	Open to learning	
9	Quietly negative	
10	Blames others	
11	Stubbornly unconvinced	
12	Enthusiastic	
13	Dejected	
14	Resentful	
15	Loudly negative	
16	Optimistic	
17	Does minimum to comply	

No	Statements	Rating
18	Withdraws	
19	Resists change	
20	Embraces change	

Now score your answers: Fill in your scores for each question in the table below, and then add the scores to get a total for each category.

Resisters		Flourishing	
Item	Score	Item	Score
3		4	
7		8	
11		12	
15		16	
19		20	
Your Total		**Your Total**	

Drowning		Quitters	
Item	Score	Item	Score
1		2	
5		6	
9		10	
13		14	
17		18	
Your Total		**Your Total**	

Now, transfer the total scores for each of the four categories onto the table below.

Team Change-Acceptance

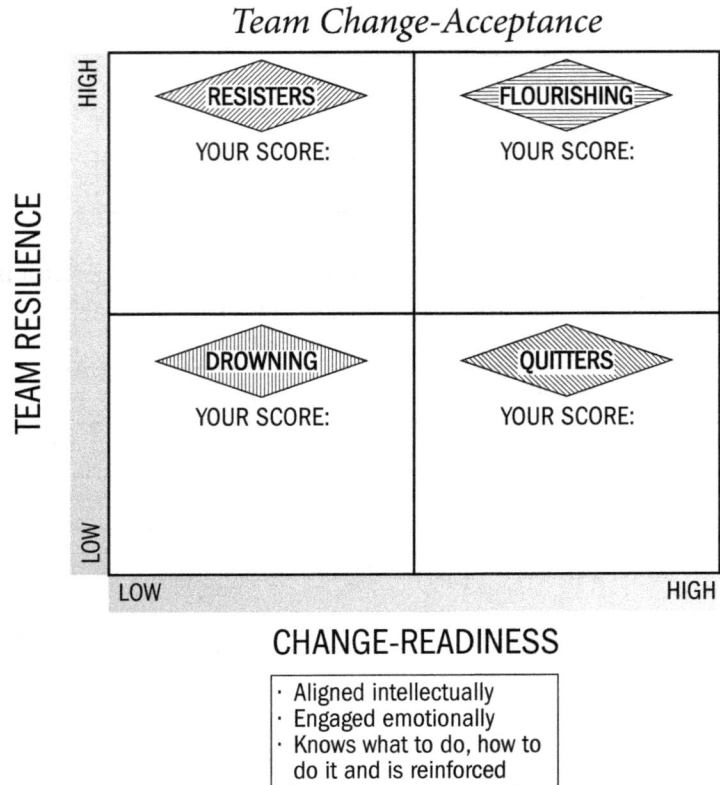

Interpreting your scores

Your scores rate the feelings and attitudes of people implementing, or being on the receiving end of, change in terms of two dimensions – team resilience and change-readiness.

The four quadrants show four simplified categories of reaction to change.

RESISTERS

They typically have medium to high resilience but with low to medium change readiness. These teams are very critical, think narrowly about the change and are stubbornly unconvinced about major aspects of the change. Consequently they are loudly negative about the change and resist it is small and even big ways

DROWNING

They typically have low to medium resilience as well as low to medium change readiness. These teams feel overwhelmed and feel that with this change, their management has let them down. They become dejected and quietly negative. They do the minimum to comply with the change.

QUITTERS

They typically have low to medium resilience but with medium to high change readiness. These teams may initially eagerly embrace the change, but later on experience implementation problems. They become disillusioned when the going gets tough, blame others and become resentful about their circumstances. Consequently they withdraw whenever they can.

FLOURISHING

They typically have medium to high resilience coupled with medium to high change readiness These teams are growing and developing; open to learning; enthusiastic; optimistic and embrace the change.

For change to be accepted, the score for your team in the Flourishing category should be higher than the combined scores for the other three categories of Resisters, Drowning and Quitters. If not, the change take-up and benefit realisation could be at risk.

These categories are shown in the diagram on the next page.

Team Resilience and Change-Readiness

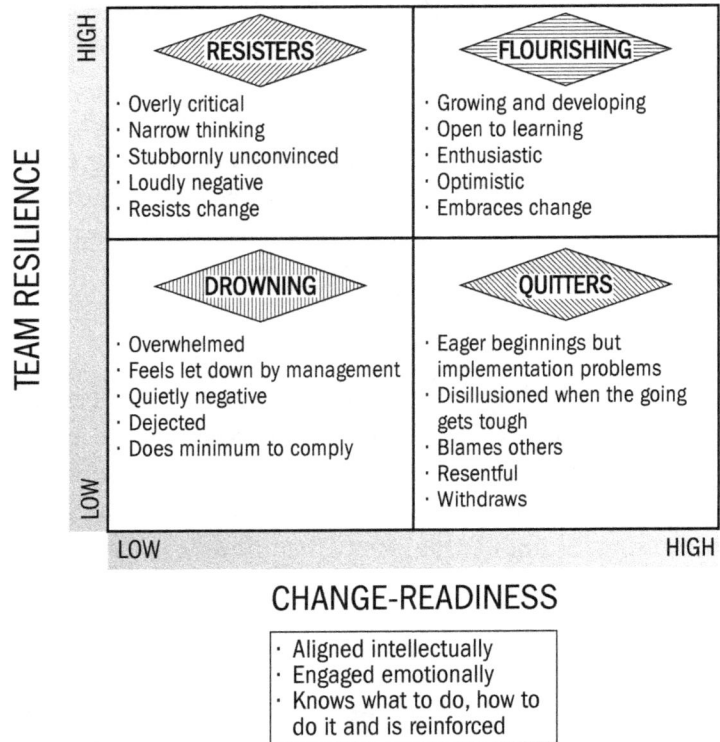

To improve the prognosis of the success of your change implementation, you should build your team's resilience and enhance their change readiness.

This chapter contains many ideas and suggestions on how to build the resilience of your teams. Find the ones that work for your team to build their inner resources and coping ability.

Strategies to enhance change-readiness

You also should enhance your team's change-readiness. This can be done by introducing support initiatives to engage your team emotionally; to align them intellectually and to reinforce new processes and behaviours required to roll out and cement the change.

ENGAGING EMOTIONALLY

This involves creating a sense of urgency about the change in the organisation. It also creates the need amongst the change recipients to engage with the change, and to understand the impact on the team.

If your team is on the receiving end of change, you should show that you understand the impact on them and how they feel. However, it's important not to verbalise your agreement or disagreement with their negative views or feelings.

So, instead of saying: 'Head office typically hasn't considered the impact on us. This is crazy!', rather say: 'I can see that the change will be disruptive and will involve more work for us. It will also put pressure on us at month's end.' Words like this will show the team that you understand the impact of the change on them.

If you can, answer the 'What's in it for me?' (or WIIFM) question for your team. If there is not much benefit to the team, or if there are mostly disadvantages to the team, don't be surprised if you encounter resistance. If this is the case, then be honest with the team, and acknowledge their concerns about the change.

Some teams have had bad experiences with organisational change in the past – to the extent they still have raw emotional wounds. If you have a team like this, you need to spend time dealing with their past experiences. You could convene workshops to let them vent their negative experiences, which will enable you to understand their feelings. Get them to write out their fears about this change and address those fears as honestly as you are able. Unfortunately, you may not be able to fully address all their fears. This often happens if their concerns involve issues which you can't address, such as top management reneging on promises or the possibility of being retrenched.

But be reassured, your sincere efforts to understand and engage your team emotionally will assist them to feel that you as their team leader understand them and are on their side.

ALIGNING INTELLECTUALLY

This involves ensuring that the rationale and business case for the change are clearly understood. This is best achieved by communicating the anticipated changed state and roll-out plan in a way that is compelling from your team's point of view. The latter is preferable to the more typical communication which is often only compelling from the Chief Financial Officer's point of view.

Keep on explaining the big picture until everyone understands the rationale and then deal with the details.

Ensure you are visible driving and supporting the change to build common belief and commitment, and ensure everyone is on the same page.

REINFORCING THE NEW BEHAVIOURS

This involves having your team trained to comply with the change. Show your leadership by being the first to attend training yourself. Help your team implement the new or changed processes and procedures.

When the change is being rolled out, introduce and monitor measures to track the ongoing implementation of the initiative. Post graphs and other tracking measures in your team's common spaces such as tea-pause areas. Create opportunities to talk about the change and how the team is doing. Give recognition at milestones. These actions will help ensure the success of the roll-out of the change by embedding the new ways of doing business in your team's day-to-day operations.

In summary, you can significantly enhance the chances of success of a change initiative by

- building your team's resilience

- ensuring their change readiness through emotional engagement and intellectual alignment

- ensuring that the required new behaviours are trained, reinforced and cemented to become part of your team's culture.

Exercises

The final exercise in this chapter, concerning building and maintaining resilient work teams, is designed to bring together the various aspects we have covered in this chapter, and to tie up any loose ends. Choose one or more of the questions from the list below to consolidate and to apply your learning to building resilient teams.

Written exercises

1. What can you do to enhance the meaning and purpose in your team?
2. Have you helped your team identify their team strengths? If not, when would be a good time to do so?
3. What plans do you have to enhance energy in your team?
4. What can you personally do to enhance the positive feelings in your team?
5. How are you handling negativity inside your team and externally? What should you do more of?
6. How do you intend to handle your next strategic planning session to ensure your team's engagement and commitment to the process?
7. What can you do to enhance your team's change-readiness and change-acceptance?

ENDNOTES

1 BlessingWhite. 2010. *Employee Engagement Report 2011*. From: www.blessingwhite. com. Accessed 3 September 2011.

2 Harter, J.K., Schmidt, F.L. & Hayes, T.L. 2002. Business-unit-level relationship between employee satisfaction, employee engagement and business outcomes: A meta-analysis. *Journal of applied psychology*, 87:268–279.

3 Coffman C. 2002. The high cost of disengaged employees. *Gallup management journal*, 15.

4 Flade, R. 2003. Great Britain's workforce lacks inspiration. *Gallup management journal*, 11.

5 Ratanjee, V. 2005. Wake-up call for Thailand, Inc. *Gallup management journal*, 12.

6 Cameron, K., Dutton, J. & Quinn, R. (eds.). 2003. *Positive organizational scholarship: Foundations of a new discipline*. San Francisco: Berrett-Kohler.

7 Seligman, M.E.P., Steen, T., Park, N. & Peterson, C. 2005. Positive psychology progress: Empirical validation of interventions. *American psychologist*, 60(5):410–421.

8 Gable, S.L. & Haidt, J. 2005. What (and why) is positive psychology? *Review of general psychology*, 9:103–110.

9 Wrzesniewski, A., McCauley, C.R., Rozin, P. & Schwartz, B. 1997. Jobs, careers, and callings: People's relations to their work. *Journal of research in personality*, 31:21–33.

10 Warner, R.B. 2000. Hot teams: What is the secret of creating magical performance? *Management today*, 15:10.

11 Blatt, R. & Ashford, S. 2006. *Making meaning and taking action in knowledge and creative work: Insights from independent workers*. Working paper. University of Michigan.

12 Buckingham, M. 2007. *Go put your strengths to work: 6 powerful steps to achieving outstanding performance* New York: Free Press.

13 Carley, K.M. & Kaufer, D.S. 1993. Semantic connectivity: An approach for analyzing symbols in semantic networks. *Communication theory*, 3:183–213.

14 Fredrickson, B.L. 2003. Positive emotions and upward spirals in organizations. *In* K. Cameron, J. Dutton & R. Quinn (eds.). *Positive organizational scholarship* (p. 163–175). San Francisco: Berrett-Koehler Publishers, Inc.

15 Cameron, K.S., Dutton, J.E. & Quinn, R.E. 2003. *Positive organizational scholarship*. San Francisco: Berrett-Koehler.

16 Tugade, M.M. & Fredrickson, B.L. 2004. Resilient individuals use positive emotions to bounce back from negative emotional experiences. *Journal of personality and social psychology, 86(2):320–333*.

17 Fredrickson, B. & Losada, L. 2005. Positive affect and the complex dynamics of human flourishing. *American psychologist*, 60(7):678–686.

18 Losada, M. & Heaphy, E. 2004. The role of positivity and connectivity in the performance of business teams: A nonlinear dynamics model. *American behavioral scientist*, 47:740–765.

19 Seery, M.D. 2011. Resilience: A silver lining to experiencing adverse life events? *Current directions in psychological science.* 20:6 390–394.

20 Dutton, J.E. 2003. Fostering high quality connections through respectful engagement. *Stanford social innovation review*, p. 54–57. Winter.

21 Dutton, J.E 2003. *Energize your workplace: How to build and sustain high-quality connections at work.* San Francisco: Jossey-Bass Publishers.

22 Cooperrider, D. & Whitney, D. 2005. *Appreciative inquiry: A positive revolution in change.* San Francisco: Berrett-Koehler Publishers.

23 Cooperrider, D.L. 1998. *Lessons from the field: Applying appreciative inquiry.* Plano, TX: Practical Press, Inc.

12

Building resilient children

Resilience enables children to grow up happy and joyful in the face of the disappointments, pain and difficulties they all experience. Resilient children are less likely to become helpless in the face of challenges; less likely to become depressed; they are more successful in persisting with problem-solving; they take appropriate risks and are better at reaching solutions[1]. Without resilience, their coping is limited, and this can eventually lead to behavioural and psychological disorders[2].

Children are taught the three R's – reading writing and arithmetic. We now know that we can teach them the other crucial R – resilience. Just as adults are able to learn to be more resilient, so, too, can children learn to be resilient[3].

This chapter provides exercises and ideas on how to help your children grow and develop their resilience[4]. It is designed to be used by a parent with their child or by the whole family, and is structured around the seven Building Resilience principles.

Some of the exercises in this chapter may sound exciting, while others may appear silly, difficult or inappropriate for your child. I suggest you experiment with the exercises to find the ones that work for you and your child. Introduce variations so they don't become stale.

Young children may have difficulty understanding the meaning of the word resilience. If so, explain it by saying it means 'to live strong or to live as a hero'. Ask them to think of such people that they know or have read or heard about.

While keeping to the objective of the exercises, allow your child's natural inclination and creativity to adapt them to what suits them and meets their needs. They will quickly give you feedback about those they enjoy and those they don't.

Exercises

Meaning is important to children. The more they can make sense of their world and what goes on around them, the easier it is for them to develop the belief that they can achieve their goals and influence their world. This belief is called self-efficacy and underpins resilient behaviours. The exercises outlined in this section will assist in deepening your child's awareness of their meaning in life and develop their self-efficacy.

> Children are a great comfort in your old age -- and they help you reach it faster, too
>
> *Lionel Kauffman*

Exercise 1: How I got through tough times

Age group: all ages

This is a useful exercise to do when your child is experiencing tough times or adversity.

1. Ask your child to remember a time in the past when they had experienced a similar tough time and triumphed.
2. Then ask them to remember how they felt at that time. Ask questions which encourage them to describe their answers in detail.
3. Then ask your child how they got through that situation. Again, ask questions to encourage them to describe the answers in some detail.

4. Finally ask them what they learnt from that experience, and how they could apply what was learned to the present tough times. Depending on the age and maturity of your child, you may need to help them generalise the learning from the past event to the present situation.

An example is that of a child who is feeling sad. She recalls a previous event that also made her sad and how she felt. She then describes what she did to get over that mood, such as going to play with a friend, reading a book, or helping mom in the kitchen. You then ask what that teaches about getting over sad moods, and highlight your child's coping mechanism. Then ask if that same coping mechanism could be used to deal with the present feelings of sadness. Help your child strategise what she could do in this situation.

Here is an example of the dialogue, using the exercise with a child who is feeling sad.

1. 'Do you remember when our dog Fluffy died? It was last year during the Christmas break when he got sick and died.'

2. 'How did you feel when I came back from the vet and told you he had died?' Listen while your child recalls the pain he felt and how upset he was at the time.

3. 'What did you do to make yourself feel better?' Listen while your child recalls what he did to get over the sadness, such as going to play with a friend, reading a book or helping dad wash the car.

4. 'Doing that really helped you get over the sadness of Fluffy dying. It was very clever of you to do those things. Do you think you could do some of those things again to help you get over this sadness?'

5. 'How can I help you do some of those things?'

Exercise 2: Identifying resilience in stories and movies

Age-group: primary school

Ask your child to identify how the hero got through difficult times. Use one or more of the seven Building Resilience principles as a structure to discuss the hero's story:

1. Connect to your meaning in life: 'What was really important to the hero? Why did they do what they did?'
2. Use your unique strengths: 'What were the hero's strengths? How were they used?'
3. Maintain perspective: 'What did you think the hero thought about so that they did not feel sad for too long?'
4. Generate positive feelings: 'How did the hero make themselves feel good? How did feeling good help the hero?'
5. Be realistically optimistic: 'What did the hero do to look on the bright side?'
6. Persevere by being open-minded and flexible: 'Why didn't the hero give up? Did the hero change?'
7. Reach out to others: 'Who did the hero help? Who helped the hero?'

Exercise 3: Creating a Meaning list

Age-group: all ages

This exercise is a collaborative activity for either a parent with their child or for the whole family together. First, each person thinks of meaningful things that they have done. It may be helpful to explain that doing meaningful things make you feel good and warm inside. Then each person in turn describes the meaningful things they have done and explains why they were meaningful for them.

1. 'Let's all think of meaningful things that we have done. In other words, things that we've done that make you feel good and warm inside. Things that made you feel happy.'
2. 'Why don't you start first, Liam, and tell us what you have done and why it made you feel so good and warm and happy. What you say is important and, if it's okay with you, I am going to write down what you say.'

Writing down each of the responses to create a Meaning list reinforces the importance of the activity. The completed list can be used later on for planning other meaningful activities.

Examples from a Meaning list are:

- hiking in the mountains
- helping collect and distribute food on World Hunger Day
- camping with the family at the seaside and taking my best friend with me
- taking tea and biscuits to the new neighbours on the day they move in
- helping the librarian place returned books back on the library shelves
- fasting as a family on our religious holidays
- helping with the school play by selling tickets and organising seating in the hall.

Exercise 4: Creating a Joy list

Age-group: all ages

Similar to creating a Meaning list, this exercise asks what brings you joy, makes you smile and fills your heart with goodness?

The exercise can be done as a family or as a parent with your child. All contributions are recorded to compile the list and then the list is used to plan further related activities.

Examples from a Joy list include

- spending time with my best friend

- helping Grandma pick fruit from her peach tree and bottle them with her

- playing a song on my guitar once I've learnt it

- acting in the school play

- exploring on my bike

- making our own paper to create Christmas cards

- cycling in bike races with Dad.

Building Resilience Principle 2: Use your unique strengths

Every child is good at something. Some are good at many things. The problem children often face is that they don't always fully understand that those special strengths are what defines them and makes them who they are. In addition, they may not see the real value of their strengths. For example, a child who is good at making and maintaining friendships may regard that strength as 'normal' or 'common to everyone'. This may also apply to a child who does not fully appreciate their strength of being athletic, always comparing themselves against others who have even more athletic ability. But, in fact, it's a wonderful gift to be able to be sustain deep relationships or to have good muscular control and coordination between eye and ball.

Your child was born with a variety of natural strengths. Using strengths feels wonderful. When your child uses their strengths, they will experience that tasks are easy, solutions are obvious, and the activity is joyful. They become so deeply engaged that it feels as though time is standing still.

As parents we should help our children identify their strengths and encourage their use at school, at home and in all other areas of their lives. These exercises will help you achieve that.

Exercise 5: Identifying your child's strengths

Age-group: all

There are two methods of identifying your child's strengths. Choose the one that suits your child the best.

Method 1: There is a free, web-based survey at http://www.authentichappiness.sas.upenn.edu. On this website you will get access to three highly regarded and researched surveys to determine your child's strengths. There is a general one for youth aged 11 to 17, one aimed specifically for children at elementary school and another for children at high school. The questionnaires are all fairly long, about 200 questions, and take about an hour to complete. Once they have completed all questions, the results can be immediately printed.

Method 2: This is a simpler, more participative, although less rigorous, method of assessing strengths. Ask your child to tell you a story about when they have faced tough times and got through them, and use that to identify the strengths. Either your child or the parent should make notes of the strengths identified.

Use dialogue such as the following:
1. 'Tell me about a time when you had difficulties at home or at school, and you got through them.' Listen while your child relates a story to you.
2. 'What do you think were your strengths that helped you to get through that?' Listen and help your child identify their strengths from the story.
3. If there are other people who are listening, such family members, ask the other people: 'What are the strengths that you heard in the story?'

An advantage of this method is that the language used to describe the strengths is the language of the child, rather than that of a survey instrument. Also, this method requires deep listening from you and others, and it's useful to model this skill for children, so that they can later learn it.

Method 3: Identifying your child's spark[5]. There are three parts to this method:
1. Find a time when you see your child is doing something well, or tells you of a time when they did something well. Reinforce that what they are

doing: 'What you're doing is really good! When you ... I think it makes a big difference to ...'

2. Talk about how they feel when they use this strength: 'I saw that you were really happy when you are doing this. What do you like about doing this? How do your friends feel when you do this?'

3. Encourage further use of the strength: 'How else could you use this strength of yours? When else could it usefully be used? Have you thought about using your strengths when you do this ...?'

Exercise 6: Identifying strengths in the movies and in storybooks

Age group: all

This fun activity develops the skill of identification of strengths in others. After having watched a movie or read a book with your child, discuss your child's experience. Ask your child to identify their favourite character or hero, and let them tell you what the strengths were and how they were used.

Then ask your child if they would like to use that strength in their own life, and, if so, in what circumstances. This may lead to an interesting conversation about either *working with* the strength, if it is an existing strength, or *working on* the strength in order to develop it, if it's not one of their natural strengths.

Exercise 7: Problem-solving using strengths

Age group: high school

When your children are facing problems, it's very tempting for you as the parent to tell the child what to do. As loving parents, we often clearly see the most effective solution and want to prevent our children making mistakes. So we give them the answer they seek. Ironically, this can lead to problems. The unintended consequence of regularly solving children's problems for them is that your child learns to ask others for solutions rather than trying to solve them on their own. Eventually, this can lead to your child not developing confidence in their problem-solving ability and remaining dependent on you.

A better alternative is to help your child learn to use their strengths to solve problems. Your guidance will initially be very useful. As your child gains confidence, they will learn to solve problems on their own.

Try the following instructions with your child:

1. 'Tell me again what the problem is and, if it's okay with you, I'm going to write down what we say on some paper.' Listen while your child describes the problem. Ask questions to ensure both you and your child have a complete understanding of the problem.

2. 'So, as I understand it, the problem that you are having is as follows ...' Summarise what you have heard your child say, listening carefully to what your child says in response. If they add additional information, or correct you, keep on summarising your understanding of the problem until they agree that you have got all the important points.

3. 'Let's now think of a different time when you have faced a similar problem that you solved. Can you think of an example?' Encourage your child to remember an example from the past. If they can't think of an example, give examples that you have seen where they have used their strengths to solve problems.

4. 'What did you do that helped you solve that problem? What were the strengths that you used that helped you solve that problem?' Assist your child to identify the process and strengths used to solve that problem.

5. 'How did you overcome all those obstacles that you had?' Again, assist your child to identify their problem-solving process and strengths.

6. 'What did you learn from the way that you solved *that* problem, which you could perhaps apply to this problem?' Assist them to apply the problem-solving process and strengths to the present problem.

7. 'I think your ideas on how to solve this problem will work. Why don't you give it a try? Is there anything I can do to help?' Reinforce your child's strategy that you think has a high probability of succeeding, and remind them of your availability to help if necessary.

Exercise 8: Using strengths in times of trauma

Age group: all

Trauma and disaster are tragedies which, fortunately, occur very infrequently to children, but when they do, they often have a significant psychological impact.

Children who experience a disaster or trauma have their sense of security and normality shattered. This is highly upsetting and may be reflected in various negative ways such as acting out, withdrawing, becoming scared of the dark or of strangers. Should this happen, there are several things you can do to reassure your child:

· Explain what has happened, encourage questions and answer them.

· Help your child explore and understand issues that affect them.

· Encourage, but don't force, your child to talk about what is so upsetting and about their feelings.

· Correct any self-blame or incorrect perceptions about the causes of the incident.

· Be available and express your love more frequently than usual.

· Limit, but don't completely exclude, access to newspapers and, in particular, TV if the same upsetting images are being shown over and again.

· Re-establish routine.

· Be patient and tolerant with your child.

· Ensure your coping behaviour and language is congruent with the message you're giving your child.

· Seek professional help for your child if there is not sufficient progress towards normality after about six weeks.

It's also important to reinforce your child's values and strengths. This will help reframe the disaster or trauma into a more acceptable way of thinking about it and, in addition, promote self-efficacy by taking action. You can do this by asking your child

• to write, paint or draw a picture to explain what happened. Listen to hear the story they are telling themselves. If it's a negative story with them as the victim, gently reframe it to a story with them coping.

- how they can use their strengths to be strong in the face of what has happened

- how they could use their strengths to assist others who are affected by the incident. If distance makes taking direct action impractical, encourage your child to compose a poem, write a letter, paint or draw a picture for those affected.

Building Resilience Principle 3: Maintain perspective

A problem can grow in your child's mind until it is completely out of proportion to reality. When this happens, it's not helpful to tell your child to stop being silly. As a parent, you should work with your child to deal with the world from their perspective. There is no shortcut to do this and it requires patience and perseverance. The exercises that follow will help you deal with your child's fears and help them maintain perspective.

Exercise 9: Choosing a strong/resilient response

Age group: all

As children grow up, they often have to do deal with upsetting situations. These include being embarrassed; bullied; getting into fights; not getting their way; not doing well at school, and being let down. The list is endless. And to make it worse for them, they feel the upsetting emotions as intensely as do adults, but don't have the adult problem-solving and communication skills to cope with them. This exercise helps your child develop problem-solving and communication skills to choose a resilient response to deal with adversity.

Preschool and primary-school children. Fold a piece of paper in half. On one half of the page, ask your child to draw a picture of the problem they are facing. Then ask them to draw, on the other side of the page, a different picture of what they want the situation to look like. Explore what it would feel like to be in the second picture. Then ask what strong actions they can take to make the second picture come true. If they don't have control over what they would like, for example if their parents are divorced and the child would like them to get back together again, gently explain that this is not possible. Then either ask again what strong actions can be taken to make a second picture come true, or gently ask them to draw another picture.

High-school children. Ask the child to describe what is happening that creates the present distressing situation. Explain that weak or defeated thinking is thinking that you are powerless; giving up too soon; thinking that everyone is out to get you. Strong and resilient thinking takes responsibility for solving problems; persists, and doesn't give up; bounces back from difficulties. Ask them to think of what weak or defeated thinking would be in this situation. Then ask them to think of what strong or resilient thinking would be in this situation. Ask what small step they could take immediately to improve the situation.

Exercise 10: Dealing with fears

Age group: pre-school

Young children can develop seemingly irrational fears. For example, your child may become afraid of dogs or swimming pools. On closer investigation, you might find that your child was surprised and upset by an aggressive, barking dog and that led to a generalised fear of dogs. Or your child choked swallowing water while bathing and that led to a reluctance to go near swimming pools.

While your child's fears may seem rather silly to an adult, they are nevertheless very real to the child. Never ridicule your child's fears. It's much more effective to help them deal with their fears by:

·   Questioning. Ask what makes them scared, and what they think will happen.
·   Reassuring. Quietly explain the facts that make their fears less scary. For example, 'I can see it looked like that barking dog was going to bite you. He was very loud. But you can see that he just barks a lot. He barks at everyone. He has never bitten anyone and won't bite you.'
·   Demonstrating. Model how you deal with those same or similar issues, and what you do to make sure you aren't scared. For example: 'When I was young I also had nightmares like you do. I sometimes even have nightmares now. Now, when I wake up from a scary nightmare, I tell myself there is no such things as goblins and witches and it makes me feel better. I then get up and have a drink of water and it makes me forget about my nightmare. You could try that too.'
·   Reinforcing. For each slight improvement your child makes in overcoming their fears, praise and reinforce the progress made.

Exercise 11: Acknowledging and learning from mistakes

Age group: all

No one likes to make mistakes, and admitting to having made mistakes can be very difficult. Yet mistakes give us the opportunity to learn from them. In fact, learning from mistakes is probably the most powerful way of learning.

This exercise helps children learn that making mistakes is part of life and that, in almost all cases, it's more important to learn from them, rather than to hide them. The exercise can be conducted as a general exercise to enhance resilience or when a specific mistake has been made and the child is battling to admit it.

Start off by giving an example of a mistake you made when you were your child's age, and the lessons that you have learned from the mistake. Explain how the lesson you learned helped you avoid similar mistakes and made you a better person.

Stress that everyone makes mistakes and that making mistakes does not make you a bad person or indicate that you are stupid. Give other appropriate, age-related, examples of people who have made mistakes, from current events, family members and books they have read.

Ask your child to explain what they have learned from a mistake they have made. Ask how they will make sure that they don't make the same mistake again. Reinforce appropriate answers by saying that you agree.

> No matter how calmly you try to referee, parenting will eventually produce bizarre behaviour, and I'm not talking about the kids.
>
> *Bill Cosby*

During this exercise, your child may relate inappropriately negative criticism that they have received from others about the mistake and which is weighing on their mind, such as 'you always do stupid things' or 'you never listen'. With younger children, dispute the criticism by pointing out the faulty logic, and reframe the criticism, such as: 'You did make a mistake, but you have learned from it and you won't make the same mistake again.' With older children, ask them how they could reframe the criticism to reflect that they have acknowledged making a mistake, and will do their best not to do it again.

Building Resilience Principle 4: Generate positive feelings

Exercise 12: The grateful game

Age group: all

Feeling grateful is a powerful and yet simple way of experiencing genuine positive feelings, even in the face of adversity. The positive feelings help to put our perception of the adversity into perspective and enhance our problem-solving ability.

In this game, the parent and child, or the whole family, write down all the things that they are grateful for. Put each item on a separate piece of paper. The pieces are then placed in a box or container. Select the rounds of the game appropriate to your child:

Round one. Each person pulls out one of the pieces of paper and draws a picture of the item. On completion, they describe the grateful thoughts and feelings they think the person must have experienced. The person who wrote the item then comments on the accuracy of the picture and description

Round two. Each person pulls out one of the pieces of paper and, without revealing it to the rest of the group, acts out a scene which describes that item. The rest of the audience guesses what lead to the feelings of gratitude.

Round three. Each person tells the listeners what they are grateful for in their lives and why they are grateful for it.

Round four. Each person tells the listeners something that happened in the past 24 hours, for which they are grateful and why they are grateful for it having happened

Exercise 13: Practising gratitude

Age group: all

There are several ways of practising gratitude on a regular basis:

- Give your child a journal or diary for recording, each evening, the things for which they are grateful.
- Write thank-you notes on a regular basis to your children, your partner and friends, and suggest your child does the same.
- Be alert to spot gratitude practised by others and point this out to your child. Reinforce the power of gratitude, emphasising the effect you think it will have on the person receiving the act of gratitude.
- When you receive praise and recognition for something that you've done or achieved, demonstrate gratitude in action by extending your thanks to the people who have helped you in the endeavour.
- Encourage your child to write a letter, expressing gratitude to someone to whom they are grateful, but have not expressed their gratitude recently. If it is possible, find a way of letting the child read the letter to that person. Face-to-face is ideal but if this is not possible, try over the phone or via Skype.
- Encourage the child to savour and be grateful for the small things they experience – playing in the park, breathing fresh air, seeing a new flower, the smell of supper cooking.

Exercise 14: The good things that are happening in my life

Age group: all

This exercise promotes positive feelings, and is particularly useful in times when there is conflict in the environment, for example between adults, or when the child is in trouble or doing badly at school. The exercise asks the child to identify, and think about, the good things that are happening in life.

Use questions to generate a conversation about the good things your child is experiencing, such as:

- What are the best things that are happening in your life at the moment?
- Why do you think these good things are happening to you?
- What are you feeling happy about at the moment?
- What can you do now that you couldn't do a little while back?
- Who are your best friends and what makes them such special friends?

A variation of this exercise is to ask your child each night before they go to sleep to tell you about the best things that happened during that day. The good feeling it produces also helps prevent nightmares.

Exercise 15: Random acts of kindness

Age group: all

A random act of kindness is something that is done out of the blue, to someone either known or unknown, without the expectation of anything in return. As a way of generating positive feelings, this exercise delights most children and adults.

The parent and child, or the whole family, discuss and decide to each undertake one random act of kindness during a 24-hour period and to meet afterwards to discuss the outcomes. At the next meeting, each person in turn describes the random act of kindness carried out, the reaction it created and how they felt.

> Few things are more satisfying than seeing your children have teenagers of their own.
>
> *Doug Larson*

Building Resilience Principle 5: Be realistically optimistic

As with adults, optimism holds many advantages for your child. It reduces the potential for depression from setbacks and disappointments. It is associated with higher achievement in academics, sports and, eventually, at work, as well as being associated with better physical health[6]. But it needs to be realistic optimism as unrealistic or unbridled optimism inevitably leads to disappointment and heartache, and could even be dangerous. The exercises that follow teach your child to be realistically optimistic in the face of life's obstacles.

Exercise 16: Building success

Age group: all

When your child is struggling to learn a new skill, this exercise will help lift their spirits and reduce the amount of time it takes to become proficient.

When seeing your child struggle and make mistakes, your natural inclination may be to point out the mistakes they are making so that they can be corrected. However, the opposite approach is much more successful, when learning a new skill[7] [8]. Rather than focusing on the things your child is doing wrong, focus on the things that they are doing right, and reinforce and build on those things. That will build your child's confidence and enhance their willingness to stay on task, even when they are struggling[9].

This exercise is appropriate for learning a new skill, such as cursive writing, playing an instrument, or mastering athletic exercises.

Ask your child questions to begin a conversation about what is going right and working as they learn their new skill:

· What do feel happy about?
· What are you doing that is working?
· How did you make that happen?
· How did you know it would work?
· How can you do more of what is working?
· Can you apply what is working to any of the other areas that you are learning?

The answers to these questions will encourage your child to apply what is working to the areas that aren't working, and this will help them generalize success from one area to other areas required for mastery.

Exercise 17: Reframing

Age group: all

The goal of this activity is to promote realistic optimism by finding a silver lining in a dark event, through reframing your child's thinking.

Preschool and primary school. For a young child, or a child unfamiliar with reframing, it is useful to construct a sentence with them and let them complete the reframing themselves:

· 'I didn't like what my friend said to me today. Normally my friend says nice things to me. An example of that is ...' Your child completes the sentence.
· 'I couldn't finish the new puzzle and that made me cross. There are other times I have been able to finish puzzles, such as ...' Your child completes the sentence.
· 'I wasn't chosen to play a game with my friends and I felt sad. I know I'm a good player like when I ... and perhaps I will be chosen next time.'. Your child completes the sentence.

High school. For a more mature child, this exercise is open-ended. Ask your child to find some positive or a silver lining in the difficulty, by asking questions such as:

· What good can come from this difficulty?
· What can you learn from this?
· What will you do differently next time you encounter a situation like this?
· Can you see some benefit from this difficulty?
· If you wanted to encourage someone else who was going through the same situation, what would you say?

> I love to play hide and seek with my kid, but some days my goal is to find a hiding place where he can't find me until after high school.
>
> *Author unknown*

Building Resilience Principle 6: Persevere by being open-minded and flexible

Children often need encouragement to build the staying power to persevere, rather than give up. This is particularly so when dealing with issues they find difficult. Perseverance is related to the desirability of their goals and their confidence they can achieve them. This section gives exercises to build perseverance, by helping your child set realistic goals, and enhances their self-confidence.

Exercise 18: Setting goals

Age group: all

Children often experience difficulty setting appropriate goals. They don't understand how to break a goal down into the steps needed to reach it, and underestimate the amount of work required for each step to reach the goal. Follow these steps with your child to establish a realistic plan to reach a goal:

1. Clearly establish the desirability of the goal in your child's mind – *not* your mind, your child's mind. If your child does not feel the goal is worthwhile, this exercise is most unlikely to succeed.

2. Help your child map out the steps needed to reach the goal.

3. Estimate with your child how long each of the steps will take to complete. Establish a date by when each step will be completed, as well as the final date for completion of the overall goal.

4. Go back to the first step, and ask what your child can do immediately to start implementing the plan.

At the end of the exercise reinforce the desirability of the goal in your child's mind and build their belief that if they stick to this plan, it is achievable.

To keep the plan fresh and exciting, put the plan in a highly visible place, so the whole family can see it, for example on the fridge door. Encourage your child to record how much time they spend each day on the plan, and record this figure against the relevant step. As soon as a step has been completed, it can be ticked off and an appropriate small celebration held.

As the plan is implemented, they may slip behind in some of the activities. If that happens, never nag as that will destroy enthusiasm. Rather keep your conversation focused on the positive feelings that will be experienced, when the goal is achieved, and focus on what small step could to be taken today to get the plan back on track.

Exercise 19: Problem-solving

Age group: pre-school and primary school

This exercise will assist young children think flexibly to identify solutions to problems and so enhance their decision-making skills.

The parent and child, or entire family, identify and write problems that they or their friends have encountered that require choices. Each problem is individually written, on a single piece of paper, and then these are put into a container.

Each takes a turn to select one piece of paper and talks about the actions that could be taken to deal with the problem. The others discuss each of the suggestions, giving the advantages and disadvantages. Useful questions are:
· What are the things that could happen f you do that?
· If you did that, how would you feel the next day?
· What are other things you could do to solve the problem?
· Who else could you go to for help?

Conclude the discussion of each problem by helping your child understand the reasons for most appropriate course of action.

While the main objective of this exercise is to develop the problem-solving ability of generating alternatives to problems, it does give you the opportunity to understand the level of your child's development and, in addition, identify and correct any faulty thinking and beliefs they may have.

Exercise 20: Making your own decisions

Age group: pre-school and primary school

As a parent, you must make many decisions for your child, for example, decisions concerning their safety, health, security and what's socially acceptable. But young children will get frustrated if they can't make any decisions on their own. This exercise helps children develop their sense of autonomy, decision-making skills and self-efficacy, all of which will boost their resilience.

Give your child as many decision-making opportunities during the day as is practical. Convert some of the decisions that you automatically make into options that you put to the child, allowing your child to make the decision. For example, ask them what they would like to wear, whether they want to dress themselves or you dress them, what they would like for breakfast, whether they would like you to help them get breakfast or not, and so on.

To balance this, you need to have a clear boundary concerning those decisions that you have to take for your child. Explain that decisions regarding safety, attending school, health, hygiene and living the values of the family, for example, are not negotiable. Always give the reason for the decision and implication of what would happen if an incorrect decision was made. When you have to make a decision yourself for your child, explain the reason why you took the decision yourself, outlining the choices you had and the decision you made.

Age group: primary school and high school

Older children are better able than younger children to consider alternatives and to make decisions on their own. As they grow up, they will be required to make decisions that are increasingly complex and difficult. This exercise is a game and helps build their decision-making ability and judgement, which will enhance children's feeling of empowerment and competence, which will in turn boost their resilience.

The parent and child, or entire family, each writes on a separate piece of paper a problem or dilemma that needs a decision. Examples are:

- What would you do if you have noticed two students copying during a test in class?
- What would you do if your friends ask you to distract the shop assistant so that they can slip a tube of lipstick into their shopping bag?

The pieces of paper are folded and put into a container. Each of the participants selects one piece of paper and, after some time to consider the response, describes how they would tackle it.

The other people in the conversation then discuss that solution, as well as offering alternative ways of tackling the problem or dilemma. Questions useful to stimulate discussion are:

· What would be the consequence of taking that course of action?
· Where could you get help in making that decision?
· What would happen if you just did nothing?
· What else could you do in that situation?
· Who else here has different ideas of what could be done in this situation?

> My mom used to say it doesn't matter how many kids you have ... because one kid will take 100 per cent of your time, so more kids can't possibly take up more than 100 per cent of your time.
>
> *Karen Brown*

The purpose of the game is not necessarily to find solutions, but rather to discuss the variety of actions that are open for solving problems and developing the process of making difficult judgements. The conversation should also include age-appropriate suggestions on where your child could go for help.

Building Resilience Principle 7: Reach out to others

Children understand that they need help from others to deal with the tough times they go through. They are less inhibited than adults in asking for help. Most also, intuitively, want to reach out to help others. These exercises help promote the attitude and skills required to be successful when reaching out to ask for, as well as to offer, help.

Exercise 21: Giving advice and encouragement

Age-group: all

As a parent it's natural for you to you want your children to succeed. Thus, when you can see they are going to make a mistake, or encounter a problem, it's tempting to tell them what to do, even before the child requests help. Over time, this can lead to stunting the development of the child's problem-solving and decision-making abilities and hinder the development of their self-efficacy.

This exercise helps parents give sufficient guidance to a child facing a problem or a difficult time, without detracting from the child's development of confidence in their own judgement and decision-making skills.

When you see a problem looming, or your child comes to you for advice on how to tackle a problem, resist the temptation to immediately tell them what to do. Rather, use the following steps to help your child develop his own solution and, in so doing, enhance overall judgement and decision-making ability:

Step 1: What do you think is the solution to the problem?

Step 2: What are the alternatives that should be considered?

Step 3: Which is the best alternative?

Step 4: How can you implement the best alternative?

Step 5: What are the risks that should be considered when implementing this alternative?

Step 6: What is the first small step you can take, right now, to implement this decision?

There are times when this approach is inappropriate, for example when your child's safety or health is at risk. Then a more direct telling approach by you is appropriate.

Exercise 22: Praising

Age-group: parents and older children

This exercise is aimed at parents as well at older children. It's about praising others.

Praising your child is good, right? It builds their self-esteem, and that helps them persist with tasks, right? Well, the answer, somewhat counter-intuitively, is not so in every case. Praise in some situations can lead to a child persisting because it encourages the child to find different solutions. Praise in other situations can lead to a child giving up in the face of obstacles, because failure is a negative reflection on their abilities[10].

Praise that highlights the process the child has followed to reach an achievement builds the child's belief that success is based on hard work and learning. An example is: 'Congratulations on winning that book prize. I'm so proud that you kept on studying during the holidays, even when your friends went out and partied. Keeping to your study schedule paid off in winning this award.' This fosters the belief that ability and talents can be enhanced and leads to children remaining on task, despite setbacks. This is called a growth mind-set[11].

On the other hand, praise that evaluates attributes of the child leads to the belief that intelligence and success comes from their innate ability. An example of this type of praise is: 'You're so intelligent; you will be successful in life', which highlights the child's attribute. Children come to believe that if they are talented and have intellectual prowess, success should come automatically. This belief leads to areas such as tasks and learning new things (that have the potential for failure) being shunned and avoided[12]. In addition, they don't rebound well from their setbacks, actually decreasing their efforts and even cheating[13]. This is called a fixed mind-set.

In summary, process praise such as 'Well done! You succeeded because you did your homework instead of watching TV' encourages a growth mind-set and is thus much more beneficial than evaluative praise, such as 'Well done! You succeeded because you're so smart', which encourages a fixed mind-set.

Thus, use process praise, relating in detail what the child did which led to the achievement, in order to assist developing a growth mind-set. A simple model that you can use, to help you give process praise, is that of What and Why, which was outlined in chapter 10. Praise the child, saying 'what' you are recognising, and then pay particular attention to reinforce outlining the 'why' aspect.

Adolescence is a period of rapid changes. Between the ages of 12 and 17, for example, a parent ages as much as 20 years.

Author unknown

Exercise 23: Dealing with backchat and disrespectful behaviour

Age-group: all

When children experience difficulties at school and at home, this often shows up in their behaviour to their parents and other adults in positions of authority. Backchat is hurtful and even bewildering to parents, who often don't know how to respond. Here are some suggestions:

It's useful to understand that even a teenage child does not have the sophisticated level of communication skills that you do. This means that you should not react to mildly rebellious comments and behaviour. Ignore rolling of eyes, stomping around and muttering when your child gets grumpy and frustrated.

This is different from name-calling, swearing, yelling, threatening and other truly disrespectful and degrading behaviour, which is in a different league and needs to be stopped.

There are four critical rules to understand and follow to cope effectively with backchat and disrespectful behaviour:

Rule 1. Do not personalise what is happening. Don't allow it to get to you. The problem is not about you; the problem is about your child. Mildly disrespectful behaviour should be ignored, and your child should only be able to get your attention when they speak respectfully to you. When they do, then you should smile, look them in the eyes and engage with them. In this way, you reward and reinforce respectful and not disrespectful behaviour.

Rule 2. When it involves unacceptable behaviour, describe it in terms of yourself: 'I'm not prepared to be talked to like that' rather than 'Who do you think you are? How dare you use that language to me!' The former keeps the control and focus on yourself, whereas the latter focuses negatively on your child and tends to escalate the argument.

Rule 3. Model the calm behaviour and respect you would like in all your dealings with your child. If you yell at your child, you must expect your child to yell at you. If you don't show respect to your child, you can't expect respect from your child.

Rule 4. You cannot change anyone's behaviour other than your own. This means that as much as you would like to, you can't change your child's behaviour. Only they can do that. Children choose their behaviour and the best you can do is to try to influence their choice.

So the next time you encounter backchat from your child, try to apply the four rules above. Afterwards, reflect on what worked and which you should carry on doing. For anything you did or said which didn't work, think of how you can respond differently next time.

Exercise 24: Encouraging others

Age group: all

Encouraging others has a positive effect on the person being encouraged as well as the person who does the encouragement. This exercise is designed to structure encouragement that elicits positive feelings in both parties.

Parent and child together identify people who need encouraging, which could also include the parents. Your child with your help, if appropriate, writes a note of encouragement to that person and which could include elements of the following:

· The person's strengths and how they can be used to deal with the trying times.

· Their belief that the person will be successful.

· Their feelings of support, affection and love for the person (as appropriate).

The note can be given, read or sent to the person or perhaps hidden somewhere to be found later as a surprise, for example, in a lunchbox or under a pillow.

> The child enters your home and for the next 20 years make so much noise you can hardly stand it. The child departs, leaving the house so silent that you think you're going mad.
>
> *John Andrew Holmes*

ENDNOTES

1 Goldstein, S. & Brooks, R. B.(eds) (2005) *Handbook of Resilience in Children*, Springer, New York, NY: Kluwer/Academic Press.

2 See reference [1]

3 E. Werner: The value of applied research for Head Start: A cross-cultural and longitudinal Perspective. In: National Head Start Association Journal of Research and Evaluation, 1997.

4   Other exercises are available at: http://www.fishfulthinking.com/ . The website contains many wonderful ideas on how to build children's resilience. (Accessed 1 January, 2012)

5   This section was inspired by the book: Benson, P.L. (2008). *Sparks: How* parents can help ignite *the* hidden strengths *of* teenagers. San Francisco , CA: Jossey-Bass. There is also a wonderful website packed with resources which you can visit for more information on this approach: http://www.search-institute.org (Accessed 1 January, 2012).

6   Seligman, M. E. P. (1996). *The Optimistic Child: Proven Program to Safeguard Children from Depression & Build Lifelong Resilience*. New York: Houghton Mifflin.

7   Johnston-O'Connor, E.J., and Kirsehenbaum, D. S. (1986). Something Succeeds Like Success: Positive Self-Monitoring for Unskilled Golfers. *Cognitive Therapy and Research, Vol. 10(1)*: 123–136.

8   Kirschenbaum, D. S., A. M. Ordman, et al. (1982). "Effects of differential self-monitoring and level of mastery on sports performance: Brain power bowling." *Cognitive Therapy and Research 6(3)*: 335–341.

9   Cooperrider, D. L., Whitney, D., and Stavros, J. M. (2003). *Appreciative inquiry handbook*. Bedford Heights, OH: Lakeshore Publishers.

10 Dweck, C. S. (2006). *Mindset: The new psychology of success*. New York: Random House.

11 Dweck, C. S. (1999). *Self-theories: Their role in motivation, personality and development*. Philadelphia: Psychology Press.

12 See reference [6]

13 Blackwell, L., Trzesniewski, K., and Dweck, C.S. (2007). Implicit Theories of Intelligence Predict Achievement Across an Adolescent Transition: A Longitudinal Study and an Intervention. *Child Development* 78 (1): 246–263.

Now attend the workshop!

The Building Resilience training is based on seven building blocks of resilience identified in recent South African research.

The workshop assists delegates to uncover their own personal answers to three key resilience questions:

1 Why not just give up when things get really difficult?

2 How do I become mentally tough?

3 What do I do when experiencing the 'dark night' of adversity?

The workshop provides delegates with the knowledge and skills to

- understand what issues undermine their personal coping and resilience
- learn tools and techniques to build their personal resilience
- maintain resilience in the face of stress at work and home.

WHO SHOULD ATTEND THE WORKSHOP?

The workshop will benefit everyone who experiences stressful life events (at work and at home) and who would like to become more resourceful and to cope better.

BENEFIT TO COMPANIES

- Staff learn the tools to resist the impact of stressful experience on their productivity; to remain task-focused; to deal with multiple demands, and to stay calm and healthy.
- Leaders and staff are better able to live in alignment with their own and the organization's values, resulting in enhanced engagement, productivity and team work.

CONTACT

Rod Warner at rodwarner7@gmail.com, or visit
www.buildingresilience.co.za

Permissions

Page 92. Dr. Rashid permission to use names and definitions of strengths from '340 Ways to Use VIA Character Strengths' by Tayyab Rashid & Afroze Anjum. Reference: Adapted from http://www.viastrengths.org/Applications/Exercises/tabid/132/Default.aspx July 16, 2008 340 Ways to Use VIA Character Strengths by Tayyab Rashid & Afroze Anjum, University of Pennsylvania, © 2005, Tayyab Rashid (Accessed 12 December 2011).

Page 179. REACH Forgiveness model. Permission given by Dr. Worthington Reference: Worthington, E. L., Jr. (2006). *Forgiveness and reconciliation: Theory and application.* New York: Brunner-Routledge. They have a website: www.people.vcu.edu/~eworth.

Page 186. Dr. Lyubomirsky for use of Best Possible Self-Exercise. Reference: Sheldon, K. M. and S. Lyubomirsky (2006). 'How to increase and sustain positive emotion: the effects of expressing gratitude and visualizing best possible selves'. *Journal of Positive Psychology* 1(2): 73-82.

Page 200. Drama Triangle permission given by Dr. Stephen Karpman (MD) Reference: Karpman, S. (1968). Fairy tales and script drama analysis. *Transactional Analysis Bulletin*, 7(26), 39–43.

Index

www.ingramcontent.com/pod-product-compliance
Lightning Source LLC
Chambersburg PA
CBHW081458200326
41518CB00015B/2300